on track ...

Dream Theater

every album, every song

Jordan Blum

sonicbondpublishing.com

Sonicbond Publishing Limited
www.sonicbondpublishing.co.uk
Email: info@sonicbondpublishing.co.uk

First Published in the United Kingdom 2020
First Published in the United States 2020

British Library Cataloguing in Publication Data:
A Catalogue record for this book is available from the British Library

Copyright Jordan Blum 2020

ISBN 978-1-78952-050-7

Typeset in ITC Garamond & ITC Avant Garde
Printed and bound in England

Graphic design and typesetting: Full Moon Media

on track ... Dream Theater

Contents

1. Acknowledgements 4
2. Introduction 5
3. When Dream and Day Unite 7
4. Images and Words 13
5. Awake 21
6. A Change of Seasons 28
7. Falling Into Infinity 35
8. Metropolis Pt. 2: Scenes from a Memory 43
9. Six Degrees of Inner Turbulence 56
10. Train of Thought 68
11. Octavarium 76
12. Systematic Chaos 84
13. Black Clouds & Silver Linings 93
14. A Dramatic Turn of Events 100
15. Dream Theater 108
16. The Astonishing 115
17. Distance Over Time 127
18. Roundup – Live/Video, Compilations, Extra Tracks, and Official Bootlegs 133
19. Bibliography 139
20. Jordan Blum's ultimate Dream Theater Playlist 142
21. Dream Theater albums ranked from best to worst 143

Acknowledgements

As always, I'd like to thank Stephen Lambe for offering me the opportunity to write this book and for showing nonstop confidence in my ability to produce something accurate, interesting, enlightening, and generally worthwhile. Similarly, thanks to various other Sonicbond Publishing writers and editors for their support and advice along the way, as well as to Tim Bowness for giving Sonicbond books a home at the Burning Shed online store.

In terms of personal contributions, thanks to all of the artists, writers, and other people in the music industry who chatted with me about Dream Theater; whether or not your responses are explicitly referenced, know that your feedback was invaluable in helping me shape my research and responses. Equal thanks to everyone who submittedpreviously published interviews, articles, and/or pieces for the photo section: Gonzalo Perkeleþorquetzacoatl, Heather Johannen, Jon Van Daal, Jorge Pozo, Pedro Matos, Rikk Feulner, Scott Hansen, Stephane Auzilleau.

Thanks to all of my friends, family, and online acquaintances whose constant interest in and advice for this project helped me remain focused and confident along the way. That goes double for my closest fellow progressive metal-loving buddies – you know who you are – for the countless conversations, debates,and laughs. Most importantly, thank you to my sister, Erica, my mother, Kandie, and my father, Jay, for their love and support in everything I do.

Oh, and I definitely want to thank you for taking the time to read this book. Whether or not our views align, I appreciate your interest and support. After all, Dream Theater's catalogue is just about as breathtaking as their influence, and they're forever among the greatest progressive acts of all time. That, I believe, is something we can all agree on.

Introduction

No other band has affected modern progressive metal as deeply or widely as American quintet Dream Theater. Formed in 1985 at Berklee College of Music in Boston, MA by guitarist John Petrucci, drummer Mike Portnoy, and bassist John Myung, the group has spent roughly thirty years repeatedly pushing new boundaries and reinventing their identity. True, predecessors such as Queensrÿche, Fates Warning, Voivod, Savatage, Crimson Glory, and Watchtower were already infusing metal foundations with prog rock trademarks like lengthy durations, heightened intricacies, and/or conceptual focuses; yet, Dream Theater were the first to fully meld influences from both genres into ground-breaking hodgepodges of quirky instrumentation, extensively complex arrangements, and high-concept songwriting. Whether subtly or overtly, they've since left their mark on just about every progressive metal act that's followed.

At first, the band was actually called Majesty. As the story goes, the trio were waiting in line for Rush concert tickets when 'Bastille Day' – from 1975's *Caress of Steel* – came on the radio. Portnoy declared its ending 'majestic' and the name was chosen. After sharpening their skills together, they decided to expand the line-up via two of Petrucci's friends from home: keyboardist Kevin Moore and guitarist/vocalist Chris Collins. From the very start – and as Portnoy revealed to Dave Everley of *PROG* magazine in February 2019 – they aimed to 'take the music as far as it would go, take the instruments as far as they would go, [and] take the composition to extremes'. He adds: 'At that time, the pure prog scene was pretty much non-existent... I was missing those kinds of bands, but I was also a full-on metalhead into Slayer and Exodus and all that stuff. When I met the other guys, we all wanted to combine the two things, like a Reese's Peanut Butter Cup'. With the group now complete, they spent the latter half of the 1980s playing shows around New York City while releasing two collections: *The Majesty Demos*, a six-track set of original material that was funded by Portnoy's grandmother and sold 1,000 copies within half a year, and *When Dream and Day Unite*, a proper studio debut with Collins' replacement, Charlie Dominici, and the now-iconic name of Dream Theater (more on that in a bit).

Although that initial album was certainly a worthwhile first step, it's often – and somewhat unfairly – overlooked because of how well its successor, 1992's *Images and Words*, captured the familiar Dream Theater sound. The main reason, of course, is that it marks the entrance of permanent singer James LaBrie, plus improvements in every facet of the band's artistry. Naturally, the rest of the decade saw them growing in creativity while increasing their levels of popularity and acclaim. Even in the face of two more line-up changes – both involving new keyboardists – Dream Theater never stopped challenging themselves, their audience, and their genre with each new record. In fact, they closed out the 1990s with their seminal fifth LP, *Metropolis Pt. 2: Scenes from a Memory*, which is commonly celebrated not only as their best work to date but also as one of the best progressive metal albums – as well as one of the best concept albums – of all time.

Expectedly, the 2000s saw the group staying true to their 1970s and 1980s forefathers in the midst of modernizing their direction even more. For instance, 2002's *Six Degrees of Inner Turbulence* arguably upped the ante from 1999's *Scenes from a Memory* in terms of presentation. Specifically, its first disc consisted of five unrelated tracks, whereas its second disc contained the forty-two-minute title suite broken into eight sections. By delving deeper into either their metal roots (2003's *Train of Thought* and 2007's *Systematic Chaos*) or their progressive rock leanings (2005's *Octavarium* and 2009's *Black Clouds & Silver Linings*), they more or less sustained their reign as the period passed.

Shockingly, the dawn of the current decade saw Dream Theater facing their most controversial era yet, as Portnoy announced his departure in September 2010. Unsurprisingly, this led to a plethora of intensely polarized reactions from fans and the progressive metal world at large that, let's be honest, have only marginally calmed down now. It wasn't too long, however, before Berklee professor and prior James LaBrie collaborator Mike Mangini was chosen as their new drummer. Nearly ten years later, Dream Theater devotees continue to compare the pros and cons of each percussionist; likewise, each of Mangini's four studio albums with Dream Theater thus far have received varying degrees of mixed responses (with 2016's flashy *The Astonishing* facing the worst feedback and 2019's focused *Distance Over Time* being championed as a return to excellence). Nevertheless, the group is arguably more popular than ever, and the amount of persistence and imagination they still show deserves respect.

Obviously, Dream Theater couldn't have achieved so much for so long without rubbing off on virtually every progressive metal peer and follower, including Haken, Riverside, Between the Buried and Me, Symphony X, Vanden Plas, and Mastodon. There are countless acts who've taken at least a little bit from the templates Dream Theater established. It's no wonder, then, why they also managed to earn dozens of awards and certifications – plus two Grammy nominations – alongside numerous references in popular culture, along the way.

No matter how you look at it, Dream Theater's impact on progressive metal is unparalleled, and that's exactly what this book aims to examine. Mixing behind-the-scenes information, original analyses, and some insights from outside experts and contemporaries, we'll go album by album – and track-by-track – through the band's catalogue to pinpoint precisely why Dream Theater's legacy and trajectory are nothing short of miraculous.

'When Dream and Day Unite' (1989)

Personnel:
Charlie Dominici: vocals
John Petrucci: guitar
John Myung: bass
Kevin Moore: keyboards
Mike Portnoy: drums
Amy Guip: cover art
Terry Date: engineer, mixing
Joe Alexander: engineer, mixing
Brian Stover: assistant engineer
Trish Finnegan: assistant engineer
Produced at Kajem/Victory Studios in Gladwyne, Pennsylvania, July – August 1988
by Dream Theater, Terry Date, and Steve Sinclair
UK and US release date March 1989.
Highest chart places: UK: none, USA: none
Running time: 51:25
Current edition: One Way Records 2002 CD remaster

The group earned a fair amount of positivity for 1986's *The Majesty Demos*. In fact, one copy made its way to Fates Warning's founding guitarist, Jim Matheos, who'd previously befriended Portnoy and who played it 'over and over again' because he 'was amazed at what they were doing'. Sadly, though, their confidence and unity didn't last very long, as Collins was fired a few months after the tape came out due to various incompatibilities (mainly, his poor vocal range and on-stage antics). Likewise, an already recognised Las Vegas band called Majesty threatened legal action if the band didn't change their designation. Thankfully, both conflicts were resolved moderately quickly, as the remaining quartet found Collins' replacement, Charlie Dominici, in November 1987, and soon had a new name – Dream Theater – thanks to Portnoy's father's love of a movie house in California. Feeling reinvigorated and self-assured, they set out to produce *When Dream and Day Unite*, an immensely promising – if dated – debut studio LP that would help kickstart a new type of music.

Clearly, signing to an actual label was an important move. Before long, they'd narrowed down the options to just two: Metal Blade and a subsidiary of MCA, Mechanic. In Rich Wilson's authorized biography, *Lifting Shadows*, then-manager Derek Simon says that they were 'ninety per cent there' with the former choice, but when Mechanic offered them 'a seven-record deal... [and] $30,000', they jumped at the chance. Today, he admits that it was an 'unfavourable' contract chosen out of inexperience and eagerness. Portnoy elaborates by stating that Metal Blade's one-record proposal was 'more of an experiment' than 'a commitment', whereas going with Mechanic guaranteed 'everything we had been striving for'.

Packed into Pennsylvania's Kajem/Victory Studios – which had just been used to make Queensrÿche's *Operation: Mindcrime*, a masterwork that Portnoy says 'was a big influence' on them at the time – they were instructed to complete the album quickly and cheaply. Producer Steve Sinclair clarifies: 'I had just recorded Megadeth's *Peace Sells... But Who's Buying?* for... $25,000 about two years earlier. That was a great album, so I thought I could make an even better album for $30,000'. Despite these pressures, as well as only being able to work between about 6:00 P.M. and 6:00 A.M., Dominici saw it as a treasured time, to say the least: 'I have hazy memories of half-naked girls running through the strange and eerie layout of the building. . . I wanted to have the same room that Geoff Tate had, hoping some of that vocal genius would be lingering and might rub off on me!'. Similarly, Portnoy reflects on how much 'potential' they all felt, noting, 'The spirits were high because we hadn't been burned yet'. By most accounts, it was a very valuable and good-natured experience.

The front cover was done by photographer Amy Guip, who reveals that it was inspired by 'a piece of artwork in college that symbolized where I felt A.I.D.S. was going at that time'. That original image featured 'a scarlet letter 'A'' being 'branded onto the chest of a photo of one of my college mates'. This friend, Steve Burman, is also used here, with the 'A' being replaced by Dominici's emblematic Majesty Symbol that has since appeared on every Dream Theater cover.

Musically, *When Dream and Day Unite* contained what the label aptly marketed as 'Metallica Meets Rush'. In retrospect, Petrucci praises it most for its robust 'spontaneity', 'fire', and 'spirit', whereas Portnoy is a bit more even-handed in disclosing that its main focus – 'the flashy playing' – prevents many of the tracks from being 'on the same level' as the rest of their discography. Along those lines, pretty much everyone involved – and everyone who's heard the record – agrees that its biggest flaws are Dominici's commanding yet limited and odd presence (which we'll discuss soon) and the generally poor sound quality. Bluntly, Portnoy deems it 'the worst produced album [Terry Date] ever made', whereas Myung acknowledges that it 'pales in comparison to our later albums' while also praising its 'sincerity'. Interestingly, Date doesn't entirely disagree, confessing, 'with the shorter time, you suffer as you have to cut corners somewhere'.

Fortunately, the record – which was dedicated to Dominici's late father and Portnoy's late mother – got plenty of encouraging reviews. In particular, *Kerrang!* writer Derek Oliver commended how its 'musical dexterity' evoked artists like the Dixie Dregs, Jeff Beck, and Neal Peart. Correspondingly, Valerie Potter of *Metal Hammer* called it 'The most original and inventive record I've heard in many a long and weary month'. While other outlets – such as *RIP* magazine – were more negative, the majority of reactions were definitely optimistic.

Those accolades notwithstanding, the LP failed to bring the group significant sales or widespread attention. Portnoy claims that this was largely due to the contract with Mechanic actually being 'crummy' because they 'did nothing with *When Dream and Day Unite* and prevented them from substantially touring or making a music video (although there were two promotional singles put out: 'Status Seeker' and 'Afterlife'). He jokes, 'We were watching Voivod and Queensrÿche doing really well and going, 'Wait a minute, we're different but not that different''. Sinclair blames MCA itself, as they felt that the songs weren't sellable enough to warrant a larger push even though 'the press and college radio were both embracing the band with open arms'. As a result, the quintet felt discouraged and 'devastated' about having their dreams of being career musicians seemingly fade away; this led to them leaving Mechanic/MCA – and parting ways with Dominici – before deciding to once again venture out as an independent instrumental act in search of a singer.

Thirty years on, *When Dream and Day Unite* can affectionately be seen as 'the blueprint' for Dream Theater's foundation. Regardless of its imperfections, Petrucci and Portnoy rejoice at how well much of the material still works in concert. This is most evident on *When Dream and Day Reunite*, a 15th anniversary live CD/DVD – recorded in Los Angeles in 2004 – during which Dominici joins them to perform the entire thing. Few listeners would consider it their favourite Dream Theater album, yet there's no denying its role in steering the band toward even better music, images, and words with their sophomore sequence.

'A Fortune in Lies' (Petrucci)

Right away, Portnoy's distinctive syncopation and Petrucci's characteristically soaring notes burst out of the speakers. Behind them, Moore's synthesized organ chords are faint but useful, as are Myung's sludgy basslines. Together, they conjure the speedy thrash metal of the 1980s more than they do any tangible progressive rock stimuli (although a moment of keyboard extravagance, coupled with some complicated rhythmic changes, do hint at a merger of Marillion and Metallica). It's not long before Dominici's squeals – a now unfashionable but not unfitting quality – take over with engrossing passion. Although Petrucci wrote it about 'an acquaintance who was arrested for theft and his subsequent experiences', there are no direct references to that incident in the lyrics. Rather, the words are obscure and slightly fantastical – 'Can you show me your gold and your silver? / A hero in frozen water' – leading to a relatively captivating and catchy chorus. As for the spoken word passage three minutes in, it comes from an unknown television prison documentary and is intensely complemented by frantic drumming and ominous synth swirls. Near the end, Petrucci delivers a flashy solo that, while surely showcasing style over substance, is undoubtedly impressive. Overall, the track is an innovative and striking way to start.

'Status Seeker' (Dominci, Petrucci)

The last entry on *When Dream and Day Unite* to be finished – but the first to be issued as a single – this one was done over just two days. Furthermore, and as Petrucci confirms, it was deliberately made to attain maximum radio airplay: '['Status Seeker'] was an example of us trying to get our style into a more accessible format'. To help accomplish this, they had Rush producer Terry Brown remix it since the original version was 'fine' but 'lacking in places' because Date was 'burnt out'. Surprisingly, Date understood the choice, remarking, 'That kind of stuff never upsets me'.

Reportedly, it was penned as an attack on those who initially dismissed Dream Theater but later pretended to have always been supportive. Dominici's scornful deliveries of lines such as 'You draw the bottom line / With a dollar sign / Change of opinion / At the drop of a dime' verify this motivation. From a technical standpoint, his voice has a more poppy personality than on the last composition, especially with the angelic harmonies. The arrangement allows Moore to shine more amid a largely sparser and more approachable footing. Specifically, the guitar arpeggios and arena rock percussion are both very inviting assets, so it works for a mainstream crowd.

'The Ytse Jam' (Petrucci, Myung, Portnoy, Moore)

In contrast, Dream Theater's first official instrumental – whose title cleverly reverses their old name – is a thrillingly decadent, if also mildly repetitive, display of melodic virtuosity. Composed during their days at Berklee, its preliminary build-up gives way to one of the group's most iconic and hypnotic guitar riffs. Portnoy smartly accentuates it with each high hat tap while Myung emulates the whole pattern. From there, Moore follows Petrucci's crunchy transitional chords and muted soloing while the rhythm section adds its own controlled complexities. Eventually, Moore continues the main riff while Petrucci adds some moody notes on top; halfway in, each of the four musicians takes a turn dishing out mesmerizingly swanky playing before testing themselves – and their audience – with an ambitiously synchronized and erratic start/stop cooldown. An emotive section comes next and, consciously or not, seems to foreshadow 'Take the Time' from 1992's Imagines and Words. Fittingly, the composition then comes full circle by essentially ending as it began to employ some typical progressive rock continuity in the process. Although Dream Theater have absolutely crafted more daring and wide-ranging instrumentals over the years, it remains a breathtaking achievement.

'The Killing Hand' (Petrucci)

Digging deeper into his figurative writing chops, Petrucci's sci-fi story deals with a man traveling back in time to learn that he's responsible for hundreds of deaths in the present. This concept, combined with its five-part structure, makes 'The Killing Hand' quite a valiant feat. Luckily, the band pulls it off well. Beginning with mournful acoustic guitar fingerpicking, it transitions into a forceful rocker not unlike something from the aforementioned *Operation: Mindcrime*. The backing chants add some emotional weight as well, and Portnoy's occasional marching beat helps Dominici immediately capture the desperation Petrucci aims for.

A handful of minor shifts happen by the midpoint of the piece, but the first major change comes five minutes in. Suddenly, it becomes trickier and faster as Petrucci and Moore spark panic prior to another reflective acoustic ballad. Afterwards, a relatively straightforward heavy section closes the track, allowing Myung momentarily to take the limelight within a few urgent measures. Honestly, it's not as satisfyingly diverse or multifaceted as it could be – and the echoey production ages it a bit – but it's still a strong precursor of things to come.

'Light Fuse and Get Away' (Moore)

It's often said that love is the most universal and common topic explored in art, so it makes sense that Dream Theater would tap into it on When Dream and Day Unite. Following an intricate yet sentimental wordless lead-in, Dominici indeed channels Geddy Lee as he laments an ill-fated romance. Naturally, the music alternates with difficulty and determination around him – effectively conveying the polarized depths that go into a break-up – but it's his graceful delivery that really impresses. Truly, Dominici's unpredictable fluctuations are surprisingly skilful on top of his bandmates' aggressive adjustments. Although Moore wrote it, the soundbite from Dominici's then-girlfriend ('I can't see where this is going') is a nice touch, too. During its second half, Moore's reverberating synths guide a marginally more atmospheric and affective detour prior to equally touching solos from Petrucci. Behind them, Portnoy and Myung keep it all steady with deceptive restraint. Without a doubt, it ends up being one of the best selections in the set.

'Afterlife' (Dominci)

Released as a single on 16 March 1989, 'Afterlife' was born as an instrumental before receiving lyrics from Collins. His departure meant that the remaining members would have to revise it yet again with Dominci. Fortunately, his exploration of mortality – while a bit cliché and basic – fits the quartet's steadfast backing nicely. In particular, Petrucci's feisty chords ebb and flow around the verses masterfully, and as always, Portnoy's syncopation is as fresh as it is appealing. As it concludes, Petrucci and Moore engage in a scorching simultaneous duel that further cements how great they work as a pair. In general, however, it's one of the most generic and unremarkable parts of When Dream and Day Unite, even if it was a crowd-pleaser in concert. By no means bad, it doesn't show Dream Theater standing out in any capacity.

'The Ones Who Help to Set the Sun' (Petrucci)

Before settling on Dominici, Dream Theater auditioned Barbara Chiovelli with this song; although they liked what she did with it, they ultimately decided that they didn't want to have a frontwoman. Former manager Andrew Ross explains that this wasn't due to sexism, but instead, because 'marketing-wise, they didn't think that could be successful'. While we may never know how that version sounded, this one is undeniably solid. It starts with the sounds of a person driving in a thunderstorm – commonly referred to as the 'Death of Spock' segment – while Moore's keyboard screeches and Myung plays a few harmonic notes. This use of natural noise would become a staple of Dream Theater music, and the concept itself – a man who falls asleep at the wheel, dreams of his death, and awakens with rejuvenated hopefulness – is somewhat similar that of 'The Count of Tuscany' twenty years later.

Beneath chimes, wind, and more harmonics, a sinisterly touching outline is played by several instruments to spark dramatic anticipation. That is, until Portnoy's grungy double bass drum signals Petrucci's razor-sharp riffs and Dominici's scarred remembrances: 'We were racing the rain / My hands held the wheel / My eyes tried to hold their place'. As usual, the group swings between unwavering accompaniments and scattered gusts of showmanship, including some thorough exchanges between Petrucci and Portnoy. On that note, Petrucci's ascending fury during his solo would also become one of his most noticeable techniques. From start to finish, the instrumentation is superb, but it's the songwriting that beams brightest on 'The Ones Who Help to Set the Sun'.

'Only a Matter of Time' (Moore)

The tense opening – courageous percussion and resolute basslines supporting Moore and Petrucci's imposing distress – easily conveys a sense of pivotal destiny. Thankfully, they uphold that ever-changing turmoil as Dominci convincingly belts out the tale of an artist stuck between artistic integrity and profitability. Lyrically, it's one of the most imaginative and dense works of the entire sequence, with a robust blend of literal and metaphorical phrases – including a reference to the album title – keeping it relatable but colourful. A standout portion comes at about the two-and-a-half-minute mark when a flurry of woeful strings brings a classical touch to the metalcore. Such startling moves would become commonplace on subsequent efforts, so it's another fine example of how much groundwork for the future Dream Theater were already laying. Likewise, Portnoy's banging of bigger drums a bit later is also resourceful. As it concludes, Dominici sings with triumph in-between victorious synth and electric guitar outbursts. It's dazzlingly flamboyant yet focused, culminating in a piercing surge of textures until they all stop at once to leave you pleasantly exhausted. It's an indisputably powerful last declaration of purpose.

Bonuses

By all accounts, the 2002 One Way Records remaster is the latest widely available version of *When Dream and Day Unite*. However, there is a 2018 red vinyl rerelease, as well as a 2012 CD import from Japan. In all cases – and despite any sonic superiority when compared to the 1989 original – the lack of any additional content is disappointing. Happily, a two-disc set of demos came out in 2004 as a part of the Official Bootleg series. We'll dig into that separately.

'Images and Words' (1992)

Personnel:
James LaBrie: vocals
John Petrucci: guitar, backing vocals
John Myung: bass
Kevin Moore: keyboards
Mike Portnoy: drums, percussion, backing vocals (1)
Jay Beckenstein: soprano saxophone (2)
Larry Freemantle: cover art
David Prater: mixing
Doug Oberkircher: engineer, mixing
Steve Regina: assistant engineer
Produced at BearTracks Studios in Suffern, New York and The Hit Factory in New York City,October – December 1991 by David Prater
UK and US release date: July 1992.
Highest chart places: UK: none, USA: 61
Running time: 57:04
Current edition: ATCO Records 2016 gold & solid red limited edition vinyl

Dream Theater – in addition to almost everyone else who heard *When Dream and Day Unite* upon release – knew that they'd made an enormously forward-thinking and skilful first LP. But, with Mechanic/MCA's lacklustre aid leading to less than desirable results – not to mention the fact that genres like grunge and rap were becoming immeasurably popular as hair metal died out – the band conceded that some big adjustments were needed for its follow-up to fully flourish. Namely, they needed to change singers and labels, no matter how frustrating, extraneous, or disheartening those processes would be. In spite of facing a lot of chaos along the way, they persevered with a vastly superior record contract and frontman, ensuring that their sophomore sequence would be as monumental as possible. To say that 1992's *Images and Words* was a step up would be putting it lightly; more accurately, the album was a colossal evolution, kickstarting what *The Prog Report* founder Roie Avin calls 'Dream Theater's reign as the kings of new progressive metal'.

Charlie Dominici's voice certainly suited *When Dream and Day Unite*, but the rest of the group remorsefully yet decisively determined that he couldn't continue with them due to – among other things – him being over ten years older and not having the look they were going for. Shockingly, Dominici was thinking of leaving, too, since the record wasn't as fruitful as he'd hoped and the rest of the band disliked his suggestions for a more streamlined style. He adds that it was like 'a marriage' that'd run its course and couldn't be saved 'through talking', so he felt it was better to 'bow out gracefully' following a final performance opening for Marillion at the New York Ritz on 14 November 1989. All these years later, he still thinks of Dream Theater as family and is happy – if not also a tad jealous – about how far they've come.

Now faced with a vocalist void, the remaining four members set out to find that perfect singer they'd been searching for all along. At the risk of unnecessary long-windedness, suffice it to say that they tried out roughly 200 people over the next two years or so. Included in that list was Fates Warning's John Arch, who'd previously critiqued Dominici's live stage presence to the band and who ultimately decided that he 'couldn't make that kind of commitment' since he had a child on the way. For a while – and reservations from outside parties notwithstanding – Dream Theater thought they'd found their answer in Chris Cintron, a spry rocker who reminded Portnoy of Kansas' Steve Walsh. That is until they got a package containing 'a glossy black and white photo, a lengthy biography and a tape' from someone who seemed to possess everything the other guys were looking for. His name was Kevin James LaBrie.

Having spent years playing with other artists – explicitly, he took over for Sebastian Bach in Canadian glam metal act Winter Rose – LaBrie was overwhelmingly and consistently extraordinary during his strenuous four-day audition. By the end of it, they 'decided that that was it and [the] search was over'. Aside from being a musical and visual match, he was chosen because unlike many of his predecessors, he was content just to sing what the others wrote for him instead of having a major say in the writing or arranging processes. Likewise, he embraced that idea that he was never going to be 'the sole focus of attention' since Dream Theater were being run primarily by Petrucci and Portnoy. Because they felt that having two Kevins in the band – in addition to two Johns – would've been overly complicated, everyone agreed to have LaBrie go by his middle name instead. The rest, as they say, is history.

With a new singer in place, it was time for Dream Theater to settle on a new record label. Coincidentally, they ended up signing with the aforementioned *Kerrang!* journalist, Derek Oliver, who now worked as an A&R man at Atco (a subsidiary of Atlantic Records). As fate would have it, Oliver's boss, Derek Shulman, was no stranger to progressive music, as he fronted one of the most unique and respected acts of the 1970s: Gentle Giant. To seal the deal, Dream Theater had to record a three-song demo with LaBrie. It featured *Images and Words* essentials 'Take the Time' and 'Metropolis', plus a leftover from the *When Dream and Day Unite* sessions called 'To Live Forever', and all of it stunned the label executives. Despite simpler rock music becoming all the rage at the time, Shulman wasn't dissuaded from signing Dream Theater, either. In fact, he confesses:

> Generally, my decisions aren't based on what other people are doing. I felt it had to be marketable or really good. And speaking as someone who signs artists and runs companies, when you see a marketplace going in one direction, you try and run in the other... I was pleased to be signing something that I personally could relate to, and who related to me not only as a record geek but as a musician who had been in a band who had done a similar thing to what they did – just touring and playing very good music.

Their two biggest roadblocks now resolved, Dream Theater were finally able to enter the studio in late 1991 to work on *Images and Words*. Regrettably, doing so proved far more perilous than expected, as producer – and former Nektar and Santana percussionist – David Prater was famously at odds with the band during the whole thing. Portnoy seems especially embittered toward him for apparently being tricked into using drum triggers; reportedly, Prater also scolded Moore for 'playing his keyboard parts wrongly on purpose to make [Prater] look stupid' – multiple members deny that Moore did this, though – and supposedly added his voice to the very end of closer 'Learning to Live' without any approval. In contrast, LaBrie and Petrucci conclude that while Pratner wasn't exactly tactful or easy-going, he 'got along fabulously' with most of the team and 'did an amazing job for us'. While there are usually multiple sides to every story, it's nevertheless astonishing that such a landmark achievement arose out of such combative circumstances.

It's also worth noting that *Images and Words* was intended to be much longer – possibly even a double album – with one discarded track standing out above the rest. Written about the passing of his mother, Portnoy's 18+ minute epic 'A Change of Seasons' was eventually deemed too much for the time being. Although he was originally hurt by the choice and even spent two hours fighting with Oliver on the phone (since Atco had given them 'every indication that it would be on the album'), Portnoy came to view it as the smart move. Likewise, Petrucci told *Prog Sphere* in 2017 that it was 'the right decision, for sure. I'm glad that [*Images and Words*] is only an hour-long record'. After all, the expanded piece ended up getting a standalone release three years later, so it all worked out in the end.

Easily one of the most iconic aspects of *Images and Words* is its artwork. Designed by renowned artist Larry Freemantle – who says that Myung was 'the key' bandmember in assisting him with the concept – it was envisioned to look like 'an old painting' with 'a collage of engravings and illustrations' that represented each of the eight tracks. That said, Moore suggests that its biggest tie is to 'Wait for Sleep', as the girl on the cover – whom Freemantle names Andrea – is holding a picture of her deceased sister. Also, 'the heart with the barbed wire wrapped around it is symbol of compassion' and, in an eerie forthcoming connection to Steven Wilson's 'The Raven that Refused to Sing', the sibling's spirit is symbolized as a bird. These days, the cover is almost as synonymous with progressive metal as Dream Theater itself.

Initially, the album didn't gain much traction; but, once a condensed version of its opener, 'Pull Me Under', was issued as a single in August 1992, everything changed. Suddenly, countless radio stations were playing it often, with their phones ringing nonstop; similarly, the accompanying music video, which the band now feels is uninspired and cheap, was equally popular on MTV's *Headbangers Ball*. After 'seven years of frustration', Portnoy says, it was 'incredibly satisfying' to become so big. As a result, the *Images and Words* tour lasted over a year and saw Dream Theater travelling internationally, recording their first live album and home video concert – *Live at the Marquee* and *Images and Words: Live in Tokyo*, respectively – and being treated like rock stars for the first time. Specifically, Petrucci notes, 'I remember there were even fans waiting at the airport. We were driven around by people wearing white gloves, and there were dinners laid on for us and so on. It was very different to what we were used to'. Likewise, Myung calls it 'one of those storybook tales'.

To date, the LP has sold over 600,000 copies, which helped it earn Gold status by the RIAA and become their only record with a Top 10 hit on *Billboard*'s Hot Mainstream Rock Tracks chart ('Pull Me Under'). It's still their most commercially successful album as well, and the amount of praise it's received over the years can't be overstated. For instance, in 2011, *Guitar World* ranked it at #7 in their Top Ten list of 1992 guitar albums; in 2013, it was named the best metal album of all time in a *Loudwire* fan-voted March Metal Madness poll; and in 2017, it placed at #95 in *Rolling Stone* magazine's '100 Greatest Metal Albums of All Time' list. Clearly, *Images and Words* was invaluable not only to the future of Dream Theater but also to the future of the genre, and fans all over the world remained awake and alert for what would come next.

'Pull Me Under' (Moore)

As we've discussed, 'Pull Me Under' – which started out as an instrumental called 'Oliver's Twist' and later appeared in the video game Guitar Hero: World Tour – is more or less single-handedly responsible for the group's massive rise. Ironically, and as Wilson comments, it would also become 'a millstone around their necks for many years to come', with fans and labels expecting them to easily recapture that lightning in a bottle with every single that followed. Obviously, that never happened, and although its swift career-boost is now seen as a fortunate fluke, the song's status as an exhilarating first impression of Dream Theater 2.0 – complete with a new singer, a new producer, and advanced craftsmanship – has never waned.

With both indirect and overt references to Shakespeare's *Hamlet* and an abrupt ending meant as a nod to the Beatles' 'I Want You (She's So Heavy)' from *Abbey Road*, the track doesn't skimp on allusions that some people might miss. Yet, every other facet of it is ceaselessly enticing enough to warrant its meteoric popularity. For one thing, Petrucci's Egyptian-esque main riff (which Portnoy, Myung, and Moore decorate with mysterious zeal) is now a rite of passage for all stylistically inclined new guitarists. Of course, LaBrie's entrance carries some of the band's most famous lyrics – 'Lost in the sky / Clouds roll by and I roll with them' – as well, and it instantly insinuates at how perfectly his theatrically silky persona fits their formula. As it goes, 'Pull Me Under' barrels through its mesmerizing musicianship and catchy choruses with the production, adventurousness, and confidence of a top-tier act, bolstering from the get-go how much development they'd made since the respectable but flawed days of *When Dream and Day Unite*. In many ways, then, *this* is the true introduction of Dream Theater.

'Another Day' (Petrucci)

Influenced by Petrucci's father's fight against cancer, this was released as a single and music video in the summer of 1993; sadly, neither took off, which is odd considering how accessible and relatable they are. The ballad begins with Moore and Petrucci playing identical chords on piano and acoustic guitar, respectively, while LaBrie issues his now-trademark grief-stricken murmurs. The softer parts sustain that tender appeal amidst delicate notes and percussion – with bittersweet saxophone interludes from BearTracks owner Jay Beckenstein instilling devastating resonance – while the heavier parts find LaBrie leaping into higher registers as the rhythmic section intensifies toward a pained electric guitar solo. That said, 'Another Day' never insults its subject matter with flagrant showiness; instead, its warm and tasteful splendour does justice to the topic while also demonstrating how adept Dream Theater were at humbler songwriting and arranging.

Chris Painter's video is a fine complement, too, as it shows the band playing in-between black and white shots of a pensive young girl – who appeared on the cover of Images and Words – and of a father and son in a hospital as they react to MRI scans. While some of its angles and transitions are a bit too early '90s, it nonetheless packs as much of a punch as the piece itself and deserves more attention than it got.

'Take the Time' (Moore, Petrucci, Portnoy, Myung)

A collaborative effort between all four longstanding members, this third entry – originally known as 'Grab That Feel' – is a response to 'the band's period of record label and singer woes'; it also uses voiceovers of Frank Zappa, The Beastie Boys, Public Enemy, Kurtis Blow, and the film *Cinema Paradiso*. Issued as a single between 'Pull Me Under' and 'Another Day' – and with a music video also directed by Painter – it was even deemed 'our 'Roundabout' or 'Bohemian Rhapsody'' by Portnoy because of its multifaceted distinction. To the dismay of all involved, however, it failed to match what 'Pull me Under' managed commercially. As with 'Another Day', though, that's surprising given how special the track is.

In a way, the trippy lavishness of its first measures foreshadows 'Metropolis—Part I', with chaotic guitar licks steering jackhammer syncopation and hostile synths. Myung then helps it settle into a friskier groove as LaBrie's verses switch between gruff, almost hip-hop attitude and thoughtful reserve. The hyperactive chorus – fleshed out with backing harmonies – is nearly as fetching as that of 'Pull Me Under'. Next, a brief glimpse of gentle introspection – 'Let my senses fall away / I can see much clearer now / I'm blind' – gives way to highly intricate instrumental asides; before long, Dream Theater recalls the chorus prior to Petrucci leading a rigorous finale with more six-string commotion. In this way, 'Take the Time' is indisputably the most ruthlessly complicated portion of *Images and Words* so far, with each player taking a stab at gripping indulgences.

'Surrounded' (Moore)

Another piano ode at heart, 'Surrounded' keeps *Images and Words*' pattern of alternating heavy and light selections in its sequencing. Moore clarifies: '[It] was just a song I arranged first as a keyboard riff. We've never done that before, where the keyboard is doing the rhythm... I really didn't think that we were going to use it when I wrote it'. Fortunately, the rest of Dream Theater decided to develop it into a tune whose exact meaning is abstract and open to interpretation, yet at the same time, its luscious sorrow can't help but attract all who hear it to some extent. In particular, Moore's piano chords and synths provide an elegant foundation for LaBrie's wispy ponderings. Eventually, Portnoy and Petrucci enter with hearty and dynamic dispositions as Moore periodically adds new shades. Sure, there's a sliver of '80s power ballad cheese to it – and it's a comparatively weak offering overall – but it's by no means wasted time. At the very least, it bests nearly everything on *When Dream and Day Unite* and its placement in-between two compositional juggernauts is quite appreciated.

'Metropolis—Part I: The Miracle and the Sleeper' (Petrucci)

By far the most sophisticated and striving thing Dream Theater had written by this point, this centrepiece of *Images and Words* is – pardon the pun – a miraculous work from start to finish. Its original title was 'Crumbling Metropolis' and Petrucci added the 'Part I' as a joke, never intending for there to be a sequel. Conceptually, he based it on an undisclosed TV documentary. While *Metropolis Pt. 2* reframes this one narratively, it has no definitive story or meaning in and of itself. Many people speculate that it revolves around Rome being founded by two competitive brothers, Romulus and Remus. Interestingly, it went through several phases and was performed live ahead of this finalized version being released as a promotional cassette in 1992. No matter its purpose or history, though, 'Metropolis—Part I' is still heralded as a magnum opus – *PROG* put it at #34 in their '100 Greatest Prog Songs Of All Time' 2018 write-up – and for good reason.

Before delving in, it must be said that much of 'Metropolis— Part I' now earns extra favour for how it ties into *Metropolis Pt. 2* melodically, lyrically, and musically. In other words, knowing how well several of these ideas would be reimagined nearly a decade later adds elation and appreciation. Nevertheless, it's downright ingenious all on its own. Right away, the sleigh bells at the start are immediately intriguing and innovative, and they juxtapose well the gloomy bass note, futuristic synth motif, threatening guitar strikes, and charging drums that surround them. Petrucci and Moore are brilliantly in synch during this first chunk, with Portnoy relentlessly dancing captivating circles around them. As for LaBrie, he gives arguably his best routine on the entire record here in terms of both performance and melodies. As such, it's already a contender for *Images and Words*' top track, and it's only just begun.

Indeed, the real magic of it comes about halfway in, when Petrucci and

Moore trade-off overwhelmingly enchanting hooks via newly vivid textures. The rhythm section maneuverers them along with spellbinding flair as well, showcasing better than ever how unmatched they are as a shared creative force. From there, Petrucci, Moore and Portnoy act as a sporadic casing for Myung's blistering and bouncy solo before the guitarist and keyboardist add their own unified wrath. After several more measures of wonderfully dizzying flashiness, Portnoy kicks off a condensed and penetrating climb toward LaBrie's dreamy resolve. By the end, you're left breathless and in awe, completely aware of how special this band is. Nearly thirty years later, 'Metropolis— Part I' is still an isolated masterpiece and the fact that it subsequently bred one of the greatest progressive metal albums of all time seven years later only adds to its admiration.

'Under a Glass Moon' (Petrucci)
Despite some challenging breaks and multilayered coatings, the formerly named 'The Battle of Jimmy Cocoa and Fish-Face' is a fairly basic stadium rocker. Everyone gives their all throughout its duration – don't get me wrong – but only Moore is truly magnetic due to his quirky embellishments (which the other players suavely enhance). The remaining aspects of 'Under a Glass Moon' are a bit by-the-numbers, especially since Dream Theater had already done tricks and turns like these previously on the album. Similarly, they'd scribed more tempting sentiments than, say, 'Beneath a summer sky / Under glass moonlight / Night awaits the lamb's arrival', so there isn't as much desire to debate what it all means. It'd stand out more if the other entries weren't so superior.

'Wait for Sleep' (Moore)
Case in point: 'Wait for Sleep', Images and Words' second to last statement and one of the group's utmost deeds in terms of evocative and refined songwriting. It focuses on how 'a girl whose sister died' deals with the tragedy since 'she's not religious'. Aside from LaBrie's heartrending recital, it was fashioned entirely by Moore, whose exquisite piano work is as infectious as it is distressing. Gratefully, his wordplay does justice to the sounds, with the closing verse – 'In with the ashes / Or up with the smoke from the fire / With wings up in heaven / Or here, lying in bed / Palm of her hand to my head / Now and forever curled / In my heart and the heart of the world' – radiating poetic grandeur. Over the years, Dream Theater would become increasingly criticised for prioritizing style over substance, but pieces like 'Wait for Sleep' testify to how superb they always were at no-frills songwriting.

'Learning to Live' (Myung)
Myung penned this endcap after the growing AIDS crisis and modified its first lines – 'There was no time for pain / No energy for anger / The sightlessness of hatred slips away' – from Ayn Rand's Atlas Shrugged. There's a playful

peculiarity to Moore's passages during the introductory jam, as well as a tantalisingly dramatic drive from the other musicians. It's here that the influence of 1970s progressive rock titans like Jethro Tull, Rush, Yes, and Genesis are most palpable. Afterwards, LaBrie's angsty sermon is hugely striking, especially with its supporting harmonies. For the most part, this template is intensified but maintained until some more spiritedly retro segues give in to tropical acoustic guitar work and shuffling percussion. Following more life-affirming and fascinating instrumentation, 'Learning to Live' niftily gives you goosebumps by reprising the core of 'Wait for Sleep' with scorching closure from Petrucci, Moore, and Portnoy stacked on top. LaBrie returns to propose some lasting thoughts before Myung's lone lead paves the way for a poignant outro that includes angelic chants. It's a beautiful method for wrapping things up and solidifying the greatness of Images and Words forever.

Bonuses

In terms of CDs, the latest offerings of *Images and Words* are 2014's *The Studio Albums 1992 - 2011* box set from Roadrunner Records and the 2011 Japanese Ltd. Edition from Wea Japan. That said, Atco put out a limited edition gold & solid red vinyl in 2016. In all cases, there are no extras, which is disappointing since Portnoy released *Images and Words Demos 1989–91* on YtseJam Records in 2005.

'Awake' (1994)

Personnel:
James LaBrie: vocals
John Petrucci: guitar, backing vocals
John Myung: bass
Kevin Moore: keyboards, co-lead vocals (11)
Mike Portnoy: drums, percussion, backing vocals (7)
John Purdell: engineer, mixing, backing vocals (6)
Duane Baron: engineer, mixing, backing vocals (6)
Prix-mo: Spoken Words (5)
Rich Kern: programming (11)
Larry Freemantle: cover art
Donald May: art direction
Dan Muro: art direction
Dennis Keeley: photography
Produced at One on One Studios and Devonshire Studios in North Hollywood, Los Angeles,May – July 1994 by John Purdell and Duane Baron
UK and US release date: October 1994.
Highest chart places: UK: 65, USA: 32
Running time: 74:56
Current edition: Music on Vinyl / East West Records America 2016 silver limited edition vinyl

As gratifying as it was for Dream Theater to finally get a breakthrough collection, it also meant that whatever came next would be deeply scrutinized by both newfound devotees and business associates. 'Suddenly, we had half a million people there waiting to hear the follow-up to *Images and Words*. Somebody once said that you have your whole life to prepare for your first album and about two months to prepare the follow-up, and that was very much the situation we faced in early 1994', Portnoy reflects. That time constraint, combined with more opposition from the higher-ups about their style, meant that the band was balancing several burdens simultaneously. Taking all of that into consideration, it's extremely commendable that what resulted – *Awake* – is so bold yet suitable. If *Images and Words* predicted the vibrant variety of *Six Degrees of Inner Turbulence*, this successor inadvertently predicted the heavier and rawer edge of *Train of Thought*. Thus, it's not as wide-ranging or enticing as its forerunner, but it still finds the group alluringly broadening their palette while continuing to establish a base identity.

Like any creative partnership comprised of strong and stubborn personalities, Dream Theater had internal conflicts from time to time. That was positively the case when *Awake* was getting underway in February 1994. Actually, they would squabble over such minute details as single notes and chord changes. Portnoy laughs, 'We would argue for days over shit like that.... You had four

21

very opinionated elements in the band. The fighting never came to blows, but there was a lot of bickering'.

Adding to those tensions was the label – now East West, which, like Atco, fell under Atlantic – because they hounded Dream Theater to make lightning strike twice by 'creating a heavier album, which they pre-supposed would be easier to market'. To be fair, this is understandable seeing as how acts like Nirvana, Pearl Jam, Alice in Chains, Pantera, and Anthrax were reaching so many people at the time. Whether consciously or not, they wound up doing exactly that via the 'more riff-based style of writing' sparked by Petrucci's new seven-string guitar and Myung's six-string bass. Even so, the lack of a 'Pull Me Under' equivalent on *Awake* disappointed the East West executives since they were more focused on the LP's monetary profitability than its creative quality.

Perhaps it's not too shocking, then, that Moore announced his separation from Dream Theater during the completion of *Awake*. As Wilson puts it, he seemed 'sullen and increasingly lonely' in the studio, giving little input and looking like 'a man going through the motions'. While just about everyone around him was saddened and stunned by the seemingly abrupt move, Petrucci took the news especially hard because they had such a deep and lengthy history. He bemoans: 'Not only were we friends but we had been playing music together for so long that I almost couldn't conceive of playing without him... Dream Theater were going in a certain musical direction, and maybe he didn't want to play that kind of music any more'.

On the other hand, LaBrie claims to have seen the writing on the wall regarding Moore's exit – with private conversations alluding to Moore's quest to 'figure out what's really important' to him in life – whereas Portnoy argues that Moore's singledom was a bitter pill to swallow in the midst of his bandmates having romantic relationships. In a statement distributed a few months later, Moore at least confirmed the former assumption by specifying that the decision was 'the best thing' for all involved since he desperately needed to concentrate on his own material. Controversially, LaBrie also reveals that he infrequently wonders 'where the albums might have gone musically if Kevin had stayed in the band and had been passionate about it'. Clearly, no one will ever know for sure, but as we'll get to shortly, his replacement undoubtedly equalled – if not surpassed – his gifts.

By and large, though, making *Awake* was far more congenial than making *Images and Words*. One of the major reasons was the entrance of John Purdell and Duane Brown as the producers. Their work on Ozzy Osbourne's *No More Tears* validated their credentials, and Oliver felt that they could help nail the required heaviness. Portnoy gloats that the pair were 'great and so easygoing', striking an ideal compromise between the actions of the previous producers by 'spending a lot of time on the sound and recording process' while also granting some occasional insights and 'an objective ear'. Petrucci concurs, revelling in how Dream Theater were free to 'express [themselves] a lot more genuinely... everybody walked away being completely satisfied with their performances and their sounds'. Curiously, they were banned from the mixing stages of *Awake* – conducted at Unique Studios in New York City – because each player unintentionally lacked objectivity and wanted his contributions highlighted more. Once Purdell and Baron were left to their own devices, they could properly create the best blend.

As for the title and look of the record, LaBrie surmises that 'Awake' is the perfect word to describe [it]', rejoicing, 'What we're basically talking about is the awareness of your existence – becoming closer and more in touch with yourself and ultimately discovering what works best for you'. It's no coincidence that the front of *Awake* resembles that of *Images and Words*, as Larry Freemantle repeated his method of integrating ideas from the songs – 'a clock face showing a time of 6:00, a mirror, and a spider encircled by a web' – into the pictures. He says that the group was very keen about what they desired. Regrettably, he was forced to use Photoshop to finish it because the company they'd used to finalize it last time, Access Images, now ceased to exist.

When *Awake* finally arrived in October 1994, it proved to be particularly divisive in Britain, with even 'the usually sympathetic *Metal Hammer*' criticizing both the record and progressive metal as 'a very adolescent notion of what 'grown-up' music might sound like'. However, American publications like *Guitar World* were more receptive to what Dream Theater were up to this time around. In any case, it landed the band their first chart placement in the UK – at #65 – and a much better result in the US, at #32. Today, Portnoy isn't shy about acknowledging the resentment he felt at how 'bands that were so anti musicianship' – namely, grunge acts – were stealing the spotlight from them. Furthermore, he considers the era to be the end of metal as they knew it.

In hindsight, *Awake* is deservedly held in higher esteem. It's been praised in numerous retrospectives on metal music in 1994, with *Rock Hard* magazine putting it at #390 in their book *The 500 Greatest Rock & Metal Albums of All Time* and *Guitar World* granting it the top spot in their 'Superunknown: 50 Iconic Albums That Defined 1994' article. At times more brooding and bizarre than *Images and Words*, it is the weaker of the two options, but it's inarguably a unique and rewarding accomplishment all the same. What's more, *Awake* serves as a fine final component of the Moore trilogy before yet another change in members – alongside *A Change of Seasons*– would formally greet the world eleven months later.

'6:00' (Moore)

The secluded and more mechanical nature of Awake is apparent from the opening synthesis of irregular syncopation and robotic keyboard patterns. Honestly, it's the first of several times that Moore channels the cold meticulousness of Keith Emerson in the set. Naturally, this harshness is enhanced by Petrucci's revved-up riffs and the spoken samples from John Huston's 1987 adaption of James Joyce's story 'The Dead'. Likewise, that tone applies to its subject matter, with lines like 'So many ways to drown a man / So

many ways to drag him down / Some are fast and some take years and years'
and 'He finally found the sound but he's in too deep' hinting at Moore's need
to leave Dream Theater for the sake of his own art and contentment. Labrie's
unexpectedly rough deliveries fit the environment faultlessly, too, and the
calmer bridge about three minutes in is a nice deviation from the compelling
shrieks around it. Overall, '6:00' isn't the marvel that 'Pull Me Under' was, but
it's definitely a good signal of the album's overarcing vibe.

'Caught in a Web' (LaBrie, Petrucci)
The second single from Dream Theater's third outing, 'Caught in a Web' is a
welcoming yet dark track that relates to deception and denial regarding societal
expectations. Apart from that, its meaning is a bit ambiguous, yet its aggression
is upheld from beginning to end. There's a malicious edge to Moore's synths,
and LaBrie sounds categorically wicked at times. The rest of the gang provides
a comparably clear-cut grounding for the chorus, plus pleasing – if also run-
of-the-mill – interwoven tapestries during the verses and instrumental breaks.
Petrucci and Portnoy's portions are expressly inviting as well, helping the piece
rise above its rudimentary majority.

'Innocence Faded' (Petrucci)
This one kind of acts as a response to '6:00' since Petrucci wrote it about
his deteriorating bond with Moore. He clarifies: 'There was a feeling of it
not being the same way it had been, and the realization that things were not
always going to remain the same'. Ponderings such as 'Distant like brothers /
Wearing apathetic displays / Sharing flesh like envy in cages / Condescending
/ Not intending to end' can certainly be interpreted along those lines. It's
appropriate that Petrucci's playing at the start induces a sense of catharsis as
if he's just come to terms with misfortune; LaBrie's airy singing, alongside the
mostly transcendental arrangement and complementary chants, is similarly
cleansing. He hits some of the highest notes of his career here – which is
obviously laudable – and the complex and/or mystical transitions that run
throughout it are dependably seamless yet substantial.

'I. Erotomania' (Moore, Portnoy, Petrucci, Myung)
The wordless first fragment of the 'A Mind Beside Itself' suite, 'Erotomania'
conjures ELP's 'Karn Evil 9' in its machine-like remoteness. Oddly enough,
it was originally part of 'Pull Me Under' before the band realized that it just
'didn't work' there; Portnoy also reports that it was written 'off the cuff' as 'a bit
of a joke and parody'. To this day, it's one of Dream Theater's most treasured
instrumentals, with clever references to the sequential two-thirds of the series
amid a plethora of quick-witted tempo and melodic shifts. Around those
sections, the group compromises between forceful and fragile temperaments
exceptionally, with Moore and Petrucci incorporating several instances of
sublime camaraderie. True, it is a dash too repetitive by the end, but there's no

refuting the strengths of its central concepts and enamouring aptitude.

'II. Voices' (Petrucci)

The volatile nature of 'Erotomania' also arouses the basis of 'Voices': mental illnesses like schizophrenia. Petrucci explains: 'It's about a psychotic disorder. The facts... are based on actual medical documents', including 'a guy who felt that his skin was inside out'. There are also religious allusions to make the song more pungent and allegorical. Myung's preliminary loop – assisted by Petrucci, Moore, and Portnoy's asymmetrical crashes – is devious and sad. A bit later, bizarre sound effects efficiently aid Moore and LaBrie's piano ballad emphasis, resulting in a riveting principal hook.

The second half of it kicks off with rapper Prix-mo reading a cautionary excerpt from *Cultural Revolution* over a disastrous backdrop. Petrucci's clean strums and Portnoy's dignified beats then chaperon LaBrie's peaceful insights. His rising bellow encloses a tightly paced wah-wah guitar solo that precedes a final appearance of the chorus and an exhilarating climax in general. Best of all, this frenzy makes the concluding segment of 'A Mind Beside Itself' even more prevailing for its stylistic juxtaposition.

'III. The Silent Man' (Petrucci)

According to LaBrie, this acoustic elegy revolves around 'communication breakdown, for instance, between a father and son. We feel that we have to play certain roles when around one of our parents, and we never really get to know the real person'. That sensitivity is encapsulated vigorously – and in strong contrast to the rage of the previous two pieces – in Petrucci's patient chords and LaBrie's meditative assertions. There's a palpable intimacy to the duo's untethered exposure, and it wisely remains classily tranquil once the strings, supplemental singing, and nonchalant percussion join in. Petrucci's brief solo is lovely as well. All in all, the whole-hearted sparsity of 'The Silent Man' makes it a great tune that once again fortifies that fact that Dream Theater doesn't need in-your-face virtuosity or extended structures to prosper.

In addition, 'The Silent Man' got its own video in early 1995 to correspond with its place as another single from *Awake* and its own EP (which also included a demo of 'Take the Time' and an otherwise unreleased instrumental, 'Eve'). A mix of B&W and colour images, its incorporation of the band playing in a barn while an old man looks into a mirror and contemplates his life is a modest but timely depiction. At first, Portnoy wanted to direct it, going as far as to drum up 'a treatment ... (basically a rough synopsis)' for the other members of the band 'using a fake name'. Unfortunately, the label only offered him a co-directing credit alongside Pamela Birkhead.

'The Mirror' (Portnoy)

A precursor to Portnoy's 'Twelve-Step Suite', it's inspired by his battle with alcoholism and is directly referenced in later material ('Repentance' and 'This

Dying Soul', for instance). Its affected synths – aligned with its gruff riffs and explosive drumming – yield a gloomily aggravated starting point. LaBrie's crotchety lead is apropos, and Portnoy's scant narration adds emotion by standing in for internal monologues he's no doubt had. Samples from the films *Falling in Love* and *Damage* meld into a serene score before the track's greatest moment – a hint at the upcoming 'Space-Dye Vest' – emerges with ingenious eloquence and then disappears just as quickly. Petrucci's wacky tenors near the end add some curiosity, too.

'Lie' (Moore)

Considering that 'Lie' – the lead single and music video from *Awake* – was initially a part of 'The Mirror', it makes sense that the two bleed into each other. LaBrie says that it arose out of 'a groove' that they used to jam to. Its prominence on the aftermath of betrayal (which could also be shrouded glimpses into Moore's state of mind) is captured well by verses like 'Doing fine but don't waste my time / Tell me what it is you want to say / You sin, you win, just let me in / Hurry, I've been out in the rain all day'. Honestly, it's largely uninteresting in every other way, with a generic metal veneer and bland melodies preventing it from feeling adequately worthwhile. Ralph Ziman's rather well-known video finds the band performing in various New York locations as the camera rushes up to them. It's a pretty typical approach for the time, and even if it's undoubtedly dated now, it's still enjoyable.

'Lifting Shadows Off a Dream' (Myung)

'Lifting Shadows Off a Dream' came from a poem Myung wrote and a two-chord progression that the band struggled to turn into a full composition. There's a nice atmosphere created by his back-and-forth movements, Portnoy's light taps, Petrucci's harmonics, and Moore's synth bedrocks. LaBrie sounds particularly breathless here, which fits, and its generally restful body and graceful words offer soothingly poignant breaths of fresh air. There's a bit of interspersed franticness, yes, yet it's almost entirely sedative and philosophical. As such, it's an often unsung hero of Dream Theater's discography.

'Scarred' (Petrucci)

The longest selection on *Awake*, it glimpses at the earthy breeziness of 1997's *Falling Into Infinity* with its preliminary pained guitar solo, tribal syncopation, and commercially appealing verses and harmonies. Naturally, there's some brasher antagonism in the mix, too, making for one of the most steadily attractive exchanges of ferocity and composure on the record. This duality is suitable since 'Scarred' was written as a commentary on depression – that is, after it was demoed to misheard lyrics to The Clash's 'Rock the Casbah'. By Dream Theater standards, it's not very demanding technically, but the constant ebb and flow of character – including some utterly revitalizing and gorgeous flashes – earns it applause even if it could do more to deserve its eleven-minute runtime.

'Space-Dye Vest' (Moore)

Marked by many as the most atypical track on *Awake*, Moore's 'Space-Dye Vest' – which was brought to the band in its completed form – is also the best of the bunch. In a chat with *RAW* magazine shortly after the LP dropped, LaBrie divulged that Moore wrote it about falling in love with a model he saw in a fashion publication: 'He carried [it] around with him for ages, but he realized that the only way the innocence could be kept, so that he could retain that love for her, was if she stayed on the page. If he'd met her, all that would have been lost. A strange song'. Ironically, Portnoy goes a step further by confirming that if they knew that Moore was leaving before they agreed to include it, it probably wouldn't have made the cut.

Its unusual origin and circumstance notwithstanding, 'Space-Dye Vest' is a magnificently inimitable and anguished ode. Built upon stylishly romantic piano chord ascensions and a fetchingly morose melody – which LaBrie reproduces expertly – it fully absorbs you in its stirring catastrophe from the onset. Its final admittances – 'And I'll smile, and I'll learn to pretend / And I'll never be open again / And I'll have no more dreams to defend / And I'll never be open again' – are especially moving. Audio clips from *A Room with a View* and *The Fifth Estate*, among other sources, enhance the theme of loneliness spurred by impossible longing; similarly, the distorted ambience and influx of drums and electric guitar seep in almost without notice because of how overwhelmingly stunning Moore and Labrie's pairing stays. Twenty-five years later, 'Space-Dye Vest' remains a one-of-a-kind gem.

Bonuses

Awake has seen many forms since 1994 and almost all of them have added nothing new to the table. However, the above-mentioned 'Eve' did arrive as a bonus disc with the original Japanese version. It begins with ethereal endurance before chimes and thoughtful piano chords introduce unswerving drumming and clean guitar licks. Aside from some electric guitar outcries toward the end, it sustains this essence to act like the coda or closing credits of a journey. Given Dream Theater's usual instrumental madness at the time, 'Eve' is unexpectedly subdued, so it's a valuable lost treasure.

'A Change of Seasons' (1995)

Personnel:
James LaBrie: vocals
John Petrucci: guitar
John Myung: bass
Derek Sherinian: keyboards
Mike Portnoy: drums, cover concept
Doug Oberkircher: engineer (1), mixing
Andy Scarth: engineer (2 – 5)
Robert Siciliano: assistant engineer (1)
Vinnie Kowalski: live engineer (2 – 5)
Larry Freemantle: art direction
Joseph Cultice: photography
Produced at BearTracks Studios in Suffern, New York and Ronnie Scott's Jazz Club
in London, January – May 1995 by David Prater
UK and US release date: September 1995.
Highest chart places: UK: 88, USA: 58
Running time: 57:30
Current edition: Music on Vinyl / East West Records America 2018 vinyl

Feeling a bit defeated by the treatment of *Awake* – as well as the departure
of yet another crucial part of the team – Dream Theater decided to postpone
working on their next proper LP. Instead, they set their sights on finding a
new keyboardist, touring as much as possible, and finally recording the one
composition that'd been hanging over them for several years: the immensely
personal behemoth known as 'A Change of Seasons'. Along the way, they'd face
a few more obstacles, but the end result would be well worth it. Demonstrating
Dream Theater's incredible knack for both constructing a side-long declaration
and characteristically yet faithfully reproducing the works of several influences
in a live setting, *A Change of Seasons* is still a fan favourite and a highpoint in
the band's whole history. Beyond that, the EP is perhaps their most important
release thus far because of how much it foreshadows their future trajectory in
the studio and on stage.

For better or worse, Dream Theater were already quite experienced in
auditioning potential new players when it came time to replace Moore. Among
the most promising candidates was Jens Johansson, a Swedish keyboardist
who'd shown great potential with Yngwie Malmsteen. As a matter of fact,
the band's management and label pre-emptively hired and announced
him as an official member without Dream Theater's knowledge, let alone
approval. Logically, that offer was quickly withdrawn. Portnoy specifies that
the rest of the band 'never really clicked with him' or knew how he'd be
'in terms of a composer or as someone who can contribute parts in verses
or choruses'. Fascinatingly, Jordan Rudess first came into the picture at this
point, too, recalling, '[*Images and Words*] was the first time I had heard any

kind of progressive metal, so I was excited and suitably impressed with their abilities'. Long story short, Rudess had also been approached by guitarist Steve Morse to join the Dixie Dregs; after considering the financial and personal responsibilities of being a new father, Rudess decided to pass on Dream Theater – at least for the time being – and accept Morse's offer. He did play with them at a gig in Burbank, California in late 1994, however.

Finally, a fellow Berklee graduate named Derek Sherinian threw his name into the hat thanks to a friend, Al Pitrelli, who also knew Petrucci. Because he 'sounded like Kevin', had played with established acts like Kiss, and shared an interest in artists like 'Ozzy, Van Halen, and Judas Priest', Sherinian was given a trial run as a live keyboardist. Unquestionably excited about and thankful for the job, he nonetheless felt some intimidation regarding the complexity and abundance of music he had to learn. In fact, in preparation for the 'Waking Up the World' tour – which began in October 1994 – he 'would play the songs at night over and over on a loop' until they became 'subliminally programmed' into his head. Another consideration was how fans would receive him since Moore was so beloved. Rather than let it scare him away or spark any sort of resentment in him, he understood and accepted that some people would be 'immediately against it'. On the contrary, though, he won over most naysayers without hindrance and was given the full-time position along the way.

Just as that problem was being solved, another was about to rear its ugly head. While on Christmas vacation in Cuba with his wife, a poor choice of breakfast caused LaBrie to suffer extreme sicknesses and prolonged vocal issues. As he recalls, 'If you've ever had food poisoning, you'll know that you wish you were dead', and the upcoming pressures of a Japanese tour to kick off 1995 certainly didn't help matters. After speaking to an ear, nose and throat specialist, LaBrie was told 'not to sing for six months to a year' – an impossibility, of course – and that 'it was literally going to be years before [he] could sing or sound like [he] had done before'. Once the tour commenced, LaBrie happily found that 'though uncomfortable, he could at least continue' and sing well enough. He still had concerns and deficiencies throughout the subsequent weeks, but he pulled through and remains profoundly thankful to his bandmates for sticking by him. By his account, his voice only came back completely around the time of *Six Degrees of Inner Turbulence*, so it's amazing that he sounds so good on *A Change of Seasons*.

After traveling to Europe from Japan – where they also endured an earthquake that killed roughly 4,000 people and measured 7.2 on the Richter scale – they stopped by Ronnie Scott's Jazz Club in London to do something unexpected. Portnoy persuaded the rest of the group to 'perform a set consisting entirely of cover versions, as well as... invite some special guests to perform alongside them in front of an invitation-only audience of around 300'. Among the extra musicians were Napalm Death singer Barney Greenway, Marillion vocalist Steve Hogarth and guitarist Steve Rothery, and even Yes guitarist Steve Howe. Although they played on tracks not included on *A Change of Seasons* – such as Metallica's 'Damage Inc.', the Beatles' 'Happiness is a Warm Gun', and Yes' 'Close to the Edge' – several other tunes by artists like Elton John, Led Zeppelin, and Pink Floyd appear on the EP. Arguably, the inclusion of these songs generally helped normalize elaborate progressive rock/ metal covers of simpler songs.

As for the title track, it finally saw the light of day due in part to the overwhelming demand from fans online. The song had been 'semi-mythical' for years – and it'd even been performed live twice in a more embryonic form – so it was only a matter of time before someone on the Ytsejam mailing list started a petition for East West Records to let Dream Theater record it. Unsurprisingly, it was extended to 23+ minutes to rival and pay homage to earlier benchmarks like Genesis' 'Supper's Ready' and Rush's '2112'. Portnoy also give details on how they decided to 'rework the whole thing and put the 1995 touch on it', including transforming lyrics and melodies. An added bit of excitement came from it being the first proper recording with Sherinian fully on board.

As alluded to previously, its dominant concept about the 'circle of life' and the notion of 'carpe diem' ('seize the day') arose from the death of Portnoy's mother. As the story goes, he was in Health class on November 16, 1984, and his teacher spoke about 'how precious life is, and how you never know when somebody you love or something in your life is going to change at any moment and when you least expect it'. That night, his mother was 'getting ready to get on a private jet to go to Atlantic City', so he kissed her goodbye and said that he loved her. Sadly, the plane crashed and she was killed, making the gesture even more serendipitous. He admits, 'If that teacher hadn't given that lesson that day, I would probably have run out the door and I would never have had a final moment with my Mom'. Ideas presented in the Robin Williams films *The World According to Garp* and *Dead Poets Society* also inspired 'A Change of Seasons'.

In exchange for letting them complete the project, Derek Oliver made a surprising demand: David Prater had to produce it. He describes how 'the commercial failure of *Awake*' made him want to 'rekindle the relationship with Prater – even under duress' because Prater was the one producer who 'fully understood what Dream Theater were actually all about'. Predictably, the group was vehemently opposed to the choice at first, but eventually, they caved and approached the situation as unbiasedly as possible. To further capture the magic of *Images and Words*, they returned to BearTracks Studios and engineer Doug Oberkircher as well.

Although the biggest rivalry during those sessions – between Portnoy and Prater –was mostly resolved this time around, Prater did manage to anger LaBrie by challenging the 'method of recording his vocals'. Prater claims that Petrucci asked him to 'do something about James carrying on like Robert Plant'; in addition, he says that LaBrie became hostile and 'agitated because he wasn't getting his performance right', leading to arguments about composite vs punch-in vocal tracking and the number of takes they needed that both parties still disagree about. At the time, they even came close to physically altercating, which Portnoy found amusing: 'There was a part of me that was really happy to see someone else really fighting with Prater because [LaBrie] had proved it wasn't just me or Kevin Moore who were having problems with him'. As with *Images and Words*, though, their combative creative processes spawned a splendidly produced record.

Larry Freemantle was brought back to do the artwork, too; naturally, it draws heavily from 'A Change of Seasons'. Featuring a child 'perched in winter snow', 'an old man on an autumn beach', and even an allusion to November 16 'in the form of a calendar', it was compiled by digitally mixing photographs. Appropriately, Portnoy was the main source of guidance as well, with 'very specific' directions for 'what he wanted and where'.

Deservingly, *A Change of Seasons* – categorized as an EP because of its brief original content and because the band and the label 'didn't want it perceived as the latest studio Dream Theater album' – fared well once released. Admittedly, it didn't soar as highly on the US and UK charts; however, outlets like *Metal Hammer*, *Guitar for the Practicing Musician*, and *Kerrang!* were majorly encouraging (even if they also stressed that only those who were already fans would really worship it). Likewise, it'd been a bit hit with fans, giving them a substantial example of how well Dream Theater could scribe their own epics while also putting their flavour on classic and progressive rock standards of yesteryear. Both of these merits would significantly impact their output forever, but they'd disputably never do it better.

'A Change of Seasons' (Portnoy)

The first of seven chapters – and several instrumental portions – that make up 'A Change of Seasons', 'The Crimson Sunrise' starts with one of Petrucci's most recognizable principal acoustic guitar arpeggios. Sherinian accessorises with apt piano chords and heavenly synth tones while high-pitched bells intermittently mirror Petrucci's notes. Suddenly, the mood becomes livelier and angrier, with Portnoy and Myung injecting a crooked rhythm to offset some truly scratchy guitar riffs. It's deliciously hypnotic and gives way to some skilfully abrupt breaks before a marginally more diplomatic passage blends into Petrucci and Sherinian's sly nods at what will be numerous recurring themes. Behind them, Portnoy and Myung enchant with precise ire until a unified burst of eccentricity births more glorious insinuations of what's to come. Hence, 'The Crimson Sunrise' is a masterful overture whose theatrical departing guitar solo segues impeccably into the next phase, 'Innocence'.

More exquisite acoustic arpeggios and restrained percussion follow LaBrie's poetic opening statement: 'I remember a time / My frail, virgin mind / Watched the crimson sunrise / Imagined what it might find'. Despite some fierce electric guitar strums and Sherinian's shrill motif, 'Innocence' remains handsomely sensitive and searching, with LaBrie's melodies and harmonies doing a wonderful job of expressing Portnoy's woeful look back on life before he lost his mother. The subsequent stage, 'Carpe Diem', is presented via a slower

acoustic route and someone whispering, 'Carpe Diem. Seize the day'. From
there, LaBrie sings musingly about the advice of Portnoy's teacher until a clip
from *Dead Poets Society* – in which a student reads from Robert Herrick's 1648
poem 'To the Virgins, to Make Much of Time' – adds thematic weight amid
bells and foreboding low synth tones. That placidness then shifts into complex
panic when the mighty rhythmic section pounces on LaBrie as he yells about
Portnoy's mother 'preparing for her flight'.

Another wild instrumental break ensues as excerpts from Jon Voight – in
1983's dramatic film *Table for Five* – play. This potion, justly called 'The
Darkest of Winters', comes across like the lovechild of *Awake*'s 'Erotomania'
and *Systematic Chaos*' 'In the Presence of Enemies - Part I'. Although the
founding trio do plenty to represent the scornful sadness of the subject matter,
it's Sherinian's evocation of genre idol Rick Wakeman that impresses most. As
it goes, his piano chords – coupled with Petrucci's sleek licks and Portnoy's
off-kilter configuration – glimpse at the adventurous spirituality of 'Learning to
Live' from *Images and Words*. There are also some really zany outbursts that
hint at what Rudess will bring to Dream Theater's chemistry during his tenure.

A euphoric epiphany explodes into the liberating fifth division, 'Another
World'. LaBrie belts out words of energized remorse – 'Tripping through
the life fantastic / Lose a step and never get up / Left alone with a cold blank
stare / I feel like giving up' – over Sherinian's idyllic organ progression. Soon,
harmonic guitar plucks, downtrodden bass notes, stubborn syncopation,
triumphant piano chords, and warm guitar picking boost the wounded
atmosphere. Given LaBrie's aforementioned health anxieties during this
time, he may be exemplifying his own grief as much as Portnoy's; either way,
his performance here is outstanding technically and emotionally, conveying
each sentiment with absolute believability. This is especially true once the
arrangement becomes more erratic to border his attacks: 'I'm sick of all you
hypocrites / Holding me at bay / And I don't need your sympathy / To get me
through the day'. Petrucci's resultant guitar solo is perfectly crestfallen yet
conquering, too, as it moves toward another incensed verse and then a quick
callback to 'The Crimson Sunrise'.

Once there, a changeover into the Floydian final instrumental movement,
'The Inevitable Summer', occurs. It's basically a highly heartfelt guitar solo over
a rhythmic reference to 'The Crimson Sunrise' – that is until it manifests into a
monstrous and industrial fusion of metal riffs and percussion over Sherinian's
piercing dominance. Some more irregular alterations and clever reprises follow
– giving 'A Change of Seasons' delightful conceptual continuity – in anticipation
of the finale, the fittingly titled 'The Crimson Sunset'. LaBrie sounds
exuberantly self-assured as scattered compositional fluctuations pilot the track
toward its ultimate purification: 'Many years have come and gone / I've lived
my life but now must move on'. Smartly, the band brings back the 'gather ye
rosebuds while ye may' line in the process, and Sherinian's staunch piano
chords enrich the sense of victory. After a quick drum fill, the piece ends where

it started, leaving you grinning at its full-circle cohesion and appreciating its place as one of the best progressive metal suites of all time.

'Funeral for a Friend / Love Lies Bleeding' (Taupin, John)
The starting point of Elton John's 1973 opus, Goodbye Yellow Brick Road, these two compositions were not written to go together. Yet, the former's investigation of the music John wanted to hear at his funeral and the latter's use of death as the symbol for a bad break-up makes them inseparable. Predictably, Dream Theater do a very authentic adaption of it. Sure, their tones are tougher overall, but they follow John's template with surprising restraint and attention to detail (well, until the metal freak-out near the end). Likewise, LaBrie does a great job matching John's phrasing and inflections. All in all, it's a bit colder and more in-your-face than the original – so it's not quite as good – but it's nonetheless an almost immaculate rendition.

'Perfect Strangers' (Gillan, Blackmore, Glover)
The same can be said for this take on the 1984 Deep Purple classic, which Dream Theater performed with Bruce Dickinson on BBC radio prior to the Ronnie Scott's Jazz Club gig. True, the otherworldly keyboard effects near the end of Deep Purple's version – as well as their classic rock textures – are gone, but in their place is something that was debatably always missing: a killer guitar solo. That addition, plus the overarching dominant and more brutal nature of it all, places an enticing new sheen on its genuine foundation.

'The Rover / Achilles Last Stand / The Song Remains the Same' (Plant, Page)
What would a set of Dream Theater covers be without the requisite Led Zeppelin? Fortunately, the quintet choose three outstanding options for their medley. At the onset, Petrucci and Portnoy nail the classic duality of Page and Bonham, respectively, and they glide into 'Achilles Last Stand' – the proggiest Led Zeppelin song – with ease. It's a tad more constricted, yes, but it's definitely a worthwhile emulation. Along those lines, LaBrie is naturally less flamboyant and expressive than Plant was on Presence (or ever during Led Zeppelin's heyday), but he comes admirably close the whole time. Myung plays with stately calculation as Petrucci does his best to channel Page's solo style, and they transition into 'The Song Remains the Same' with matching meticulousness. Honestly, LaBrie gets a bit overbearing and incoherent at this point, but his uninhibited enthusiasm is alluring.

'The Big Medley' (Water, Livgren, Mercury, Perry, Schon, Morse, Rutherford, Banks, Collins)
Essentially, it's a hodgepodge of a half-dozen prized rock tunes that receive equally brief yet respectful consideration. First up is Pink Floyd's 'In the Flesh?'

with Petrucci, Sherinian, Myung, and Portnoy providing faultless impersonation of the preliminary portion. LaBrie's airy authoritativeness and echoed commands are awesome as well. Swiftly, an abridged copy of Kansas' 'Carry on Wayward Son' detonates with every element – except the singing – accounted for; afterwards, the 'Can't do this to me, baby' section of Queens' 'Bohemian Rhapsody' – complete with an exact recreation of Brian May's solo – reels into Journey's fervently romantic 'Loving', Touchin', Squeezin'. LaBrie's timbre is especially suitable for this one. A wordless rendering of the Dixie Dregs' 'Cruise Control' appears next and is quickly swallowed by the concluding homage, Genesis' 'Turn It On Again'. Portnoy's sprightly syncopation shines most before LaBrie thanks the cheering audience. While shovelling six songs into a ten-and-a-half minute combo unavoidably makes some of it seemed rushed, 'The Big Medley' is a jaw-dropping nod to a handful of Dream Theater's most beloved forebears.

'Falling Into Infinity' (1997)

Personnel:
James LaBrie: vocals
John Petrucci: guitar, backing vocals
John Myung: bass, Chapman Stick, backing vocals
Derek Sherinian: keyboards, backing vocals
Mike Portnoy: drums, percussion, backing vocals
Doug Pinnick: additional vocals (7)
Kevin Shirley: engineer, mixing
Rich Alvy: assistant engineer
Barbara Lipke: assistant engineer
Dave Swope: assistant mixing
Tony May: photography
Paul La Raja: photography
Storm Thorgerson: design
Peter Curzon: design
Sam Brooks: design
Produced at Avatar Studios in Manhattan, New York,June – July 1997 by Kevin Shirley
UK and US release date: September 1997.
Highest chart places: UK: 163, USA: 52
Running time: 78:12
Current edition: East West Records America 1997 CD

Ever since the release of 'Pull Me Under', Dream Theater were continually pressured to fashion more mainstream music. Despite proving how praiseworthy and popular their lengthy and intricate material can be with *A Change of Seasons*, this burden lingered when they began scribing the successive collection. As Wilson writes, the group 'were creating songs at a frantic pace, [but] they constantly had to endure the ignominy of having their carefully crafted demos repeatedly rejected by the record label moguls'. With new faces demanding contentious things behind-the-scenes – as well as more skirmishes brewing between the members – the making of their fourth full-length effort could've been smoother, to say the least. Equally, the finished product has always been the most divisive album of Dream Theater's early days (well, at least since LaBrie entered). Even the band disagrees on whether or not its relative accessibility is the result of external obligations or internal artistic decisions. No matter the conditions, *Falling Into Infinity* – which was going to be named *Stream of Consciousness* until they decided that it was a 'pompous' title– is more often than not a step down from *Images and Words* and *Awake*. However, its few flickers of excellence and its commitment to a fairly atypical milieu make it an underrated anomaly upon reconsideration.

At this point, East West Records became part of Elektra Records, with Sylvia Rhone running the show as its president. Thus, Oliver partially blames her for dictating *Falling Into Infinity*'s path: 'In my opinion, she would have dearly loved to have dropped Dream Theater…. she was clear that this time around they should come up with some shorter, snappier tracks so that radio could get behind the band again'. While Petrucci may insist – via a 2014 chat with *RockBook* – 'we wrote the kind of album we wanted to write', there's no denying the sting he felt when demos like 'Raise the Knife' and 'Where Are You Now' were rejected by Oliver in March 1996. Similarly, Portnoy is empathetic toward Oliver for being caught in the middle between Dream Theater and his bosses, but he still feels 'terribly disappointed' that Oliver didn't 'stand behind' them more instead of getting 'consumed by the machine'. Over the years, the other players have voiced similar grievances. Although a few discarded songs would eventually come out one way or another – including a 20+ minute prototype entitled 'Metropolis Part II' –one must wonder what the LP would consist of had Dream Theater been given unadulterated control over its selections.

For Sherinian, this was his first fully realized opportunity to be a part of the writing process, so he was observably excited about and devoted to it. Musically, Portnoy reflects, he was more than up to the task as someone 'who enjoyed jamming and giving ideas'; yet, when it came to lyrics, the other members had to increase their involvement. He also chimes in regarding how much hate Sherinian gets for the polarizing content on *Falling Into Infinity* by clarifying, 'His input had *nothing* to do with the change in direction. He was willing to write a twenty-minute epic just as much as he was to write a four-minute commercial song … Derek never imposed himself on us but was always willing to contribute wherever we wanted it'. Reasonably, Sherinian also responded to those who questioned his role with at least a tinge of annoyance: 'The bottom line is I'm here, I'm going to lay down some shit for the next record, and hopefully you'll like it. And if you don't, well, that's too bad'. In his defence, Sherinian – like his bandmates – rarely pushes himself in terms of complexity, but he never fails to add something useful and emblematic to the recipe.

Worsening their shared anxiety was the parting of co-managers Jim Pitulski and Rob Shore after the downward spiral of their corrosive partnership. Shore says that their 'personality clash' was a consequence of having 'too many cooks in the kitchen'. With their company, Roundtable Management, now expunged, Dream Theater were uncomfortably forced to pick a side; this inevitably led to arguments over loyalties and what's best for the group. Specifically, Petrucci sided with Shore while Portnoy preferred Pitulski, adding, 'It was kind of like if two parents get divorced, the child shouldn't have to decide who gets custody!' There were also discussions of leaving both men behind in favour of 'a bigger management company' so that they could 'quadruple' the band's following, as Sherinian explains. When Shore was finally chosen, Pitulski sued 'in an attempt to recoup some of his losses'. Unfortunately, the involvement of lawyers and added hassle of it all nearly drove Portnoy to break up the band altogether.

Obviously, that didn't happen, as Dream Theater continued working on the project. However, more changes at the label meant that a few trusted people – namely, Oliver – were replaced. Others, such as 'radio promotion people, the publicity people and marketing guys' were also let go, leaving Dream Theater with an assortment of strangers who had little interest in knowing and supporting them. Portnoy is explicitly critical of Oliver's stand-in, Josh Deutsch, for only caring about tunes 'that radio would play'. Nevertheless, Deutsch agreed to let them make *Falling Into Infinity* as long as a producer could be brought in to streamline it. Numerous names were thrown into the hat by the group – including Trevor Horn, Kevin Gilbert, and Paul Northfield – but in the end, Kevin Shirley got the job.

Portnoy comments that both parties were – at least initially – unenthusiastically open to working together. Whereas Shirley became more interested after seeing them live in Europe around Christmas 1996, Dream Theater remained largely reluctant toward his influence during the pre-production phase. With duration and monetization limitations pouring in from Elektra, the planned double disc was scaled down to a single one and Pro Tools was used to 'transform the sound and approach of many of the tracks'. These included 'Burning My Soul', 'Take Away My Pain', and 'Lines in the Sand'. 'It was the first time in the band's history when the songs were being re-written for us', Portnoy reflects, while conceding that he started to question his need and ability to steer so much of the Dream Theater vehicle. Shirley presently refutes the notion that he was working 'under any orders' from Elektra, correcting: 'It was just something I thought that I could do ... To be honest, I don't think the band were in the best shape at the time. They were struggling a lot with themselves ... and I think that I was one of the things they reached for that they thought may fix it'. At the very least, Myung and Sherinian now commend Shirley for his assistance and attitude during the process.

Dream Theater's resistance toward outside input was further tested when Shirley brought in a guest songwriter – Desmond Child – to help revise Petrucci's 'You Not Me'. Given Child's background with artists like Bon Jovi, Kiss, Cher, and Aerosmith, it's no shock that Shirley thought he could make the piece a hit. Portnoy, in particular, was sceptical, calling it 'a really tough pill to swallow' and feeling 'really bothered' that Child rewrote the song with only Petrucci instead of the whole team. In contrast, Petrucci was 'absolutely interested' in learning all he could about the craft from an 'established, respected professional'. He also recalls his trip to Child's home in Florida being very pleasant and eye-opening, so while he's more unwilling to let people tell him what to do today, he doesn't entirely regret the collaboration.

Luckily, finally making *Falling Into Infinity* was, according to Portnoy, an 'amazingly good time'. In fact, it even led to him having 'a great relationship' with Shirley afterwards. Part of the reason why it was so fulfilling for the members is that they had access to myriad instruments, such as 'two drum sets ... a dozen different amps and guitars ... [and] all these keyboards and a Mellotron organ'. He also reckons that the recording was thrillingly tentative since it saw them tracking the sequence 'song-by-song as opposed to instrument-by-instrument' so that each composition would 'have its own identity'. Myung mentions how this method allowed them to 'explore the nature of each song' more than they ever had. Although they questioned using a peripheral talent – Child – during the creation period, they welcomed the chance to use a friend and favourite singer, King's X vocalist/bassist Doug Pinnick, to bring more life to 'Lines in the Sand'. Petrucci, Sherinian, and Portnoy also had a bit of fun deeming themselves the Del Fuvio Monks – 'a secret organization based on mockery, bitter diatribe, and sardonicism', laughs Sherinian – when they provided backing vocals.

As an indirect sign of how much Dream Theater were becoming a leading name in modern progressive music, legendary genre designer Storm Thorgerson was brought in to help with the artwork. With the title in mind, he conjured up 'a bunch of his sketches based on that theme, and the results were amazing', smirks Myung. To achieve the main image, Thorgerson went as far as constructing a real platform and placing the model(s) 'in the sea off Camber Sands on the south coast of England'. He illuminates: 'We only actually used one platform, and we then took two shots before reversing them back in the studio.... But it is actually someone sitting on top of the platform. I think they were two different guys, and they were probably friends in order for it to be cheap!' Fascinatingly, he also mentions that the cover was somewhat stimulated by a Gary Larson *Far Side* cartoon in which 'a birdwatcher [is looking] through his binoculars at this bird that is about to attack him ... the main idea was that you're looking at the person, who is looking at the other person, who is looking back'. Regardless of how the music itself has aged, it endures as one of Dream Theater's most striking covers.

Upon release, *Falling Into Infinity* sold decently in America but 'failed to even hit the top 75 in the UK'. Wilson indicates that the 'somewhat muted reaction' from fans bothered Dream Theater more, though, as it was the first time they were chastised by their audience for supposedly 'selling out in an unashamed attempt to appeal to the mass market'. By and large, critics agreed, resulting in a few prickly reviews and interviews, to put it mildly. For the most part, the band agrees that the LP was an overt attempt to get more listeners, but they contest the suggestion that they lost any artistic integrity along the way since they've never shied away from penning 'mellow songs or poppy songs' if apropos. Portnoy attributes the wrath from a few 'trend-obsessed' British metal magazines, specifically, to their fawning over 'emerging bands such as Korn, Foo Fighters or pop-rockers such as The Stereophonics'.

Recently, online publications like *Proglodytes* and *Progressive Music Planet* have bestowed acclaim and contextual defence on *Falling Into Infinity*, and rightly so. It's far from a great record, but it is a satisfactorily enjoyable and experimental entry in Dream Theater's arsenal. As Portnoy honourably surmises, 'We did everything we could do to try and give [Elektra] that type of record, and if they failed to do anything with it, then as far as I was concerned, we'd done our share'. Thankfully, they'd more than bounce back a couple of years later, with an expanded return to an earlier narrative yielding an unforgettable masterpiece.

'New Millennium' (Portnoy)

High-pitched bells and Sherinian's mesmerizing pattern kick off this dig at Elektra and the music industry in a larger sense. More dynamic futuristic entwinements generate a rebellious yet spacious blueprint for LaBrie's slithering decrees and spiralling rebuffs. Bizarrely, its ruminating resentments make it come across like the older sibling of *Train of Thought*'s 'This Dying Soul'. Halfway in, a trance-like section takes over, permitting attitudes like 'Swallow pride before it swallows you' and 'Don't dare bite the hand that's starving you' to radiate Portnoy's criticisms with matter-of-fact strife. The instrumentalists then play around Sherinian's central melody with breezy flair, with Myung and Petrucci taking it over one point while Portnoy relentlessly guides them with resourceful fitness. Petrucci also adds some demonic tones later on, fortifying 'New Millennium' as one of the most tonally wide-ranging and striving offerings on the record.

'You Not Me' (Petrucci, Child)

At first, this one was known as 'You Or Me', and Portnoy claims that it was going to be discarded before Shirley brought in Child to fix it up. Sadly, this single is still nothing to write home about. Sure, the chorus is catchy enough, but nearly every element is peculiarly stale and generic. The performances are great, don't get me wrong, but there's nothing distinguishing about it aside from Petrucci's solo. Instead – and unsurprisingly given Child's background – it fares too far toward dumbed down, radio-friendly rock. An enjoyable song but one that was already beneath its creators.

'Peruvian Skies' (Petrucci)

On the other hand, 'Peruvian Skies' is among the best inclusions on *Falling Into Infinity* when it comes to core songwriting. One of two pieces in the set that deals with child abuse, its subjugated Floydian vibe is irresistible from start to finish. Petrucci's mildly psychedelic acoustic fingerpicking and electric leads are quite fetching, and Myung's technique – which he says was directed by Shirley telling him to 'play with a Roger Waters mindset' – is unflashy yet vibrantly characteristic. As for the rest of the band, Sherinian's delicate piano interjections and Portnoy's carefree drumming suit the arrangement perfectly.

Undoubtedly, LaBrie's heartbroken velvetiness is another stellar component, as he sings of a fictional girl named Vanessa being abused by her father with utmost sincerity. Lines such as 'Battered and bruised / Always confusing / The love that she's losing for hate' really drive home the situation. While the track would be great if it remained this way, the rapid swing into emotive metal madness meaningfully symbolises the dismay of the topic. Petrucci effectively evokes the squealing anguish of David Gilmour, too, which is a nice touch.

'Hollow Years' (Petrucci)

A pinnacle cut from Dream Theater's early period, it was also the lead single from the LP. Portnoy and Petrucci introduce it with relaxing repentance via reserved percussion and longing European acoustic schmaltz, respectively. Fans speculate that it's about the end of a heterosexual relationship, with each person walking away from each other. Lyrically, there's plenty to verify that interpretation, and once again, it's LaBrie's melodies and harmonies that make it so gorgeously cherishable. Sherinian uses his keys wisely as well, accentuating different passages without ever trying to steal the show. In every way, then, 'Hollow Years' is a superb and timeless composition.

Yet again, the label was keen to make a music video to help boost sales and attention for the record. Having been down that road a few times before – and considering the $100,000 price tag – the group weren't entirely on board. Filmed in Toronto by Axel Baur, its barely saturated glimpses of the band and extras mulling around the city pensively certainly embody the right spirit; even so, it received little airplay from MTV or elsewhere.

'Burning My Soul' (Portnoy)

'Almost written directly to Derek Oliver', as Portnoy confesses, 'Burning My Soul' is rife with metaphors about how label executives were trying to control Dream Theater. It was initially called 'Carnival of Clams' and matures with sinister concentration. Every timbre – including LaBrie's natural singing and its memorable robotic counterpart – is malevolent, adversarial, and even a bit carnivalesque. On that front, it's a successfully unique and intrepid dig at those around them. Conversely, it's not very gratifying beyond that, with barely any nuance or depth beyond its superficial indignation. The solo near the end is tremendous, though, and its motorized effects help it stand out

'Hell's Kitchen' (Sherinian, Myung, Portnoy, Petrucci)

Born as the middle section of 'Burning My Soul' before Shirley separated the two, 'Hell's Kitchen' – named after the neighbourhood that contained Avatar Studios – is a decent instrumental at best. Its aura of transitional calmness would definitely work better in the midst of the previous piece; on its own, there's not adequate substance to warrant its duration. Portnoy's lively syncopation over Petrucci's pleading guitarwork is impactful – and Myung and Sherinian successfully pepper it up – but it's not diverse or engaging enough to merit its own spotlight. The way it bursts into the next track is cool, though.

'Lines in the Sand' (Petrucci)

It's a deserved fan favourite from Falling Into Infinity whose original moniker,

'Cat's Tail', was smartly rejected. In an interview with Guitarist, Petrucci discloses that 'the main riff came from something that Derek had written and we had started working on during some of the soundchecks on tour'. Indeed, Sherinian's glossy tone – matched with wavering ambience, devilish guitar spikes, and peppy rhythms – produces a larger-than-life ether at the start. The arrangement remains friskily purposeful and intricate before and around the forthright verses, with Myung's bass downright growling at points. The use of intersecting vocals is quite fruitful, too, especially when Pinnick complements LaBrie's gripping chorus with his trademark lower register. The chilled-out reprieve halfway through – in which Petrucci delivers a bluesy solo over redemptive piano chords and percussion – is a winning detour as well. The remainder of 'Lines in the Sand' endearingly upholds that demeanour with enhanced edge as it brings back recognized musical and vocal necessities. It's a highlight of the record, for sure.

'Take Away My Pain' (Petrucci)

In the beginning, this tribute to Petrucci's late father was 'far slower, simpler and more emotive' than this official form. So much so that Portnoy still holds resentment toward Shirley for what he did to it: 'It was the most heart-drenched, emotional statement that John Petrucci ever made ... Kevin just turned it into a Caribbean trip to Disneyworld'. Startlingly, Petrucci is more accepting of what it became, primarily because of how Shirley encouraged him to use his wah-wah pedal with more spontaneity, resulting in 'an approach that was so different, was very cool and wouldn't have otherwise come out'.

As it stands, 'Take Away My Pain' undoubtedly exudes the tropical essence that Portnoy critiques, with muted guitar licks, light synths, and bouncy drumming aiding LaBrie's poised singing. That said, it better captures the underlined meaning during the more intense and impassioned chorus. The poignant bridge in the middle is easily the superlative moment, however, with LaBrie urgently asserting, 'His final scene / The actor bows / And all those years / Are gone somehow' in conjunction with lovely interlocking instrumentation. Obviously, Petrucci's subsequent solo is as virtuosic as it is moving, helping to repurpose what remains in the process. In other words, some of it is marginally incongruous, but none of it strictly detracts from Petrucci's message.

'Just Let Me Breathe' (Portnoy)

Another one of Portnoy's unbounded jeers at the music business, 'Just Let Me Breathe' begins intriguingly enough with a climbing guitar line over Petrucci and Myung's synchronized perseverance. Petrucci and Sherinian then embellish with spiteful riffs until LaBrie vindictively tells off inferior contemporaries and infuriating higher-ups: 'A daily dose of eMpTyV / Will flush your mind right down the drain / Shannon Hoon and Kurt Cobain / Make yourself a household name'. Beyond serving as a general tell-off to various people around them, these words are explicitly meant as a retort to alternative rock band Blind

Melon, who told *Guitar for the Practicing Musician* that *Images and Words* is 'the kind of music you listen to right when you start to get public hairs'. Never one to tolerate such disrespect, Portnoy naturally had to fire back. Afterwards, Sherinian and Petrucci unite yet again for aggressive flare-ups that – intentionally or not – conjure the central two-note interval of 'Wait for Sleep'. It's inarguably one of the most no-holds-barred bits of showmanship on the album, and the track is surely elevated because of it.

'Anna Lee' (LaBrie)
The second song in the sequence to revolve around battered youths, LaBrie's 'Anna Lee' was influenced by an article he read in which a girl named Natalie was the victim of sex trafficking. Appropriately, it's a coolly paced ballad with modest acoustic guitar swipes, luscious piano chords, and angsty melodies portraying somber observations. At certain points, the band achieves a stadium rock energy akin to, say, Queen or Van Halen; yet, the touching foundation persists until the end. It's the type of composition that makes an impression as it plays but fails to linger in your memory once it's done.

'Trial of Tears' (Myung)
All things considered, *Falling Into Infinity* wraps up with its top submission. Myung states that he presented a 'semi-finished' demo to Dream Theater that went through 'many different stages' before getting to this point. While you may think that 'Trial of Tears' is about the involuntary repositioning of Native Americans in America during the mid-1800s, he enlightens, 'It deals with ego and my perception of it, and understanding how it can cage you and really alter your perspective'. There are also hints at regret and the Biblical notion of 'love thy enemy', all of which proved to be 'therapeutic' for him to finally get off of his chest.

The first segment, 'It's Raining', conveys naturalistic sounds with its sparse bass and guitar notes, periodic percussion, and sparkling environment. Sherinian adds synthetic strings once it kicks into gear, and LaBrie's multilayered chorus – 'It's raining / raining / raining on the streets of New York City' – is unassuming but enthralling. Similarly, the post-chorus is effectually empowering vocally and musically, while the bridge is capped off with welcomingly uncanny keyboard textures. The next chapter, 'Deep in Heaven', is a wordless voyage that's first dominated by Petrucci's speedy tricks and Myung's tidy pizzazz. Sherinian and Portnoy take over after a while, though, with their own valiant splendours. In total, it's a bit self-serving and extraneous, but it does a fine job of displaying their abilities before a demoralised acoustic guitar configuration hosts the conclusion, 'The Wasteland'. Gusts of wind, browbeaten piano notes, and steadfast beats cater LaBrieas he retools the earlier chorus with sorrowful ingenuity. It's a rivetingly distressing coda that cements *Falling Into Infinity* as an uneven but underappreciated part of Dream Theater's lineage.

'Metropolis Pt. 2: Scenes from a Memory' (1999)

Personnel:
James LaBrie: vocals
John Petrucci: guitar, backing vocals, programming (7)
John Myung: bass
Jordan Rudess: keyboards, choir arrangement and conducting
Mike Portnoy: drums, backing vocals
Theresa Thomason: additional vocals (7, 11)
Mary Canty: additional background vocals (7)
Mary Smith: additional background vocals (7)
Jeanette Smith: additional background vocals (7)
Sheila Slappy: additional background vocals (7)
Carol Cyrus: additional background vocals (7)
Dale Scott: additional background vocals (7)
Clarence Burke Jr.: additional background vocals (7)
Terry Brown: voice of the Hypnotherapist (uncredited)
David Bottrill: voice of Edward (uncredited), mixing, engineer (1, 9, 10, 12)
Doug Oberkircher: engineer
Brian Quackenbush: assistant engineer
Michael Bates: assistant engineer
Kevin Shirley: mixing, assistant engineer (2 – 8, 11)
Rory Romano: mixing, assistant engineer (2 – 8, 11)
Shinobu Mitsuoka: engineer
Eugene Nastasi: assistant engineer
Lili Picou: art direction and design
Dave McKean: cover illustration
Ken Schles: still life photography
Andrew Lepley: house photography
Produced at BearTracks Studios in Suffern, New York,1999 by Mike Portnoy and John Petrucci
UK and US release date: October 1999.
Highest chart places: UK: 131, USA: 73
Running time: 77:06
Current edition: Music on Vinyl / Elektra Records 2019 orange and gold mixed vinyl

On the surface, *Falling Into Infinity* did everything it needed to be the breakout success Elektra was pressuring Dream Theater to make. Ironically, it had the opposite effect; it sparked ridicule and disenfranchisement from many fans while failing to bring in adequate new ones or sell especially well. As a result – and after some more hardships – the band decided to stick to their guns moving forward by attaining almost absolute autonomy over their music, image, and the like. The most immediate result of this resolution, *Metropolis Pt. 2: Scenes from a Memory*, is by and large the antithesis to its predecessor. A magnificent tale overflowing with self-indulgently difficult music and an absorbing, inventive, and emotional bit of fiction at its heart, this extravagant sequel to *Images and Words'* greatest track is the zenith Dream Theater endeavour, plain and simple. While many artists tend to overestimate the weight of their work, Portnoy hits the nail on the head when he calls it a masterpiece and 'the ultimate Dream Theater experience at *every* level – musically, lyrically, conceptually and production'. At the risk of sounding hyperbolic, *Scenes from a Memory* is more than just their best work to date and one of the top story albums in all of popular music; it's quite possibly the greatest progressive metal record of all time, too.

Such a triumph wasn't achieved without dissension, of course, and the end result is made even more astounding by the fact that Dream Theater almost disbanded after *Falling Into Infinity*. You see, Portnoy remained irritated about his stifling lack of authority since Elektra started calling the shots; this justified disgruntlement, coupled with a rising strain between him and Petrucci over management choices, balancing their professional and personal lives, and giving in to the label's demands, began to really wear on him during the 'Touring into Infinity' venture of late 1997. Speculatively, they even stopped talking to each other for several weeks, and Portnoy admits, 'When you are an active alcoholic you end up saying a lot of stupid things that you end up regarding afterwards'. After playing with Slayer and Pantera in Finland in June 1998 – and feeling envious of their off-stage comradery – he went off on tour manager Bill Barclay for not stopping at a McDonald's on the way back to the hotel. Portnoy says that the trivial incident was merely 'the straw that broke the camel's back', and he planned to make a subsequent show – recorded in Paris for the *Once in a LIVEtime* release–his last. He expounds, 'I realized I couldn't be in a band that doesn't have control over its own artistic voice ... We were going through so much bullshit and changes ... I felt John was giving in to a lot of the industry stuff with just me fighting it, that those guys were being swayed and it was too much for me'.

Mercifully, he agreed to stay until the tour finished, and in the process, Dream Theater were able to reconcile most of what ailed them. For one thing, they were persuaded by Frank Solomon and Bruce Payne – both of whom were involved with Deep Purple at the time – to let the pair co-manage them after Shore left a few months prior. Petrucci warned them that Dream Theater might break up anyway, but they were successfully persistent and confident in their promise to help fix things. One of their first tasks was to make sure Elektra didn't interfere with the music anymore. 'Plus we wanted to be able to self-produce ourselves, with me and John calling the shots', Portnoy mentions. At last, he and Petrucci were recognized as the leaders of Dream Theater – which their bandmates were completely fine with – and given far more sovereignty to dictate their future.

In reconsidering that direction, the duo made the tough choice to tell Sherinian that he was out due to persistent incompatibilities. Chiefly, Sherinian's increased gaudiness on stage started to cause problems. As Wilson writes, he was a modest figure upon joining; however, once he felt like an embedded and crucial member, he started 'wearing flashy and unbefitting clothes', as well as 'festoon[ing] the keyboard area with lava lamps and a rug', among other tapestries. Sherinian even admits that he went this route to become more famous and desirable. No one else on stage had any decorations, and Petrucci later remarked, 'Derek, you know, all this stuff up here looks a little out of place'. Rather than scale back his set-up, they controversially spread it around the stage.

Furthermore, they started representing themselves as two other bands – Nightmare Cinema and Nicky Lemons and the Migraines – during the sets to bring a bit more fun to their concerts. The former alter-ego was fairly innocuous, as it merely meant that they'd switch instruments while performing Deep Purple's 'Perfect Strangers'; however, the latter really bothered devotees since it involved Sherinian acting as the obnoxiously pretentious frontman. To do so, he wore 'a bright yellow feather boa around his neck, with the rest of the band belting out rapid, punk-influenced numbers'. Reportedly, Portnoy still sees it as just a bit of fun but also speculates that 'James and John Petrucci look back and cringe'.

Although Sherinian's role as a musician wasn't an issue, his other antics became too much for the other guys. Portnoy clarifies: 'When you are on tour it's all about the performance, and at that point, Derek was really playing the role of the rock star'. Whereas everyone else had families by this point – whom they'd bring with them on the road – Sherinian was single and 'constantly trying to pick up chicks', too. Lastly, many fans never warmed up to him replacing Moore. Cumulatively, these factors forced his bandmates to let him go via a telephone conference in early January 1999. Sherinian was stunned, as they'd just been discussing plans for the next project as if everything was totally fine; in retrospect, though, he understands the decision and is on good terms with them to this day. In fact, he and Portnoy currently play in a project called Sons of Apollo.

Obviously, Petrucci and Portnoy didn't want to let on that Sherinian was being fired while they were still touring, but they'd had a replacement ready to go for a while: Jordan Rudess. He, Portnoy, and Petrucci – alongside revered bassist Tony Levin –continued to build immense personal and musical chemistry while working on their second LP as instrumental supergroup Liquid Tension Experiment. Portnoy remembers: 'One night, we kind of hypothetically asked him if he would join again if he had the opportunity'. Having, regrettably, turned down the chance after Moore left, Rudess wasn't about to make the same mistake twice, so he enthusiastically and humbly said 'absolutely', and the rest is history. Although they felt 'horrible' pulling the rug out from under Sherinian – pun intended – Portnoy knew that they needed to bring in Rudess 'for the sake of the band's survival'.

With a new line-up and a freeing new balance of power in place, it was finally time to start proper work on *Scenes from a Memory*. Two major steps were moving into the comforting and congenial BearTracks studio to ensure the right environment as they wrote, and creating an 'inspiration corner' of beloved narrative sequences – such as Pink Floyd's *The Wall*, Marillion's *Misplaced Childhood*, Genesis' *The Lamb Lies Down on Broadway*, The Who's *Tommy*, and the Beatles' *Sgt. Pepper's Lonely Hearts Club Band* – to guide them. Upon accusations of plagiarism or unoriginality, the band adamantly spell out that they, as well as virtually all artists, draw from what they like. Portnoy adds: 'We just wanted something that we could refer to, not steal from'. For Rudess, it was the first time he'd truly delved into acts like Iron Maiden and Queensrÿche, so he was grateful on that front as well. Although he 'walked into the studio with a ton of recorded musical ideas' for *Scenes from a Memory*, Portnoy 'was not thrilled' and said that Dream Theater should 'write everything together'. In the end, they used some of what Rudess brought but not everything.

Naturally, they pulled from both prior 'Metropolis' compositions to flesh out this one, which proved somewhat challenging since, again, the *Images and Words* centrepiece wasn't written to have a successor or even make literal sense. Bluntly, Portnoy reflects, 'I don't even think John [Petrucci] knew what ['Metropolis—Part I'] meant ... we actually had to make sense out of those old lyrics by shaping the new ones around them'. As for the cast-off 'Metropolis Pt. 2' suite, which Petrucci now sees as 'sloppy' and 'horrible', elements of it made their way to tracks like 'Overture 1928', 'One Last Time', and 'The Dance of Eternity'. Likewise, 'scraps of songs that had been leftover from as far back as the *Awake* sessions were also dusted off and utilized'.

Dabbing in hypnosis, reincarnation, murder, politics, and disastrous romance, the plot of *Scenes from a Memory* is kind of ingenious(especially considering its twist ending). In the simplest terms, the story finds a young man named Nicholas visiting a hypnotherapist about his visions regarding a fatal 1920s love affair between Victoria Page and two brothers: Senator Edward Baynes – 'The Miracle' – and Julian Baynes – 'The Sleeper'. In the end, it's revealed that just as Nicholas is Victoria rebirthed, the hypnotherapist is really Edward coming back to murder her once again. Honestly, it's a startlingly beautiful and harrowing account, and aside from using the film *Dead Again* as support, Petrucci did a lot of probing to do justice to the themes:

> Mike and I had talked about a couple of things, we had the initial idea and that got more focused on a story about a past life. So I began to read books about that subject, went to the library to research the time period to try and get some names and places that would set the scene. I picked up some hypnosis audio CDs and things like that to get the right kind of dialogue used in those types of sessions ... I guess the music was already written at that stage.

For the first time, a Dream Theater record would be self-produced, too, which was exciting and a little intimidating for the leading pair. Nevertheless – and with Oberkircher serving as their engineer once more – they carried on confidently knowing that no outside producer would be able to capture their vision perfectly or allow them the space to 'have everything set up, walk in, write and maybe record something, maybe not'. Portnoy attests:

> I always felt that there were too many chefs in the kitchen as it was. You already had at least four and sometimes five people interjecting opinions and we would sometimes spend days, weeks or even months banging out four bars of music and arguing over one note. We would finally resolve it within ourselves only to have some sixth guy – who had nothing to do with the writing of it – suddenly chuck it out the window. That rips your heart out.

Without a doubt, they do an exceptional job on this first attempt. Unfortunately, though, mixing it wasn't so easy. First, David Bottrill was given the task after proving capable with his treatment of recent King Crimson and Tool LPs. Initially, Dream Theater approved of what he did, but once Shirley told Petrucci that it 'doesn't sound bad but it doesn't sound especially good', the guitarist asked him to remix it in only two days. Despite not having enough time to redo four pieces – 'Finally Free', 'The Dance of Eternity', 'One Last Time', and 'Regression' – Shirley succeeded and the collection was ready to release.

It's worth mentioning that Dream Theater were immovable about not publicizing the fact that the record was a sequel until it was out. Avin divulges: 'Throughout the promotional process ... the use of 'Metropolis' as part of the album title was left unrevealed, using only *Scenes from a Memory* as a working title'. Portnoy elaborates by saying that the advanced single edit of 'Home' removed 'any of the musical references to 'Metropolis'.

As the aforementioned concept albums demonstrate, just about every musical masterpiece has an iconic cover. *Scenes from a Memory* is no exception. Originally, Portnoy proposed using a 'layout like a playbill': 'the yellow box on top with 'Dream Theater' in black with just a single image that would have been representing reincarnation or murder'. Ironically, it was the label who convinced them to aim for something more artistic and unique. Enter Dave McKean, whose illustration of 'an old man's face, made up of a million different old fashioned photos', was deemed 'perfect' by Portnoy. Sadly, it was already commissioned for a *Sandman* graphic novel called *Brief Lives*, but McKean was happy to create something new based on the same style. Specifically, he unveils, the man's face would 'be made up of smaller snapshots from that person's life'. To do it, he blended 'a painting in acrylic' with photos from the band and his own family scrapbooks. Rather than see it as one of countless assignments he's had over the years, McKean recognizes its greatness by still including it in his portfolio.

Fearlessly and appropriately, they decided to play the entire sequence during the ensuing Metropolis 2000 world tour – which lasted over a year – including projected footage of dramatized scenes. Arguably the other biggest American progressive rock band at the time, Spock's Beard, filled many of the opening slot, too. A few hitches notwithstanding, it was going smoothly – that is until Terry Brown got wind of Dream Theater implementing his studio voice clips as the hypnotherapist during the concerts. His lawyer demanded a large amount of money as compensation for the seemingly unauthorized usages. Portnoy claims that Brown was well aware of how his samples would be used, whereas Brown insists that he was only providing guide vocals and not final takes. Regardless, they had to pay him off to avoid further legal action. The last performance of the American run – done with a choir and actor Kent Broadhurst as the hypnotherapist – was recorded at the Roseland Ballroom in New York on August 30, 2000. It was later issued as the *Live Scenes from New York* CD and the *Metropolis 2000: Scenes from New York* DVD.

Although the immediate chart placements might convince you otherwise, *Scenes from a Memory* received a lot of love from the press. That should come as no surprise to anyone who's heard it, and at the time, Portnoy wasn't shocked, either: 'If you look at history, concept albums were usually the peak of a band's career'. Today, it's sold over half a million copies and continues to be heralded by critics and fans as one of the all-time best progressive rock and/or metal records. Above all else, *Scenes from a Memory* validated every risk Dream Theater took to make it and redeemed them in the eyes of virtually everyone who doubted them following *Falling Into Infinity*. The only downside of crafting something so exceptional is being expected to outdo it the next time around. Once the 2000s hit, though, another intrepid new format and some substantial turbulence will help them come very close.

'Scene One: Regression' (Petrucci)

Act I begins with a clock ticking back and forth between stereo channels, which is brilliantly effective in making you feel like you're undergoing hypnosis alongside Nicholas. The hypnotherapist's countdown and directions are direct but comforting in creating a sense of security. In-between, a glimmer of 'Home' is applied, as well as some choral bellows akin to Pink Floyd's 'The Great Gig in the Sky'. As he finishes, Petrucci, Rudess, and LaBrie materialize with humble and gentle warmth. The former's acoustic motif – which every Dream Theater fan who's also a guitarist inescapably learns to play – is sublime in its own right; yet, its ability to blanket LaBrie's verses so dreamily makes it even prettier. Speaking of LaBrie, his bittersweet recitations convey tender and universal yearning. He sets the scene well by detailing how his 'subconscious mind / Starts spinning through time / To rejoin the past once again'. Almost inaudibly, Rudess follows them with ornamental horns. LaBrie's final words – 'Hello, Victoria / So glad to see you / My friend' – are charmingly cordial as they confirm that this isn't the first time the two of them have met. It's a spotlessly classy, informative, and beguiling way to begin, and like much of the LP, it runs into the next track with cunning seamlessness.

'Scene Two: I. Overture 1928' (Petrucci, Portnoy, Myung, Rudess)

If not for its colleague several spots down the line, 'Overture 1928' would be the best instrumental of Dream Theater's first decade. Following a mechanical release, reversed sound clips, and a single keyboard stroke that recalls the start of 'Metropolis— Part I', Portnoy and Petrucci's climbing unified fury stampedes toward entrancing razor-sharp riffs and spirited rhythms. Myung and Petrucci join forces for a speedy descent before Rudess' angelic phrase dances around colourful syncopation. Two taps from Portnoy invite the return of Petrucci's reign underneath a stunning solo from Rudess, whose tone and technique alone show an advancement in the group's chemistry. Luminously, Petrucci interrupts with bawling incitements of a few of Scenes from a Memory's chief themes as piano, synths, drums, and bass support him; afterwards, more hypnotic guitar lines give way to hellish yet mesmerizing rhythmic breakdowns and riffs. Then, Petrucci rises out of the ashes with lightning-fast hustle as Dream Theater build anticipation toward a tight climax that's ricocheted –

'Scene Two: II. Strange Déjà Vu' (Portnoy)

– as 'Strange Déjà Vu' appears.Crunchy guitar chords and animated drumming escort LaBrie as he sings with cryptic tenacity about being led to a house where Victoria appears in a mirror. He asks, 'Young child / Won't you tell me / Why I'm here?' implying that he's been 'drawn to' this place countless times before. His backing falsetto enhances his desperation. Suddenly, a panicked shift in the arrangement accompanies his realization that 'there's something tearing at her soul' that she needs to tell him about. Then, LaBrie pleasantly vocalizes as Victoria on top of a twisty yet therapeutic backdrop of hearty syncopation and decorative synths, among other timbres. Her final admittance – 'I'm not the one the Sleeper thought he knew' – is an intuitive nod to the *Images and Words* forbearer.

After a calm transition, Dream Theater get hyper-aggressive via Petrucci's commanding lead and Portnoy's double bass drum inflections. Of course, Myung keeps pace without limitation. Nicholas returns to gruffly bemoan, 'Metropolis surrounds me / The mirror's shattered the girl', as well as declare his need to connect with Victoria again. An abrupt classical piano break segues into Nicholas' alteration of Victoria's dirge. Admissions like 'Tears my soul into two / I'm not the one I thought I always knew' and 'Uncanny, strange déjà vu / But I don't mind / I hope to find the truth' show his dedication to discovering and solving her story.

Although they'll do it even better as *Scenes from a Memory* carries on, 'Strange Déjà Vu' categorically exhibits growth in songwriting and instrumentation, as well as their ability to interweave the two within a single piece.

'Scene Three: I. Through My Words' (Petrucci)

A minute-long piano ode, it's equally exquisite and traumatic lyrically and musically. Rudess stylishly garnishes his purposefully repetitious three-note seed to capitalize on LaBrie's unremitting epiphanies. Nicholas feels a bond and duty to Victoria unlike he's ever felt before, as he realizes just how unbreakably linked they are. He vulnerably sings, 'All that I take with me / Is all you've left behind / We're sharing one eternity / Living in two minds', solidifying the recognition that he *is* her and that he needs to put things right. As a showpiece for how discerningly and unpretentiously wholehearted Dream Theater can be, 'Through My Words' is a paramount composition.

'Scene Three: II. Fatal Tragedy' (Myung)

The plot thickens as Nicholas begins to uncover what exactly happened to Victoria all of those years ago; similarly, *Scenes from a Memory* truly signals Dream Theater's evolution of wacky showmanship at this point, as 'Fatal Tragedy' presents a kind of boundless yet spellbinding sophistication never before attained in their catalogue. Rudess and LaBrie's 'Through My Words' bleeds into the first part of it, with Nicholas still lamenting his uncertainties. A heavier score arises once he meets a trustworthy 'older man' who tells him that Victoria's murder 'was talked about for years'. LaBrie's rising outcry – 'She passed away / She was so young' – is quite genuine, and as usual, Petrucci and Rudess complement each other with captivating counterpoints.

Ghostly croons mask a quick interlude that turns into an alluring declaration – 'Without love / Without truth / There can be no turning back' –during which Petrucci and Portnoy provide backing vocals. Next, Rudess' gothic organ chords juxtapose the rest of the players' sporadic surges with engrossing unanimity. Following some more reprisals, a ferocious whirlwind of instrumentation takes over. Petrucci's coarse and irresistible riffs steer relentless rhythms until Portnoy's contribution branches out over Rudess' dizzying keynotes. It's a downright addictive display of odd textures and odder measures, and the ways in which Petrucci and Rudess go back and forth with their manic and bizarre solos are incredible. Eventually, everyone comes together for a collaborative climb of complexity, ending with a handful of exuberant percussive taps, the reappearance to a major guitar part, and the return of the hypnotherapist. He coolly informs Nicholas, 'Now it's time to see how you died / Remember that death is not the end / But only a transition'. In doing so, he concludes Dream Theater's most zany yet organised arrangement thus far.

'Scene Four: Beyond This Life' (Petrucci)

It launches with the most hectic portion of the whole record: a ruthless torrent of authoritative percussion, bass playing, and guitarwork – with screwball keyboard accents as a side dish – that instantly gets under your skin. Quickly, it gives way to tranquillity as Myung maintains the main theme beneath airier musicianship and LaBrie's chilling account of the homicide. The otherworldly noises around them add to the sense of unease and confusion as the tune becomes increasingly irritated. In a way, it's among the most mainstream metal moments on *Scenes from a Memory*, yet its advancement of the storyline and moderate revisions keep it absorbing.

A soft bridge consisting of acoustic arpeggios, more peculiar effects, and a prophetic statement – 'Our deeds have travelled far / What we have been is what we are' – comes into view. Petrucci takes over with a foreboding melody prior to offering another blistering solo as a segue into the ensuing outrage. More attractive hostility surrounds LaBrie's details of Victoria ending the relationship and being killed as a consequence. The soft bridge is then expanded to state, 'All that we learn this time / (What we have been is what we are) / Is carried beyond this life'. Once again, Petrucci and Portnoy's supplemental chants complement LaBrie well.

From there, Rudess instigates another madcap jam by taking the spotlight with plenty of melodic finesse. A tempo shift incites an equally charismatic wah-wah solo from Petrucci before Rudess returns with quirky horns and magical flamboyance over the bewitching precision of his bandmates. Behind them, the core motif is toyed with in different key signatures. It culminates in a breakdown straight out of Frank Zappa's playbook; more breathtaking virtuosity effortlessly subsequently invites LaBrie's matter-of-fact cue of the bridge. All in all, it's another jaw-dropping fusion of songwriting and score that proves why *Scenes from a Memory* is leaps and bounds beyond what preceded it.

'Scene Five: Through Her Eyes' (Petrucci)

As the title implies, this companion to 'Through My Words'– issued as a single on May 30, 2000 – is born of the same ilk but expands upon its cohort's DNA. Thomason's initial hums imply that Victoria is literally with Dream Theater as Petrucci's bluesy screeches and Rudess' heavenly choir coat the landscape. Portnoy's shakers prompt Rudess to echo his part from the earlier piece as acoustic strums chaperon LaBrie's silkily solemn reflection on Victoria's death: 'Now that I`ve become aware / And I`ve exposed this tragedy / A sadness grows inside of me / It all seems so unfair'. Once again, he captures Nicholas' mindset – about seeing 'the writing on her stone' and feeling 'like part of me had died' – with masterful authenticity. Gorgeous harmonies enrich the consequent melody: 'And I know what it's like to lose someone you love / And this felt just the same'. It leaves him going back to the start and contrasting the family he has with the one Victoria never got. LaBrie's grief-stricken murmurs at the end raised up by matched melancholia from everyone else enhances the already emotionally taxing gem. Although it can seem a tad cheesy and sugary on its own, within the context of *Scenes from a Memory*, 'Through Her Eyes' is divinely devastating.

'Scene Six: Home' (Portnoy)

This sexualized survey of Julian Baynes' drug and gambling vices – and the start of Act II – is filled with Middle Eastern dashes akin to Led Zeppelin's 'Kashmir', as well as drops of proto-djentire. Petrucci's introductory notes fuse with eerie tape loops and Indian timbres to spark an exhilarating soundscape. His hypnotic main riffs growl assertively beneath Portnoy's fetching syncopation, ultimately exploding with marvellously dirty magnetism. As Julian, LaBrie mightily announces his inescapable addictions: 'Lines take me higher / My mind drips desire / Confined and overtired'. His soaring testimony of 'This city's cold blood calls me home' bonds the track to 'Metropolis Part I', which is cool, and Rudess' faint electric piano chords instil more tension. Likewise, Petrucci's quick ascension toward LaBrie's purging concession – 'The city – it calls to me / Decadent scenes from my memory / Sorrow – eternity / My demons are coming to drown me' – is utterly thrilling. LaBrie does an excellent job conveying Julian's conflicted psyche.

Myung takes over Petrucci's central pattern during Rudess' mystical contemplation. Over them, Edward emotionlessly adds another wink to the *Images and Words* ancestor when he states, 'I remember I was told there's a new love that's born / For each one that has died'. He copies Julian's melody but repurposes the title to suit his own ulterior motive of stealing Victoria away from him: 'Living their other life / Is getting them nowhere / I'll make her my wife / Her sweet temptation calls me home'. We also realize that – just as Julian and Edward are the 'Sleeper' and 'Miracle', respectively – Victoria is the figurative 'Metropolis', as LaBrie once again conjures 'Metropolis Part I': 'Victoria watches and thoughtfully smiles / She's taking me to my home'.

As compelling as these sections are – especially with all of that continuity linking the 'Metropolis' arc – the real brilliance of 'Home' comes during its second half. The opening ambiance is brought back alongside sounds of gambling and sex, juxtaposing Julian and Edward's simultaneous misdeeds. Obviously, it's very provocative and suspenseful. Soon, its mounting tautness is freed through Portnoy's domineering beats and Rudess' electrifying solo. Of course, Petrucci gets his turn at bat with a correspondingly daunting outburst as the rhythm section continues its transfixing irregularities. Fittingly, Nicholas chimes in with his own take on LaBrie's principal phrase – 'Her story – it holds the key / Unlocking dreams from my memory / Solving this mystery / Is everything that is a part of me' – before a frenzied raga prompts more fascinating cultural complications. Niftily, Petrucci's feedback and the initial sounds of 'Metropolis Part I' move us into the greatest progressive metal instrumental of all time, 'The Dance of Eternity'.

'Scene Seven: I. The Dance of Eternity' (Petrucci, Portnoy, Myung, Rudess)

Named after the closing line of 'Metropolis Part I', it's said to have over 100 time signature changes. That distinction is one of many reasons why 'The Dance of Eternity' is Dream Theater's instrumental masterwork, as well as an immeasurably influential composition. Its enrapturing, unpredictable, and plucky quirks expertly reuse many neighbouring themes while externally laying the foundation for countless genre brethren over the past twenty years.

The industrial pounce that kicked off 'Overture 1928' returns beneath more disorienting reversed sound collages. Soon, Myung's hellish bass line supports

Portnoy and Petrucci's synchronized militaristic assault. Then, Rudess sprinkles puzzling garlands over infectiously off-kilter riffs and rhythms. It's basically the musical equivalent of a carnival funhouse, and each moment is a methodically yet playfully contagious. A hasty piano break, a rapid bass line, and some ELP-esque electronic keyboard notes are spread out amongst the perpetual frenzy. It continuously adds exciting new segments in-between the established ones, all the while growing anticipation for some sort of apex. Fortunately, it's delivered through Rudess' vivacious vaudevillian piano breakdown, whose atypical boldness bolsters how much freshness and experimentation he brought to *Scenes from a Memory* and Dream Theater overall.

More flashy and trance-inducing savagery ensues, with Myung letting loose like never before around Rudess, Petrucci, and Portnoy concurrently driving toward a shared discharge with a level of lurid exactness that leaves you speechless. Another callback paves the way for more impeccably orchestrated structural collapses – including a sort of jazz fusion detour around the five-minute mark – until a final kooky disruption and some conclusive guitar and drum blasts resolve into the next entry in the sequence. Without question, 'The Dance of Eternity' remains mind-bogglingly creative and complex no matter how many times you hear it, and no progressive metal instrumental made in its wake – by Dream Theater or anyone else– has ever definitively topped it.

'Scene Seven: II. One Last Time' (LaBrie)

Elegantly morose piano chords ready Nicholas' moving investigation into the murder. The official report states that Julian killed Victoria and then himself, with Edward finding their bodies and giving an anonymous witness testimony. However, as LaBrie dejectedly verbalizes, 'It doesn't make any sense / This tragic ending / In spite of the evidence / There's something still missing'. Behind his soulful clamours, Portnoy, Rudess, and Myung keep it simple while Petrucci's cyclical notes evoke apt misfortune. As Victoria, LaBrie disconsolately sings about laying down with Julian 'One last time / Until we fade away'; afterwards, a restful transition tips off a sensitive solo from Petrucci and then an uplifting bridge finds Nicholas celebrating the 'many clues' he's found in Edward's old house. It's a luscious slice of triumph and cleansing since Nicholas now knows the truth and can put things right. Or, at least so he thinks.

'Scene Eight: The Spirit Carries On' (Petrucci)

With its lovely melodies, poetically purifying lyrics, and enveloping context, 'The Spirit Carries On' is an easy contender for the best song Dream Theater has ever written. Once more, LaBrie and Rudess make a flawless team, as the former's wispy quandaries and the latter's somber but curing piano arrangement are immensely powerful. Myung trails behind them with quaint notes while Petrucci's relaxed acoustic strikes and Portnoy's conquering syncopation make you feel every bit of restorative acceptance that Nicholas does. After all, his bond with Victoria could represent the connection anyone shares with a loved one who's passed on; therefore, his eloquently liberating verses and comforting chorus – 'If I die tomorrow / I'll be all right / Because I believe / That after we're gone / The spirit carries on' – resonate beautifully with every listener in some way.

As if the track weren't enough of a tear-jerker already, Victoria sends him a motivational farewell prior to a trendily grief-stricken solo from Petrucci. It's awe-inspiring, as is LaBrie victoriously modifying his part of 'Regression' to reflect how much he's learned and grown due to his journey. Petrucci's rhymes here are particularly accessible yet meaningful: 'Victoria's real / I finally feel / At peace with the girl in my dreams / And now that I'm here / It's perfectly clear / I found out what all of this means'. The band's unassuming playing behind LaBrie is perfectly congratulatory, too, and the spiralling choir escalates the life-affirming grandeur as it ends. Unfortunately, all of that goodwill instantaneously becomes heartbreaking in retrospect once the hypnotherapist reveals what his plan was all along.

'Scene Nine: Finally Free' (Portnoy)

Like most great concept albums, *Scenes from a Memory* goes back to the start upon completion. Brown wakes up Nicholas as Petrucci fingerpicks his portion of 'Regression'. Rudess adds festive orchestration as the sounds of someone driving away in a car plays. Next, bells motion ominous acoustic arpeggios, clasps of thunder, and threatening strings to hint at the betrayal to come. An encircling piano passage greets Edward as he candidly recounts murdering his brother and Victoria. What's more, he gloats about cleverly framing his brother by falsifying a murder-suicide note: 'This feeling inside me / Finally found my love / I've finally broke free / No longer torn in two / I'd take my own life before losing you'.

After Rudess brings back his downtrodden construction for a moment, the music becomes happier and fuller as Victoria proclaims her plan to run away with Julian and 'break free of the Miracle'. It's quite catchy, and Dream Theater shrewdly reprise the aforementioned memo with a different last line – 'He'd kill his brother if he only knew' – to add more predictive misfortune to their fates. Like angels in a Greek tragedy, LaBrie, Portnoy, and Petrucci harmonize about how she and Julian almost got away with it. Sadly, more menacing bells and guitar riffs – as well as cricket chirps and screams – cascade as shots fire and Edward demands, 'Open your eyes, Victoria' before running away.

Suitably, 'One Last Time' comes back briefly before another profound Petrucci solo kicks off arguably the most desirable hook on the whole record. Above eager synths and guitar lines, LaBrie details their deaths, imaginatively connecting the past with the present by remarking, 'A blinding light comes into view / An old soul exchanged for a new / A familiar voice comes shining through'. In keeping with the trend, Nicholas now recites the note with yet another poignant alteration: 'No longer torn in two /I learned about my life by living through you'.Honestly, it's difficult not to get a bit choked up as his final communication to Victoria – 'We'll meet again, my friend / Someday soon' – flows over the grungy outro.

In an ideal world, that would be the end of the tale and both Nicholas and Victoria would retain this happy ending. Of course, that doesn't happen. Instead, Dream Theater pull a twist worthy of The Twilight Zone by having us eavesdrop on Nicholas as he arrives home, puts on a televised news report, pours himself a drink, plays a big band rendition of the start of 'Finally Free', and immediately gets killed by the hypnotherapist (reincarnated as Edward). He even commands, 'Open your eyes, Nicholas' to make the reveal unmistakable. In one last instant of ingeniousness, the concluding measures of static move directly into the beginning of the group's next LP, Six Degrees of Inner Turbulence. That feature is just the cherry on top of the tour-de-force sundae that is Scenes from a Memory.

'Six Degrees of Inner Turbulence' (2002)

Personnel:
James LaBrie: vocals
John Petrucci: guitar, backing vocals
John Myung: bass
Jordan Rudess: keyboards, orchestral arrangements
Mike Portnoy: drums, backing vocals, co-lead vocals (1, 8)
Howard Portnoy: gong drum (4)
Doug Oberkircher: engineer
J.P. Sheganowski: assistant engineer
Kevin Shirley: mixing
Claudius Mittendorfer: assistant mixing
Ken Schles: photography
Dung Hoang: illustration
Ken Schles: still life photography
JMatic: art direction
May Redding: stylist (photography)
Produced at BearTracks Studios in Suffern, New York,March – August 2001 by Mike
Portnoy and John Petrucci
UK and US release date: January 2002.
Highest chart places: UK: none, USA: 46
Running time: 96:17
Current edition: Music on Vinyl / Elektra Records 2016 orange vinyl

With the creative and critical successes of *Scenes from a Memory*, Dream
Theater entered the new millennium at the height of their game. Their fanbase
was bigger and prouder than ever, the press showered them with praise,
and internally, they felt unparalleled artistic contentment and capability.
Understandably, such a situation was both elating and nerve-wracking, as it
meant that everyone involved – the band, the label, the media, the audience,
etc. – likely anticipated something even more audacious and satisfying with the
follow-up. So, how does one try to best a magnum opus? For Dream Theater,
it was to eventually take another page from their progressive rock forefathers
by condensing a conceptual suite into an album-long track. Coupled with
five other thematically rich selections, the forty-two-minute beast elevates
Six Degrees of Inner Turbulence to being another aspiring, enduring, and
significant benchmark in Dream Theater's backlog. It doesn't surpass its
predecessor, but its winning commitment to a striving format and an amplified
array of styles earns it prominence all the same.

Although it's still packed with made-up accounts, *Six Degrees of Inner
Turbulence* is easily the group's most overtly personal and socially conscious
album thus far. Various forms of mental illness, familial resentment, and stem
cell research are all explored. Most importantly, its opener, 'The Glass Prison',
kicks off Portnoy's multi-album 'Twelve-step Suite' that's inspired by his battle

with and salvage from alcoholism. He'd been dealing with the disease for many years by the dawn of the 2000s, yet it – alongside his use of cocaine as a crutch and his self-confessed perfectionism and OCD – finally reached its tipping point during the current touring cycle. As he explains:

> For so many years, I kept it in check ... I was never a day drinker, and would always wait until the end of the night... toward the end I was drinking earlier in the day while the opening band were on, and I would get onstage already half-crocked... I would find myself at the meet-and-greets after the show with a bottle of Jack Daniels, and being rude to fans and things like that.

His bandmates noticed this behaviour to a degree but never fully comprehended the extent of his problems. Luckily, they were as supportive and understanding as possible, encouraging him to quit drinking on his 33rd birthday, stay committed to attending AA meetings no matter what, and refrain from being around alcohol as much as possible. Reportedly, Petrucci would even confiscate all of the booze in Portnoy's hotel rooms as soon as they arrived. Logically, Portnoy wanted to use his talents and platform to help himself – and any applicable listener – heal. He illuminates: 'I had an idea of writing a song that was kind of in three sections ... it seemed to me like writing about all 12 steps in one song would have been just short-changing the concept'. Rather, he elected to document the first three steps of recovery in 'The Glass Prison' and then devote one song on each of the next four LPs to the remaining nine.

At first, Dream Theater wanted the record to be significantly different musically from what preceded it. In fact, they considered delving into world music, with Petrucci bringing in a friend who was 'an expert in all kinds of ethnic music, especially like Indian music' to lead them. Portnoy reminisces: 'What we were going to do was that each song would represent the style or flavour of a different country. We did take a couple of those master classes and learned some different, weird African rhythms and it was interesting'. Ultimately, they abandoned the idea in part because of Steve Vai had just put out a similarly schemed LP – *Alive in an Ultra World* – and because a recent Pantera concert convinced them to change directions.

By late June, they'd completed five songs for *Six Degrees of Inner Turbulence* and chose to take a brief break to recalibrate and do other things, including non-Dream Theater live performances. Upon reconvening – and with only three weeks left to do it – they planned to make the titular sixth and final track another venture in the vein of 'A Change of Seasons'. With Petrucci directing Rudess to create the happiest and saddest things he could – which blossomed 'many of the themes' that were used – they'd only set out to max out the runtime of a single disc. However, their unbridled eagerness to keep adding prized passages led to *Six Degrees of Inner Turbulence* being twice as long and the need for two discs to hold the entire collection. They thought about presenting it as one unbroken piece, but as Portnoy shares, they 'decided to index it because after a few listens, the novelty of seeing the CD timer reach 42:00 would wear off and it would become very annoying to have to scroll through the whole song to find a particular section'.

In typical fashion, LaBrie was brought in to record his vocals once virtually all of the instrumentation was recorded. He flew into New York City on September 10, 2001; obviously, the events of the following day made Dream Theater reevaluate their priorities and itinerary.LaBrie remembers: 'I was at the Paramount Hotel about three miles from the site ... So I was pretty freaked out, and it took like two hours to get through on the phone to my family and everyone else'. The tragedy also negatively affected the distribution of and discourse around Dream Theater's latest live release, *Live Scenes from New York*, but we'll save that for a future discussion.

Once the metaphorical and literal smoke settled, they got to mixing *Six Degrees of Inner Turbulence* with Shirley and securing the artwork. As Wilson describes: 'The white backdrop was decorated with a yellowing paper effect, a child's doodles, and scrawled handwriting which was far removed from the more embellished, progressive rock styling of earlier albums'. According to artist Dung Hoang, Portnoy 'wanted a stark, white look and something more artistic and painterly'. That involved using acrylics and oil to build layers, as well as hiding references to the number six throughout the entire booklet to symbolize both the title itself and its place as Dream Theater's sixth studio project.

Despite a few selections absolutely deserving to be issued as singles and music videos, none were. 'A lot of the press and media – whether on TV or radio – have a stereotype that's attached to our name. They're not even going to bother listening to the single we deliver because to them, we represent a certain style and audience', Portnoy justifies. Having attempted numerous times to appease that part of the industry, they felt that their time, effort, and money would be better spent improving things like concerts and DVDs for diehard devotees.

Thankfully, *Six Degrees of Inner Turbulence* was prosperous anyway, with many of the band's usually favourable outlets championing them yet again. Even a magazine no one anticipated to care about Dream Theater – *Entertainment Weekly* – said that 'its very existence leaves you gaping in open-mouthed, saucer-eyed awe'. Although some admirers hadn't been able to internalize the material by the time the World Turbulence tour kicked off in mid-January 2002, they soon came to learn and appreciate it, too. Predictably, many discussions were had over which disc is superior, but the majority of fans came to adore the cumulative effort after a handful of intense listens.

The World Turbulence tour was also notable for giving rise to a new live Dream Theater gimmick: complete recreations of classic older records when they play two consecutive nights in a city. The practice started at the February 18 and 19 shows in Barcelona, where Portnoy worked in a cover of Metallica's

Master of Puppets; later, Iron Maiden's *The Number of the Beast*, Pink Floyd's *The Dark Side of the Moon*, and Deep Purple's *Made in Japan* would also get the full Dream Theater treatment. Naturally, some attendees were upset about paying to see Dream Theater play someone else's music, leading to disgruntled posts on internet message boards. In response, Portnoy wrote a scathing denouncement of such reactions on his official website, including the following excerpts:

> I cannot believe some of the crap I am reading ... Myself and some of the other band members are truly surprised (well actually, maybe not!) and frankly disgusted at the immature and unappreciative behaviour of some of the fans who couldn't handle our choice of set-list and album cover[s] ... Was the other 2 hours of DT material that night NOT ENOUGH???? Or what about the 3 hours of different DT material played the previous night?

He later spoke in a friendlier and more collected tone about putting the shows out as part of an official series: '[It] is simply to pay tribute to some of the bands and albums that shaped us, and perhaps introduce a new generation of Dream Theater fans to our roots... I wouldn't be doing my job if I didn't offer our fans around the world a chance to hear these unique shows'. At the very least, these recitals humbly demonstrate once more how willingly and skilfully able the quintet are at paying homage to their forebearers.

It wouldn't be an early Dream Theater LP without a change in members being talked over – if not enacted – and this time, LaBrie was the one in question. He'd been increasingly chastised by concertgoers and reviewers for his on-stage presence, and his bandmates soon openly shared those same qualms. Portnoy admits: 'There were aspects of both his singing and his presentation that we knew were probably holding us back', adding that they now preferred vocalists like Thom Yorke and Bono over folks like 'Geoff Tate, Steve Perry, and Bruce Dickinson'. Whereas they were initially pleased to have LaBrie removed from the creation process and merely appear to record vocals when needed, they now wanted him to be more involved and less isolated from the figurative musical family. Petrucci also remarks that LaBrie seemed disinterested in his position. After nervously scheduling a conference call with him – Portnoy refers to it as 'a shape-up or ship-out kind of meeting' –they were delighted to see him being wholly receptive to their concerns and to improving however he could. LaBrie comments: 'To be honest, it was what I needed.... I'd been in such a rut for so long, I almost needed a reality check or something to snap me out of that trance.' Part of the process required having him work with a vocal coach, get in shape and play an active role in the writing sessions for everything after *six Degrees of Inner Turbulence*. Although a cluster of fans still rebuke LaBrie as a singer, most of them – myself included – agree that Dream Theater simply wouldn't be Dream Theater without him.

Six Degrees of Inner Turbulence remains one of the group's most rewarding

records. The first set of tunes are among their most vividly adventurous
and rousing to date, whereas the epic finale is essentially their *Thick as a
Brick*: a masterfully entwined chain of segments that traverses a multitude
of varied formulas and philosophies before returning home with seductive
resourcefulness. Such a sundry disposition also makes it Dream Theater's
Magical Mystery Tour, and like the Liverpudlian foursome, they'd return a year
later with a more concise, return-to-roots train of thought.

'The Glass Prison' (Portnoy)

It's dedicated to Bill Wilson – the co-founder of Alcoholics Anonymous – and
directly correlates to the starting points of the AA program. As Portnoy clarifies:
'[T]he first step in the first section of the song is admitting being powerless, the
second step is needing the help of others ... The third section is being willing
to turn your life over to a higher power and handing over your will'. He also
acknowledges that its multifaceted assembly is a tip of the hat to 'Mouth for
War' by Pantera and 'Holy Wars ... The Punishment Due' by Megadeth.

The static that concluded *Scenes from a Memory* welcomes us to this
exploration of the initial three parts of Portnoy's multi-album model:
'Reflection', 'Restoration', and 'Revelation'.A bell periodically rings as scruffy
bass notes purr beneath Petrucci's clean fundamental motif. Before long,
Portnoy accompanies them with unstable beats, resulting in a stirringly
anxious build-up to Rudess' piercing emulation of Petrucci's riff. From there,
its unrestrained wrath definitely exemplifies the impact of the aforementioned
pair of metal messiahs; this antagonism is upheld as Portnoy and LaBrie trade-
off verse lyrics, with the latter using a distortion filter to seem distant. It's a bit
bland melodically, but the sheer strength of it all keeps it mesmerizing. Along
the way, Rudess' hearty and odd digital timbre add an invigoratingly bizarre
coating right before the catharsis of the sing-along chorus. The last lines of this
opening portion – 'Chasing a long lost friend / I no longer can control / Just
waiting for this hopelessness to end' – are touchingly enlightening in terms
of what Portnoy was going through. Likewise, the subsequent reprise of the
starting instrumentation alongside police sirens is a stimulating segue into the
next movement.

The sludgy chords and DJ-esque record spinning that start 'Restoration'
are an unconventional pair, to say the least, but it somehow works. Similarly,
Portnoy's growls – something he controversially does throughout his career –
and the animalistic background chants complement LaBrie's unfriendly lead
to produce a surprisingly effective hellish musical representation of Portnoy's
inner fight. Rudess' pouncing organ uproars deepen LaBrie's soothing angst –
'Help me / I can't break out this prison all alone' – as the rest of Dream Theater
trudge along with demonic determination. He and Portnoy continue their
crotchety back-and-forth dialogue, personifying Portnoy's cognitive dissonance
over the relentless score. Smartly, they echo the 'Help me' fragment before
diving into a furiously unhinged and eccentric instrumental break. Petrucci

and Rudess interchange showy expertise before uniting to support a short solo from Myung, which is placed around more frenetic ruptures. It's a completely captivating marathon that surely points to the unapologetic aggression of *Train of Thought*.

After a swift breakdown, Portnoy's nonstop percussion and LaBrie's catchy gratified insights introduce 'Revelation'.It's the shortest and simplest portion of 'The Glass Prison', acting more like a bolstering coda than an immense journey; yet, the stationary arrangement is enjoyable enough to make LaBrie's confessions sufficiently provoking. On that note, his verses are spotlessly desirable, with an ultimate resolution – 'I turned around, saw a light shining through / The door was wide open' – that caps off the track superbly and makes you want to see where the 'Twelve-step Suite' goes afterwards. It was also wise of Dream Theater to end it here, with the sound of glass shattering, instead of with the lengthy drum solo they'd demoed.

'Blind Faith' (LaBrie)

Revolving around the manipulative and authoritative clout of religion, 'Blind Faith' swells with orchestral warm-ups and prolonged violin-effected guitar yelps at first. It fruitfully cements an uneasy setting on which Petrucci places his mellow outline. Hassle-free syncopation and piano intervals join the fray as LaBrie's snarky inquisitions unfold. More vibrant characteristics are incorporated, generating a breezily effervescent ether that recalls *Falling Into Infinity* and foretells *Octavarium*. The forceful chorus is met with a rougher foundation and more backing vocals, and the words that follow – such as 'Yeah, I have it all / The bigger house / An iron fence to keep you out' – are apt jabs at the exclusory corruption commonly found in organized piety.

A loving bridge with mimicking guitarwork – 'And still life pushes on / With or without you' – offers palpable craving and empathy. In-between extra reassuring riffs, Myung preserves the theme as Petrucci and Portnoy let loose. Shortly thereafter, Rudess gifts both a sudden yet ravishingly symphonic piano deviation and a couple of friskily agitated solos, each with vastly different tones. Expectedly, Dream Theater carry back the pre-chorus, chorus, and inaugural instrumentation to bring 'Blind Faith' full circle. While a trace too wearisome overall, it's almost entirely exciting, moving, and dynamic, with Rudess once again displaying crucial resourcefulness.

'Misunderstood' (Petrucci)

There are multiple interpretations of what this one is about, ranging from more commentary on Christianity to how an artist like Billy Joel can, as Petrucci explains, 'go from being in front of a million people to back in his hotel room all by himself'. In any case, it's a very good track whose serene start – brushes of acoustic guitar and weird sound effects beside LaBrie's pensive meditations – soon grows into a prettily peaceful yet gloomy atmosphere. Menacing guitar arpeggios and strings play a major role in this progression, and the multilayered chorus is accentuated by Portnoy's shaker. Colourful kinks pervade as we move closer to the defiant and fighting chorus, with probing melodic changes and combatively poetic wordplay adorning the environment in the interim. Halfway in, Petrucci's stacked solo – which he reversed twice in the control room – is downright creepy, especially with Rudess' supernatural strings around it. In fact, it's debatably the most daringly uncanny division on Six Degrees of Inner Turbulence. That said, 'Misunderstood' mostly plays it safe from this point onward – which isn't a knock against it – by referring to previous parts amid additional nuttiness from Rudess and Petrucci. It's redundant and tedious by the end, yes, but it nonetheless showcases just how brazenly investigational Dream Theater were at this stage. It's a shame that the cassette version of the record condensed some of that staunch lunacy.

'The Great Debate' (Petrucci)

Undoubtedly one of the most polarizing pieces Dream Theater ever cut, it features Portnoy's father, Howard, on the gong and was originally named 'Conflict at Ground Zero'. Obviously, they changed it to 'The Great Debate' after 9/11 and to better reflect the subject-matter: an unbiased and timely statement about stem cell research. Galloping bass and drums – among other elements – frame a series of voiceovers from various pundits, newscasters, and the like about the topic. While it's far from the first time the band has employed soundbites to augment a song, it's feasibly the most apropos thus far since it clues listeners into the exact discussions Dream Theater are responding to.

About three minutes in, feverish guitar riffs unveil two verses that cleverly juxtapose opposing but equally legitimate viewpoints. In doing so, they instantly demonstrate how the argument – like so many others – is filled with grey areas and can't be reduced to one-sided, black and white judgments. Plus, the robotic effect on LaBrie's voice makes him sound suitably emotionless and objective. As a result, he's expressly potent and hopeful when he unaffectedly belts out the ensuing hook: 'Turn to the light / Don't be frightened of the shadows it creates'.Later, and in great contrast, he menacingly sings, 'Are you justified / Justified in taking / Life to save life'. These aligned temperamental twists from all involved cunningly find Dream Theaterarticulating the divided answers to stem cell research *within* the mood swings of the tune.

This topsy-turvy set-up is sustained pending a fleeting and tender bridge – 'We're reaching / But have we gone too far' –that goes into an intimidating voiceless conduit for more punchy assertions. LaBrie's murmurs become boisterous when he decrees, 'Miracle potential / Sanctity of life / Faced against each other / We're divided'. As he modifies the earlier hook to reflect a new mentality, the arrangement is stilted and pouncing – that is, untilRudess and Petrucci take over by spicing up their emblematic wildness with heightened sentimentality. Around them, the rhythm section is complex but controlled, and the addition of angelic voices right before the main riff returns is a nice touch. More voiceovers appear, too, to possibly insinuate that the 'Great Debate' will continue despite the need for amicable compromises. Whether or not Dream Theater – or any artist – should be so political is in the eye of the beholder, but there's little doubt that they accomplish their task exceptionally here.

'Disappear' (LaBrie)

The first disc of *Six Degrees of Inner Turbulence* ends with this overwhelmingly calming yet distressing ballad about death. Specifically, LaBrie says that he penned it after 'seeing a young couple in a mall. They looked like newlyweds, and for most people, including themselves, they had the whole world and many years in their possession. I had a striking thought: 'What if all of this came to [a] crashing halt when one of them is found to have a terminal disease? How would the one left behind deal with and express their experience and loss?'' Previously known as 'Move On', it was totally omitted from the cassette version of the album, which is tragic since it's the best bit of songwriting in the whole package.

Rudess' regal piano chords, paired with the inexplicable noises around it, make the composition feel simultaneously dreamy and nightmarish. It's instantly and tastefully unsettling; fortunately, though, his alignment with Petrucci's acoustic guitar strums – which channel those of 'Scene One: Regression' – are splendid. Together, they harvest a sunnily sorrowful grounding for LaBrie's reverberating search for closure: 'Why, tell me the reasons why / Try, still I don't understand / Will I ever feel this again? / Blue sky, I'll meet you in the end'. It's an unforgivingly upsetting yet universally felt ode for anyone who's longing for someone they've lost.

Heavenly synths and supplementary eeriness – including cellos played backwards – prevail as Portnoy comes in at the second verse. LaBrie stays earnestly mournful, reciting brutally blunt miseries around flourishes of harps and other arresting components. Thankfully, he finally finds solace as the music intensifies: 'So I'm moving on / I'll never forget / As you lay there and watched me / Accepting the end, I knew you were scared / You were strong / I was trying'. The interlocking voices at this moment enrich its meaningful muscle, leaving only a last instrumental callback between LaBrie's healing and the inevitable self-reflection that commences after Six Degrees of Inner Turbulence is done. Even writing about it gives you a lump in the throat – trust me – so suffice it to say that the enchanting heartache of 'Disappear' is far-reaching and timeless.

'I. Overture' (Petrucci, Portnoy, Myung, Rudess)

Composed mostly by Rudess – with Portnoy, Petrucci, and Myung working around 'his keyboard parts since his parts were recorded first' – it was the first thing Dream Theater created for 'Six Degrees of Inner Turbulence'. Interestingly, Portnoy approached his contributions 'like that of an orchestral player... by doing things like multiple marching snare drum overdubs and bass drum and tom patterns with orchestra cymbals'. As for how it comes across, well, it bests virtually every other progressive metal overture of 2002 – namely,

Symphony X's turn at bat for 'The Odyssey'– due to its fertile and versatile fusion of foretelling themes.

It starts off with irate philharmonic opulence, meshing stubborn metal and succulent ceremonial trademarks as it hints at upcoming melodies. There's an air of sophisticated classiness to it that few, if any, of their peers could match; in other words, it's a perfect amalgamation of Dream Theater's recognized recipe and centuries-old classical works. Its gesture toward 'War Inside My Head' about one-third through is arguably the peak of that balance, and the lush tranquillity that follows delivers a stunning divergence. As it winds down, a tricky united oscillation from Myung and Portnoy signals Petrucci's imposing licks as the 'Solitary Shell' and 'About to Crash' suggestions play out. It wraps up by triumphantly announcing 'Losing Time/Grand Finale', too, so it by and large indicates motifs in chronological order. From beginning to end, it's as cohesive and creatively go-getting as you'd hope.

'II. About to Crash' (Petrucci)

This one deals with a girl who has bipolar disorder and battles with her alternating states. Rudess' fancily resilient piano chords softly appear out of the aftermath of 'Overture' and are quickly met with infrequent destruction from his bandmates. LaBrie shares her story with rewarded springiness and eye-catching compassion, using pertinent metaphors to manifest what she and an unspecified male counterpart – probably her father or doctor – go through. The relatively straightforward music is majorly worrisome, yet it becomes lightly jovial as LaBrie details her upbringing. Still, it's a hauntingly relatable chronicle so far, especially in learning how she tried so hard to be 'the perfect teenage girl' despite being so unhappy and 'los[ing] her mind'.

An intriguing and inventive rotation happens near the end, with everything changing mid-chorus into a sterner and more buoyant transformation from her depression to her mania: 'Much to her advantage / She resumed her frantic pace / Boundless power / Midnight hour / She enjoyed the race'. Petrucci's bawling solo is made tenser by the thrust of the other players, and it seamlessly slows down – with kind-hearted support from Rudess and Portnoy – to squeeze more sadness out of the situation and further allude to 'Losing Time/Grand Finale'.

'III. War Inside My Head' (Portnoy)

This dive into PTSD– resulting from the Vietnam War – was written alongside 'The Test That Stumped Them All', which is why the two sound so similar. As for its brief length and why it cuts off when it does, Portnoy says, 'It's just the way it came out'. Appropriately, it charges in full-bodied, with panicky percussion and riffs – from Petrucci and Rudess in sync – exhibiting the horrors of battle. Subtle flamboyant qualities, such as horns, add a slightly debauched funhouse vibe, too. LaBrie is grim in describing what the person went through in the jungle: 'A free vacation / Of palm trees and shrapnel

Above: John Myung looking mysterious while his Majesty bandmates smile in the dressing room of L'Amour, Brooklyn in 1986. *(Dream Theater; provided by Scott Hansen)*

Below: Dream Theater embodying the token 1980s metal look in a 1989 promotional photo for *When Dream and Day Unite*. *(Photo by Chris Carroll)*

Left: Although many fans consider *Images and Words* the true start of Dream Theater, their debut album is a worthy predecessor, and Amy Guip's design remains provocative and interesting. (*One Way Records*)

Right: Nearly thirty years later, Larry Freemantle's cover for Dream Theater's sophomore record is still one of the most iconic in all of progressive metal. (*ATCO Records*)

Left: Freemantle once again incorporated imagery from the songs to create *Awake*'s eye-catching collage. (*East West Records America*)

Right: James LaBrie bringing his trademark passion and style to the stage in 1992. (*Photo by Edwin Van Hoof*)

Left: Likewise, John Myung plays with modest concentration at the same gig. (*Photo by Edwin Van Hoof*)

Right: John Petrucci rocking abstract artwork on his guitar in 1992. (*Photo by Edwin Van Hoof*)

Right: Former keyboardist Derek Sherinian looking mildly annoyed before a performance in 1994. (*Photo by John Harrell*)

Below: A calm, cool, and collected Dream Theater – sans a keyboardist – pose for a 1994 promo shot. (*Photo by William Hames*)

Below: An earlier shot of Dream Theater (with former keyboardist Kevin Moore) looking frustrated yet focused in the studio in 1994. (*Photo by Michael Johansson)*

Right: We see a united group with individual styles in this 1997 promotional image. (*East West Records America; photo provided by Scott Hansen*)

L - R : MIKE PORTNOY, JOHN MYUNG, JAMES LABRIE, JOHN PETRUCCI, DEREK SHERINIAN

PHOTO CREDIT : JOHN FALLS 1997

Below: Dream Theater pose with friends Steve Howe (Yes), Steve Hogarth (Marillion), Steve Rothery (Marillion), and Barney Greenway (Napalm Death) at Ronnie Scotts Jazz Club, London, in 1995. (*East West Record Americas; photo provided by Scott Hansen*)

Left: Drummer Mike Portnoy, photographer Joseph Cultice, and Freemantle drew from *A Change of Seasons*' title track to conceive its evocative cover. (*East West Records America*)

Right: Although 1997's *Falling Into Infinity* is underwhelming, if also underappreciated, there's no denying the fascinating design by genre legend Storm Thorgerson. (*East West Records America*)

Left: *Metropolis Pt. 2: Scenes from a Memory* is almost certainly Dream Theater's greatest achievement, so it's only fitting that the cover looks just as mesmerizing. (*Elektra Records*)

Right: In contrast to the complexity of earlier albums, the imagery here is charmingly reserved, abstract, and almost child-like. (*Elektra Records*)

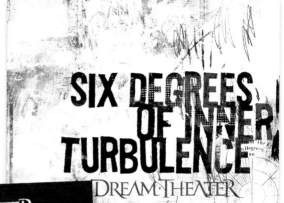

Left: The band purposefully went darker and dirtier with 2003's *Train of Thought*, and that lack of colourful playfulness is surely expressed by the artwork, too. (*Elektra Records*)

Right: This album marked the start of Dream Theater's collaboration with artist Hugh Syme, who brings a tasteful and earthy symmetry to the look of *Octavarium*. (*Atlantic Records*)

Above: A brighter and sleeker Dream Theater welcome the new millennium in this 2002 promotional photo. (*Photo by Ken Schles*)

Right: Keyboardist Jordan Rudess tips his hat to us during the *Train of Thought* writing sessions. (*Photo provided by Scott Hansen*)

Left: Dream Theater and crew take a breather together during the Summer 2004 tour. (*Photo by Rikk Feulner*)

Right: A glimpse at the Octavarium Orchestra making magic at New York City's Hit Factory. (*Photo provided by Scott Hansen*)

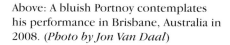

Above: A bluish Portnoy contemplates his performance in Brisbane, Australia in 2008. (*Photo by Jon Van Daal*)

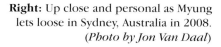

Right: Up close and personal as Myung lets loose in Sydney, Australia in 2008. (*Photo by Jon Van Daal*)

Above: The 2008 Brisbane show also sees Petrucci nailing every note. (*Photo by Jon Van Daal*)

Above: An ecstatic crowd thoughtfully watches Dream Theater do their thing in Lisbon, Portugal in 2009. (*Photo by Pedro Matos*)

Left: Rudess uses an eccentric instrument to suit his eccentric playing during a 2009 show in Melbourne, Australia. (*Photo by Jon Van Daal*).

Right: Syme adds touches of insect bizarreness to an otherwise classy symbolization of 2007's *Systematic Chaos*. (*Roadrunner Records*)

Left: *Black Clouds And Silver Linings.* An appropriately poignant and artsy cover to accompany Portnoy's uneven last stint with the group. Intentionally or not, the blue sky in the doorway even links it to its follow-up, *A Dramatic Turn of Events.* (*Roadrunner Records*)

Right: *A Dramatic Turn of Events.* Emerging from the trials and tribulations of replacing Portnoy with Mike Mangini, Dream Theater certainly had to do a tough balancing act. Luckily, this 2011 re-emergence exceeded expectations. (*Roadrunner Records*)

Above: A double dose of Rudess at a 2014 concert in Portugal. (*Photo by Pedro Matos*)

Above: Bathed in pink, Rudess reveals an even quirkier instrument at that same Portugal show. (*Photo by Pedro Matos*)

Left: LaBrie returns to belt out a beloved tune in Portugal. (*Photo by Pedro Matos*)

Above: Mangini is poised to deliver percussive thrills in this 2014 shot from Sydney. *(Photo by Jon Van Daal)*

Below: At the same time, we look up at Myung being a master of his craft. *(Photo by Jon Van Daal)*

Above: The band waves goodbye to a packed house of adoring fans in Portugal in 2017. (*Photo by Pedro Matos*)

Left: Wildman Petrucci sizes up a solo during the 2017 Sydney stint. (*Photo by Jon Van Daal*)

Below: They clearly brought visuals to match the music at this 2017 Portugal performance. (*Photo by Pedro Matos*)

A.C.O.S-- 1 (THE CRIMSON SUNRISE)
        2 (INNOCENCE)
THE MIRROR/LIE

BURNING MY SOUL
ANOTHER HAND/KILLING HAND

JUST LET ME BREATHE
CAUGHT IN ALICE'S 9-INCH TOOL GARDEN

PERUVIAN SKIES
PULL ME UNDER

LINES IN THE SAND

TAKE AWAY MY PAIN
A.C.O.S. -- 4 (THE DARKEST OF WINTERS)
THE YTSE JAM
LEARNING TO LIVE
A.C.O.S. -- 7 (THE CRIMSON SUNSET)

METROPOLIS PART 1

Left: An impressive and intriguingly arranged setlist from a 1996 concert. (*Photo provided by Scott Hansen*)

Above right: One can only imagine what it must've been like to join them on their 1997 European tour. (*Photo provided by Scott Hansen*)

Right: A cool token from Dream Theater's February 2002 show in Amsterdam. (*Photo by Stéphane Auzilleau*)

Left: Not a bad price to see Dream Theater support *Train of Thought*, right? (*Photo by Heather Johannen*)

Left: A colourful ticket from the historically significant – and totally awesome – first Gigantour. (*Photo by Gonzalo Perkeleporquetzacoatl*)

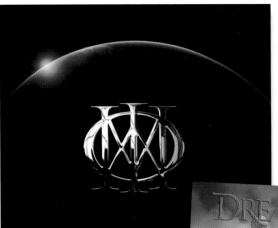

Left: The cover to Dream Theater's self-titled 2013 LP is about as exciting and memorable as the music is represents. (*Roadrunner Records*)

Right: Despite its flaws, *The Astonishing* doesn't get the credit it deserves, and its artwork does a fine job of making you feel like you're a part of the plot. (*Roadrunner Records*)

Left: To prog or not to prog, that is the question Dream Theater ask as their latest studio record displays a futuristic nod to Shakespeare's *Hamlet*. (*Inside Out Music*)

/ Trading innocence for permanent psychotic hell'. In contrast, his chorus rises enticingly with Portnoy's backing singing. It's certainly not a favourite movement of 'Six Degrees of Inner Turbulence', but it is undeniably successful in encapsulating the gravity of its topic into a persuasive track.

'IV. The Test That Stumped Them All' (Portnoy)
A madcap cyclone of rhythms, guitar playing, and quirky keyboard accents guides us into this depiction of a man trying to remedy his schizophrenia. Although faster, it very much conserves the uninviting metal edge of its predecessor – in a good way – with a simple and satisfying rhyme scheme in the lyrics. LaBrie discusses the tests and trials that the doctors put him through, with a modest yet attractive chorus instantly getting stuck in your head. What's most interesting about 'The Test That Stumped Them All' are the vocal exaggerations Dream Theater use to represent the people around the patient. Exchanges like 'The boy is simply crazy! / Suffering from delusions / We honestly think that maybe / He might need an institution' find LaBrie adopting a melodramatic persona while Petrucci and/or Portnoy counter with falsetto replies. It's a novel and absorbing way to enlarge the theatricality. Petrucci and Rudess' solos roughly midway into it are strong, of course, but not as unique or essential as some of the others they include in the sequence. In total, it's a great glimpse into Dream Theater's most unstoppably harsh side, as well as a staggering juxtaposition to the song that comes next.

'V. Goodnight Kiss' (Portnoy)
Portnoy enlisted his family – wife Marlene, son Max, and daughter Melody – for the voices heard on this piece about a mother who's lost her child[ren] and is suffering from post-partum depression. It's the most ambient and delicate part of the disc, with barely more than Petrucci's seemingly underwater guitar chords assisting LaBrie's operatic lamentations at the start. Rudess' perverted strings and imperial piano playing enhance the sense of trauma, too, while Portnoy's shy taps maintain the momentum. It presents a good stylistic change for the work – with stirring connections to 'Overture' from Petrucci – and the final segment of spoken hospital ordeals is quick-witted and remarkably disturbing.

'VI. Solitary Shell' (Petrucci)
Deftly diffusing the tautness that arose from the ending of 'Goodnight Kiss', Petrucci's acoustic guitar hustle is an unconcealed homage to Peter Gabriel's charming 'Solsbury Hill'. This time, Dream Theater are detailing a youth with schizoid personality disorder or some form of autism, with Rudess' playful overtones insinuating childlike wonderment. LaBrie sings with omniscient sympathy as he tells the tale of a boy who 'was considered somewhat odd / Kept to himself most of the time / He would daydream in and out of his

own world / But in every other way, he was fine'. It's surprisingly upbeat and radiant, actually, with a lavish instrumental passage two-thirds through that sees Portnoy and Myung team-up for start/stop dominance around Rudess' celebratory cycle. Petrucci also gets the spotlight with an unperturbed, Grateful Dead-esque acoustic guitar solo before the guys come together for a growing ascent toward resolution. All in all, it's an outstanding piece of the puzzle.

'VII. About to Crash (Reprise)' (Petrucci)
Told from the perspective of the aforementioned anguished girl, this return starts off with exhilarating hunger. Petrucci's chainsaw licks move around the direct rhythms with merry independence, and LaBrie does an excellent job portraying her ecstasy: 'I'm alive again / The darkness far behind me / I'm invincible / Despair will never find me'. It's impossible not to get swept away by its energetic glory. Naturally, they revise the chorus from 'About to Crash' as they go, leading to a wonderful wedge of instrumentation in which Rudess and Petrucci go all out with multiple characteristically white-knuckle timbres. In particular, Rudess' solo after the militaristic collapse from Portnoy and Myung – while quite short – is one of his most hypnotically pleasurable add-ons ever. As it comes to a close, it recalls 'Overture' with awesome tenacity, revealing yet again why Dream Theater is pretty much matchless when it comes to tying together several themes to make an awe-inspiring culmination.

'VIII. Losing Time/Grand Finale' (Petrucci)
Dissociative identity disorder, more commonly known as multiple personality disorder, gets the focus here. The majestic endcap of 'About to Crash (Reprise)' is carried over prior to 'Losing Time' taking its place as a soothing ballad ornamented by fuzzy guitar arpeggios and shuffling syncopation. LaBrie paints a caring portrait of how isolated and lost the sufferer is – 'She doesn't recall yesterday / Faces seem twisted and strange / But she always wakes up / Only to find she'd been miles away' – and the chorus oozes weighty desperation and yearning as the score gets more robust.

The track becomes a tad more optimistic when 'Grand Finale' kicks in, with LaBrie assuring his audience: 'Hope / In the face of our human distress / Helps us to understand the turbulence deep inside / That takes hold of our lives / Shame and disgrace over mental unrest / Keeps us from saving those we love'. He then alludes to each of the previous 'degrees' as the music shifts slightly toward a more selfless and appreciative attitude. Given how much stigmatization and misfortunate still surrounds mental illness, this message is still undeniably vital. It concludes with a drum fill and gong hit, fading out by extending an E major chord into the silence. This same chord starts the next album, Train of Thought, continuing the continuity between records that Scenes from a Memory started in addition to capping off one of the best progressive music suites of the 2000s.

Bonuses

The Japanese edition of *Six Degrees of Inner Turbulence* contains a radio edit of 'Solitary Shell'. Predictably, it removes the instrumental jam entirely and instead adds two guitar chords after Portnoy's drum fill. It's not as good as the proper version, but it makes sense why this version was made.

'Train of Thought' (2003)

Personnel:
James LaBrie: lead vocals
John Petrucci: guitar, backing vocals
John Myung: bass
Jordan Rudess: keyboards
Mike Portnoy: drums, backing vocals
Eugene Friesen: cello (5)
Doug Oberkircher: engineer
Dan Bucchi: assistant engineer
Brian Harding: assistant engineer
Kieran Pardias: assistant engineer
Yohei Goto: assistant engineer
Kevin Shirley: mixing
Jerry Uelsmann: artwork, photography
Anita Marisa Boriboon: art direction
Produced at Cove City Sound Studios, Pie Studios, The Hit Factory, and Beat Street Studios in New York City, March – September 2003 by Mike Portnoy and John Petrucci
UK and US release date: November 2003.
Highest chart places: UK: 146, USA: 53
Running time: 69:21
Current edition: Music on Vinyl / Elektra Records 2016 grey and white vinyl

Having pushed themselves into magnificently ambitious territory – as well as fulfilled a few progressive rock prerequisites – with *Scenes from a Memory* and *Six Degrees of Inner Turbulence*, there weren't many untested artistic avenues left for Dream Theater to traverse. Hence, their next studio undertaking saw them do what many other acts before them have done once they've conquered the boundaries of experimentation: they honed their influences and reassessed their tactics into a revitalized back-to-basics declaration. That's not to say that *Train of Thought* is uninspired or lacking in complexity (far from it), but rather that it largely substitutes the reflective storytelling and glitzy timbres of its precursors for a bleaker and less fantastical guise teeming with insidious mercilessness. It's a different course of action for sure – and a definite turn-off for some – but its abundance of top-notch melodies and vicious musicianship places it as one of Dream Theater's most consistent and adrenaline-charged offspring.

They began writing it in early March 2003 –choosing without hesitance to make it 'unashamedly brutal, based on the notion of creating a 'classic' heavy metal album' like the ones they were replicating on the road – and finished everything but the vocals in less than a month. In an interview with *Metal Edge* magazine at the time, Portnoy said that they wanted to make it feel like live performance rather than overly produced, as well as 'a little easier to digest'.

He adds: 'We also looked at all the tunes from our catalogue that always go over great live, and it's always the real heavy, grooving songs ... We wrote [the songs] in a rehearsal studio with the amps on eleven, and wrote them as a live band before translating them to tape'.

Although he wasn't opposed to that direction, Rudess was still in the midst of his heavy metal education, and he wondered how much he could contribute to a style that typically prioritizes guitar, bass, drums, and vocals over keyboards. Luckily, he soon realized the role he should play:

[It] took me a while to get used to what was going on, and it was a little bit of a shock to be thrust into the dream that the boys had for creating a metal album. It wasn't a personal dream, but it was their dream and I wanted to relate to it. When we first started, I wasn't really sure what to do or how to position myself ... That just meant that I had to walk out of the room sometimes just to get a sonic break. Just to refresh myself and bring my composer mind back to the table ... I ended up making a lot of sounds that were just really grungy and heavy, and when you listen to them it's hard to tell what it is. It could be a guitar or anything ... I've now got this collection of heavy stuff that goes so well with the guitar.

As for LaBrie, he was determined to take a more active role in the creation of *Train of Thought* following the stipulations and concessions he established with Portnoy and Petruccia few months earlier.After all, he was glad to be given the ultimatum of – as Wilson puts it – 'shape-up-or-ship-out' since he, too, felt the need to do more than just offer a lyric or vocal melody on occasion. To that end, he says it 'created a renewed sense of belonging and camaraderie' within Dream Theater because he was there for every step in the process, even if he did little more than voice his thoughts on the music that the other four guys were coming up with.

The writing of *Train of Thought* would've remained quick and smooth if not for a harrowing – yet undeniably humorous in hindsight – mishap that, ironically enough, became news around April Fools' Day. To make a long story short, a man named Anthony Mendez had spent about a month going around New York City pretending to be Portnoy; he even knew 'intimate business and family details' and 'managed to steal wallets, credit cards, cell phones, house keys, and whatever else he could get his hands on'. Predictably, he also ordered gear from drum companies on behalf of Portnoy. Even Savatage guitarist Chris Caffery – now with Trans-Siberian Orchestra – was momentarily fooled by him at a bar one day. Caffery remembers: 'He held phone conversations on my phone with supposed mutual friends ... I got into a room with this guy ... and knew something was up. He was still hammered, but he was not a good drummer'. Mendez was finally captured as Dream Theater were working on the record's penultimate track, the instrumental 'Stream Of Consciousness', forcing them all to stop and rush to the Queens Police Station. He was 'charged with criminal impersonation in the second degree and grand larceny in the fourth degree, with bail set at $100,000' before being jailed. (He returned three years later for a less successful second attempt.)

Shortly after Mendez was apprehended, they entered Cove City Studios—and then Pie Studios a bit later – to work on recording and overdubbing the music. As they were finishing up, they were asked to do a co-headlining tour with Queensrÿche that summer. Portnoy reflects: 'It actually worked out good that we took a six-week break to do [it], because we needed that period to write the lyrics'. For better or worse, the situation would impact the songwriting on *Train of Thought* more than they'd anticipated. Basically, Queensrÿche were unfriendly and detached, demanding that they close the show every night. In addition, then-guitarist Mike Stone insulted Petrucci by insinuating that he needed help as a guitarist. Resourcefully, Petrucci filtered these 'behind-the-scenes difficulties', among other grievances, into opener 'As I Am'.Unsurprisingly – given their tempers – Portnoy and ex-singer Geoff Tate continued their feud for years afterwards.

After laying down LaBrie's vocals, they instructed Shirley to mix it all with Metallica and, oddly enough, nü-metal newcomers Mudvayne in mind. By the end of September, it was completed at The Hit Factory and ready to receive its title and artwork. Of the former component, Portnoy rightly boasts: 'It just seemed totally fitting, given the power and aggression of the music. It felt like a steamroller – like a train just running you over'. As for the imagery, he wanted a lack of colour to reflect the darkness of the tunes. Upon discovering the work of retired visual artist Jerry Uelsmann, Portnoy 'had the art directors at Elektra investigate the possibilities of working with them ... we were able to use his gallery work, and went through hundreds of photos and found some that tied with the lyrics'.

Dream Theater took great care not to let fans know much about *Train of Thought* before it came out that November. This was partially due to how online speculation – such as the type *Scenes from a Memory* and *Six Degrees of Inner Turbulence* received – can result in 'no room for the imagination once the record comes out', as Portnoy remarks. Although warranted, this nonetheless meant that devotees were divided upon hearing it. Specifically, some 'found the uncompromising heaviness ... suffocating, and lamented the loss of the musical light and shade that had always balanced previous albums'. Many of those naysayers have no doubt warmed up to it since then, but their gripes remain valid considering how much of an anomaly it remains nearly twenty years later.

On the other hand, the press were almost entirely positive, with more unexpected outliers voicing their support. For instance, *The Washington Post* jokingly warned, '*Train of Thought* is the classic metal album that no classic metal band could ever pull off. Wear earplugs if you must, but the rest of us will go deaf in bliss'. Congruently, pop culture juggernaut *IGN* declared: 'They've gotten a lot heavier this time out, and I welcome it'.The subsequent

2004 tour – during which they recorded the *When Dream and Day Reunite* commemoration/redo alongside Charlie Dominici and Derek Sherinian, plus *Live at Budokan*– was also met with encouraging reviews and barely any trouble on or off stage.

Anyone who prefers Dream Theater's frank hostility over their whimsical flights of fancy probably regards *Train of Thought* as a favourite, and for good reason. Its instances of shallow noodling and undeservedly elongated track durations aside, the LP is persistently alluring because of tight and enthralling commitment to its specialized sound. In nailing their vintage aesthetic, they made something infectiously brisk, outspoken, and lingering. In that sense, it's perhaps the last truly great Dream Theater album, and its comparable uniqueness from the rest is something we all should honour.

'As I Am' (Petrucci)

Literally picking up where *Six Degrees of Inner Turbulence* left off, the only single from the record, 'As I Am', is fearlessly – if also adolescently – confrontational from the start. Lyrically, it's Petrucci telling Dream Theater doubters and cynics, 'We are not going to change for people that try to mould us into a formula. We are just doing what we do, and hopefully people appreciate it'. On the contrary, the sentiment 'For those who understand / I extend my hand' is meant as a thank you to the loyal and open-minded fans. Some awkwardly on-the-nose wording notwithstanding, it's hard to deny the cleverness of the pre-chorus: 'I've been trying to justify you / In the end, I will just defy you'.

Sonically, it's endlessly thrilling and catchy. Petrucci's opening harmonics and strikes, matched with Portnoy's breakneck syncopation and Myung's guttural hums, instantly wakes you up to the refined provocations that await. True to his word, Rudess' layers are frequently hard to pinpoint, but his starry intonations during the more tranquil and alluring transitions are surely valued. His synths also build expectancy for a hyperactive and choppy guitar solo that, despite servicing technique over mood or melody, is still damn impressive. Portnoy's ensuing drum fill is just as imposing, and LaBrie nails his atypical hostility the whole way through. Cumulatively, it's a kickass way to kick off *Train of Thought*.

'This Dying Soul' (Portnoy)

This is the second entry into the 'Twelve-step Suite', covering the fourth and fifth parts: 'Reflections of Reality (Revisited)' and 'Release'. Astutely, it also looks back at 'The Mirror' from *Awake* a few times, such as with the line 'Hello mirror/ So glad to see you, my friend / It's been a while' (of course, this is a nod to the wistful conclusion of 'Regression' from *Scenes from a Memory* as well). Its initial blizzard of jackhammer percussion and guitar riffs is completely tantalising, with the song's signature mystical lick excelling as one of Dream Theater's most spellbinding. Similarly, Rudess' foreshadowing of a key vocal section is exciting.

Like the previous tune, the equilibrium between tolerant and tumultuous moments during this first half is cool, too, with gentle verses leading to defiant counterpoints. As for the chorus, it's delightfully adhesive. The same can't be said for LaBrie's cringe-worthy distorted raps, but the sheer fluidity with which the group fluctuates between motifs makes up for it. Lastly, the piano-led tie to the next movement is peacefully moving, closing with a link to the previous entry in the saga – 'All your sins will only make you strong / And help you break right through the prison wall' – that can't help but put a smile on your face.

Some tricky modulations give way to the less personable 'Release'. The oscillations between stereo channels prevents it from being totally lifeless, as do the instrumental jolts. Draped in Rudess' spectral tones, LaBrie then appears like a foreboding phantom to warn, 'You can't hold onto your secrets / They'll only send you back alone'. Extra reprisals combine with fidgety new breakdowns as Rudess and Petrucci implement tacky showmanship that's self-indulgent and extraneous, yet breath-taking nevertheless. It's no wonder why even diehard listeners were pushed away by these exhaustingly abrasive measures; however, those who like their Dream Theater hectic and thematically booming no doubt bow down to 'This Dying Soul'.

'Endless Sacrifice' (Petrucci)
It's the most hospitable selection thus far and speaks about the troubles of being on the road for too long. Petrucci enlightens: 'Whether you're in a band or in the military, it is being away and longing for your spouse and children. On both sides there is sacrifice'. His introductory acoustic arpeggios align with the relaxed rhythms, piano accompaniment, and shimmering keyboard phrases to convey restless aching. LaBrie is proportionately downhearted as he bemoans the passage of time and distance, telling his loved ones: 'I'm so far away / And so alone / I need to see your face / To keep me sane / To make we whole'.

The main hook is fairly generic, to be honest, but it does accurately epitomize Petrucci's exasperation. Rudess' symphonic response is a commanding connection between it and fresh crestfallen verses. Further on, the Metallica influence really shines within an offbeat instrumental arrangement that also comprises Kansas-esque keyboard outcries and archetypally spiralling time signature swipes. Rudess' jesting orchestral flare-up six-and-a-half minutes in is a great testament to his light-hearted charisma, too. He and Petrucci take turns ruling the landscape before conjoining in a confounding loop of proficiency. Right as LaBrie returns, they also coalesce for a tremendously fretful riff that amplifies enthusiasm. From there, the quintet runs through a few indispensable portions one last time, solidifying 'Endless Sacrifice' as another majorly engaging facet of the disc.

'Honor Thy Father' (Portnoy)
Although they've since reconciled, Portnoy is full of vitriol and spite in this attack against his stepfather. Bearing in mind that the man threw him out of the

house after he came back from Berklee – among other discretions – Portnoy's need to vent is reasonable. Right away, he, Myung, and Petrucci blast off into scornful metal misery. A snappy bass slogan escorts LaBrie and Portnoy's dual beliefs: 'You pretended I was your own / And even believed that you loved me / But were always threatened by some / Invisible bloodline that only you could see'. Rudess and Petrucci embellish Myung's lead, sparking one of the most addictively intense jiffs of chaos on *Train of Thought*. Like 'This Dying Soul' – and no matter how therapeutic the words are for Portnoy – LaBrie's rap is still peculiar. Happily, the hasty mantra 'On and on and on and on it goes' is pleasingly motivating.

He stays fixated on firmly telling off his foe with mentions of trying to 'make amends' and getting his 'piece of mind when you hear this song'. It's not expressly compelling melodically, but his performance is spot-on as the others develop their gruff accommodations. A rapid and appealing conversion of pace and purpose, 'Watch the way you talk / Don't cross the crooked step', indirectly makes it clear that the track isn't about Howard Portnoy. In a traditional Dream Theater method, conceptually related clips from several films and TV shows – Magnolia, At Close Range, Ordinary People, The Royal Tenenbaums, and Oz– play over more dulled ferocity. They're soon replaced by climbing keyboard puzzles that are terminated to make way for Petrucci's crunchy stabs, which waver between stereo sides with absolute displeasure. Additional warlike turmoil reroutes to past extracts to wrap it all up in a belligerent bow. 'Honor Thy Father' may be too wooden and weird every now and then, but it generally stands out due to its raw reactions and intricate violence.

'Vacant' (LaBrie)

Outside of providing a necessary respite from the daunting chunks of lethal sophistication that precede it, 'Vacant' is gorgeously pleading in and of itself. LaBrie wrote it about his daughter, who fell into a coma just before turning seven-years-old. Miraculously, she recovered, and in a 2009 forum post on his website, he expounded:

> The Doctors told my wife and I, she might have had a stroke. While they were about to do a Cat-scan Chloe came out of it. It was a miracle and never again did she have incident with this type of situation. The Doctors never did give us a full diagnosis as to what really happen. Quite honestly I think they were just as baffled as us. Nothing before or since has ever left me feeling as distraught or helpless. [*sic*]

Exquisitely supported by cellist Eugene Friesen, Rudess and Petrucci synchronize the same downtrodden keynote as LaBrie sings with as much gravely smooth conviction as ever. His demoralised spirit exudes from each expression, making his final quandary in particular – 'She's losing control / What can I do? / Her vacant eyes / Black holes / Am I losing you?' – almost unbearable because of the story behind it. It may be Dream Theater's simplest composition to date, but it's also one of their most handsomely harrowing.

'Stream of Consciousness' (Petrucci, Portnoy, Myung, Rudess)

The sole instrumental on *Train of Thought* – and the group's longest yet – gets its title from the original name for *Falling Into Infinity*. As they were working on it, they created a contest for fans to make up their own finished songs based on the charts and multiple section descriptions – like 'Crimson Setup', 'UK Rise', and 'Straight Groove x2' – that Portnoy posted online. The winner would get an autographed copy of the album, the latest Ytsejam Records releases, and a few tickets and backstage passes to a 2004 show. Plus, their track would be 'played during the 'house music' before each show'.After receiving over fifty entries, they put the best seven – including ones from two genre siblings, Linear Sphere and Redemption – on a compilation CD through the Dream Theater International Fan Club.

'Stream of Consciousness' itself is built like the continuation of 'Vacant', with a minor modification of the previously mentioned keynote serving as its centre. In a way, it signifies all of the motley moods LaBrie may have been feeling about his family's situation. After a shy start, Rudess' stately horns add some life to the otherwise enjoyably drab discourse. Likewise, the bouncy diversion at the three-minute mark further cements how well he and Petrucci work as foils and colleagues around Portnoy and Myung's concentrated basis. For the most part, the remaining time is spent retooling these ideas around scattered sensationalism and trickles of virtuosic slices. It's all terrifically interconnected and poignant– don't get me wrong – but it gets tiresome by the end, as it fails to feature enough diversity to rationalise its length. Sadly, this problem marks the beginning of a periodic trend for Dream Theater moving forward, so it's far from the last time a solid blueprint is not sufficiently succinct or multidimensional. Even so, it's a fabulous inclusion as a whole.

'In the Name of God' (Petrucci)

It's likely Dream Theater's most contentious and forthright critique of religion, as it looks at the intersection of extreme fundamentalism and physical attacks. Petrucci explains: '[Leaders] say that it's in the name of God, and if you do this, you'll be saved. It's a kind of backward way of thinking, twisting the fate of religion in order to attain a violent end. These people have done mass suicides, killed individuals and groups of people'. Unfortunately, these practices don't seem to be stopping any time soon, so his commentary is no less important now.

An ominous acoustic guitar arpeggio heralds pulverizing rhythms and riffs as LaBrie speaks in simple rhymes about the illogicality of it all. After some choir croons, piano dirges, and shaken percussion, the enormously gripping and germane chorus – 'Listen / When the prophet speaks to you / Killing / In the name of God / Passion / Twisting faith into violence / In the name of God' – chimes in. Afterwards, a snug bypass activates new, marginally altered musical and lyrical criticisms. It's not long until a perkier segment, 'Blurring the lines / Between virtue and sin / They can't tell / Where God ends / And mankind begins', adds more wounded rumination.

A scant and tribal trajectory – complete with secret bit of Morse code that translates to a vulgar Portnoy catchphrase – takes over. Myung's snarling pattern steers cosmic notes, restful drumming, and slithering narration about 'Hundreds of believers / Lured into a doomsday cult'. This is commonly thought to reference the Branch Davidians who were killed in during the Waco, Texas siege of 1993. Petrucci's jagged lashes, an unanticipated computerized interruption, and LaBrie's nearly inaudible shouts increase the tension. Petrucci successively builds toward a tastily elaborate start/stop enigma – not unlike the one that'd jumpstart *Systematic Chaos* in 2007 –before he and Rudess enter into some superfluous shredding.

Thankfully, 'In the Name of God' gets back on track when celestial squeals and histrionic beats rejuvenate the chorus. Bells and synths set off piecing questions – 'Does following faith / Lead us to violence?' – prior to bestowing a relevantly unruly outro as voices recite 'The Battle Hymn of the Republic'. It dies out gradually, making Rudess' brief piano coda as evocative as possible. It's also worth noting that he plays the last note – F, which also opens *Octavarium* – with his nose. Altogether, it's a thoughtful gem and a first-rate way to cap off the record.

Bonuses

Curiously, only Korea got a special edition of *Train of Thought*. Its second disc, entitled 'Selections from *Live Scenes From New York*', holds seven of the original twenty-five tracks: 'Overture 1928', 'Strange Déjà Vu', 'Home', 'The Spirit Carries On','Just Let Me Breathe', 'Caught in a New Millennium' (a blend of 'Caught in a Web' and 'New Millennium'), and Liquid Tension Experiment's 'Acid Rain'.Because we'll be talking about the entire thing later, we'll say no more about them now.

'Octavarium' (2005)

Personnel:
James LaBrie: lead vocals
John Petrucci: guitar, backing vocals
John Myung: bass
Jordan Rudess: keyboards, Haken Continuum Fingerboard, lap steel guitar
Mike Portnoy: drums, backing vocals
Elena Barere: concert master (7, 8), violin (2)
Ann Lehmann: violin (7, 8)
Katharine Fong: violin (7, 8)
Katherine Livolsi-Stern: violin (7, 8)
Catherine Ro: violin (7, 8)
Laura McGinniss: violin (7, 8)
Yuri Vodovoz: violin (7, 8)
Ricky Sortomme: violin (7, 8)
Carol Webb: violin (2)
Richard Locker: cello (2, 7, 8)
Jeanne LeBlanc: cello (7, 8)
Vincent Lionti: viola (2, 7, 8)
Karen Dreyfus: viola (7, 8)
Pamela Sklar: flute (7, 8)
Joe Anderer: French horn (7, 8)
Stewart Rose: French horn (7, 8)
Jamshied Sharifi: conductor, string arranger
Jill Dell'Abate: orchestral contractor
Doug Oberkircher: engineer
Ryan Simms: assistant engineer
Colleen Culhane: assistant engineer
Kaori Kinoshita: assistant engineer
Michael H. Brauer: mixing
Hugh Syme: art direction, design, photography
Produced at The Hit Factory, New York City, November 2004 – February 2005 by
Mike Portnoy and John Petrucci
UK and US release date: June 2005.
Highest chart places: UK: 72, USA: 36
Running time: 75:44
Current edition: Atlantic Records 2014 CD reissue

Love it or hate it, *Train of Thought* was incontestably a bold move for Dream
Theater, as it risked splitting the fanbase and critical consensuses like never
before. To an extent, that's exactly what happened; yet, it eventually won over
many of its initial detractors and grew quite a dedicated following. Above all else,
it was a total triumph in terms of the band fully injecting the fortes of their '70s
and '80s metal forefathers into their recipe. Therefore, the sensible next step

was to more transparently pay respect to the other half of their DNA – antique progressive rock – within what Rudess calls 'a classic Dream Theater album' that's 'quicker to appreciate'. In a nutshell, the fruits of that labour, *Octavarium*, blend the saturated pigmentation of *Images and Words* and *Six Degrees of Inner Turbulence*, the user-friendliness of *Falling Into Infinity*, and the embittered snapshots of its predecessor into a highly likeable bundle. Admittedly, it's their most uneven LP in almost a decade – with at least two disposable pit stops that point to more shortcomings on the horizon – but it usually thrives.

Octavarium marks both the end of Dream Theater's nearly fifteen-year contract with Atlantic Records and the final record recorded at The Hit Factory before it closed in April 2005. Sentimentality, sales, and artistic freedoms aside, they weren't really upset over the former situation since they still felt that the label wasn't providing adequate promotional support or respect for the group's longevity and sustained quality. True, Atlantic did put out a promo of two songs – 'These Walls' and 'Panic Attack' – ahead of time, but that didn't stop Dream Theater from eventually moving to Roadrunner Records for the next studio outing. As for the end of The Hit Factory – where many other notable acts, like Michael Jackson, Madonna, Bruce Springsteen, Beyoncé, Paul Simon, Stevie Wonder and John Lennon, also passed through – procedures were moved to Hit Factory Criteria Miami for cheaper and easier operations. As for the building, it was turned into luxury condominiums in 2006.

As Rudess confirms, they'd already decided to 'really [go] back to creating a real band effort, as well as [draw] upon ... various stylistic influences' when they began writing the LP. In part, they also wanted to 'make it less complex for people' so that the audience could 'latch on to [certain songs] faster'. Always on the defensive, Portnoy pushed back against the now-common accusation that they were selling out: '[W]e write songs like that because we have that side to us. We love bands like U2 or Coldplay, as well as liking shorter songs ... I mean, writing long songs is easy for us – it's the short ones that are difficult'. Petrucci acts more as a mediator in declaring that *Octavarium* was meant to explore all of their sides in one set: 'I think in general the feeling was that we wanted the songs to be very strong. When we were writing, we actually stripped the sound down and sat there with piano, guitar and vocal to make sure that the melodies and structures were interesting to us and sounded original'. Naturally, their newfound universal cordiality made the scribing sessions almost entirely tension-free.

Whereas past ventures presented faux classical touches, *Octavarium* permitted Dream Theater to work finally with a real orchestra. On February 16, 2005, over a dozen musicians – conducted by fellow Berklee alumni Jamshied Sharifi and chosen 'because of their sight-reading ability' – flooded into Studio One and were able to 'nail music they'd never seen or played before in a maximum of two takes'. For as much praise as Sharifi and his crew deserve, he's quick to shower an equal amount back onto the music they were embroidering: 'When it's good, the players feel that quality, feel there

is a reason to be there and they are that much more inspired. And talking to
the players afterwards, they all had a great time on that session'. Three pieces
in total include the orchestra, with the most substantial being the side-long
closing title track that's directly stimulated by Yes, Genesis, and Pink Floyd,
among other seminal artists. 'We wanted it to have a real prog treatment, and
that changes the way you orchestrate it and the types of parts you come up
with ... The cool thing is that Jordan had all of those major influences', Petrucci
rejoices. To grasp those retro tinges, he and Rudess aimed for '[*magic*]chords
that were melodic but a little bit strange at the same time'.

Even more subtle is Portnoy's plan of writing the sequence 'in ascending
chromatic key'. He describes: '[T]his is our eighth studio album ... [with] five
live albums in between. If you look at a keyboard octave, you have eight notes
leading from A to A, and then the five black notes, the incidentals, in between.
So I looked at our album structure kind of the same way'. Starting with
'Sacrificed Sons' in the key of E, they carried the gimmick to each of the other
seven tracks and included half step 'sound effects' to link them.

Of course, the trademark that began with *Scenes from a Memory* – having LPs
segue into each other – carries over one last time since 'The Root of All Evil'
extends out of from *Train of Thought's* 'In the Name of God'. By this point,
though, Portnoy felt pigeonholed by his cool idea, so he decided to close
the loop and make *Octavarium* 'a cycle within itself' by having 'Octavarium'
conclude with the devilish piano intervals that start 'The Root of All Evil'.

Having already wowed people with the covers of many Rush staples – not
to mention Fates Warning's *Perfect Symmetry* and Megadeth's *Countdown to
Extinction*– Hugh Syme was brought in to do the artwork. After discussing how
'everything you do in music' yields 'either a cluster or triad', he and Portnoy
settled on modelling the back-and-forth physics principle of Newton's cradle.
Other ideas – such as an octagonal maze, a spider and an octopus – wound up
in the booklet, and the back image of a girl avoiding the spheres was conceived
'just to make the inertia believable', Syme says.

Gratefully, both the sales and reception of *Octavarium* fared better than
those of *Train of Thought*. Specifically, it sold close to 30,000 copies in America
alone during its first week, with *Billboard*, *Metal Hammer*, and even *Kerrang!*
revelling in its 'sound of undisputed champions effortlessly asserting their
supremacy'. Chart-wise, it did well internationally, landing top five spots in
Sweden, Italy, and Finland, as well as top ten spots in Denmark, Japan, and
Norway. More recently, both *Classic Rock* and *Loudwire* coincidentally ranked
it as the eighth-best Dream Theater studio work, while *Prog Sphere* placed it
as the sixth. Perhaps most importantly, LaBrie claims that it's 'full of the things
that have brought Dream Theater to what we are ... There is an incredible
sound, feel and atmosphere to it. I truly think it's great'.

Almost immediately after it came out, they started playing live again.
Among the most significant of these treks were their co-headlining stints with
Megadeth as part of Gigantour and more nights of 'An Evening with Dream

Theater', where they'd perform for roughly three hours each evening and include full renditions of Pink Floyd's *The Dark Side of the Moon* accompanied by Theresa Thomason and 'the original film clips' that Pink Floyd used in the 1970s. Portnoy clarifies: '*The Wall* is probably my favourite album of all time ... but it's such an exhausting experience, and it would have been a major undertaking – not just for us but for the audience – to endure'. To his surprise, a fair amount of concertgoers were unfamiliar with and underwhelmed by the material. 'When we did Metallica or Iron Maiden the prog fans probably hated it. In doing an album like *Dark Side* ... the metal fans are probably going to be bored to tears', he concedes. Expectedly, they received commendation for staying faithful to the arrangements.

On April 1, 2006, they played a special 20th-anniversary show at Radio City Music Hall in New York City. The first part of the night consisted of stuff they'd been playing during the tour; however, the second and more unforeseen portion saw them come back from intermission alongside Sharifi's thirty-piece orchestra that contained many of the same people as *Octavarium*. Petrucci divulges that it took 'several months' to plan it all, as they had to decide on the setlist ASAP and then let Sharifi know if they were 'going for a grandiose, epic, movie-sounding thing or ... a more sensitive quartet type of thing'. Sharifi necessitated working with the same concertmaster as on *Octavarium*, Elena Barere, to help them learn about ninety minutes of music in only 'a six-hour rehearsal' the previous day. Once again, Kevin Moore declined Portnoy's request to be a part of the gala. Outside of a few technical, timing, and financial hiccups, the event was everything they'd hoped it would be. That summer, it'd be released as one of Dream Theater's most beloved live documents, *Score*.

Even with a borderline dud or two, *Octavarium* is memorable, distinctive, and worthwhile. It's relatively benign and a touch cheesy in spots, but its strengths considerably outweigh its weaknesses as it recaptures the enchantments of pioneering progressive rock within Dream Theater's updated palette. In that way, it's a comprehensive acknowledgment of not only how far the band has come since forming in 1985, but also of the formative 1970s names who got them there. Today, it's also easy to view it as a calmer and more vivid intermission between the bedlam of 2003 and the systematic chaos of 2007.

'The Root of All Evil' (Portnoy)

Octavarium starts with chapters six and seven of Portnoy's 'Twelve-step Suite', 'Ready' and 'Remove', respectively. Its menacing mash-up of footsteps, percussive escalation, guitar echoes, and wavering digital varnishes – collectively inspired by Pink Floyd's 'Welcome to the Machine' – is niftily overwrought. Once that anxiousness breaks, Petrucci's launches into one of his greatest winding lynchpins in years while everyone else keeps up their stride. With Portnoy's low-end mimicry, LaBrie is rebellious yet remorseful in sneering: 'Never could have just a part of it / I always need more to get by / Getting right down to the heart of it / The root of all evil has been running my

79

whole life'. They linger on that magnetic nastiness some more – with Rudess' cavernous piano and mysterious synths aggregating malice and plugging space – to set-up an immeasurably fetching hook: 'Take all of me / The desires that keep burning deep inside / Cast them all away / And help to give me strength to face another day'. LaBrie's voice is extraordinary here.

The 'Remove' sector takes offs with grungy gusto as it pilots its way toward alluding to both 'The Glass Prison' and 'This Dying Soul' with inventive and dexterous ingenuity that gives you goosebumps. Then, Rudess' twitchy mechanical wizardry and Petrucci's grounded flashiness glide through a horde of ruthless foundations. Gratifyingly, LaBrie's hook and Petrucci's earliest riff return and then fade out as closing piano work offers a peek at the 'Medicate (Awakening)' stage of 'Octavarium'. It's a crafty way to close 'The Root of All Evil', the latest example of why Portnoy's 'Twelve-step Suite' unremittingly benefits the albums on which it resides.

'The Answer Lies Within' (Petrucci)

The sounds of nature act as an F♯/G♭ segue so that 'The Answer Lies Within'– which Petrucci purportedly wrote for his children – can resolve to G minor. Relating back to Dream Theater's goal of fashioning more accessible choices that highlighted songwriting over-complication, this is the best of that bunch on *Octavarium*. It's a tad sappy, sure, but LaBrie and Rudess soar as a sparsely solemn pair at the start. Correspondingly, Petrucci's life-affirming guidance is unpretentious and heartening, as are his acoustic strums beside Portnoy and Myung's graceful complements. Obviously, the strings beautify it, especially in-between the brighter bridge – 'You've got the future on your side / You're gonna be fine now' – and the chorus. By no means is it their finest ballad, but it's certainly not their worst, either, and it's hard not to feel uplifted by its luscious simplicity.

'These Walls' (Petrucci)

It's one of Dream Theater's most insatiably riveting configurations, due mostly to Rudess' mesmerizing keyboard motif that follows a G♯/A♭ pitch bend and shrieking guitar revs. Dealing with the irritation of not reaching your creative potential, 'These Walls' also profits from Petrucci's spacey arpeggios and a nuanced verse melody. The pre-chorus, aided primarily by conquering syncopation, is compellingly urgent. There's an intoxicating essence of dread and determination to it all, with a tastefully emotional guitar solo and some concluding orchestral bombast enhancing its dense and luminous perseverance. The ending transition – a hodgepodge of chimes, wind, heartbeats, and ghostly tones – is particularly effective as well.

'I Walk Beside You' (Petrucci)

Ticking clocks bleed into this preliminarily promising but excessively sugary power ballad. To be fair, everything up to the chorus is bland but okay; it's the crux of the track that veers too close to flowery radio-friendly wholesomeness for comfort. The lyrics are as superficial and insipid as those of countless pop stars, and the instrumentation is hardly more daring than the cookie-cutter slop of many mainstream rock darlings.Even at their most scaled-down and maudlin, Dream Theater are capable of far better than this.

'Panic Attack' (Petrucci)

Amazingly, they redeem themselves with this engrossing – if also overly extended – C minor excursion into alarm and fretfulness that was featured in the 2008 video game Rock Band 2. It'd work fine as an instrumental, mainly because it's ruled by one of the most iconic and astonishing bass lines of Myung's tenure. Portnoy and Petrucci pack on fitting fury to contest him, and they also back up LaBrie's effectively freaked out verses. Rudess' choir and piano intermediately glimmer with stylish panache, too, and the fortified rhythmic willpower aptly embodies commotions like 'Rapid heartbeat pounding through my chest / Agitated body in distress'.Halfway in, LaBrie's falsetto fright – 'Run / Try to hide / Overwhelmed by this complex delirium' – boosts the authenticity of his enactment and sees him sign off so that the rest of 'Panic Attack' can rain down a dizzying influx of guitar and keyboard aguish. Throughout it all, Portnoy and Myung function as a wickedly changeable backbone, making the inevitable reappearance of the chorus exceedingly satisfying. As it closes out, a carnivalesque chord bursts out of the left and right stereo channels as a bizarre programmed C♯/D♭ progression moves into 'Never Enough'. It's an indisputable highpoint for Octavarium.

'Never Enough' (Portnoy)

It's penned by Portnoy as a heated retort to the minority of listeners who were constantly unhappy with what the group did. In a chat with Brave Words & Bloody Knuckles, he inferred: 'To me, one of the most frustrating things about the internet is all the whining, bitching, complaining and dissecting that our fans do over every single thing ... it's very frustrating for me personally because I'm constantly tearing myself away from my family to give more and more'. Thus, its blunt words – notably, 'What would you say / If I walked away / Would you appreciate / But then it'd be too late / Because I can only take so much of your ungrateful ways / Everything is never enough' –are dutifully understandable and unafraid. That said, 'Never Enough' is almost entirely by-the-numbers by Dream Theater standards, with its most attention-grabbing aspect being motivated by the electronic vehemence of Muse's 'Stockholm Syndrome'. Rudess' automated tapestries are arresting and they do give rise to stupendous multilayered guitar work from Petrucci, but apart from that, there's little here that's tempting.

'Sacrificed Sons' (LaBrie)

Brought about by a D♯/E♭ collage of pitiful strings, static, and voices that go from jumbled to judicious, 'Sacrificed Sons' broaches the September 11,

2001 devastation with tender tactfulness. Portnoy kindly manoeuvres gloomy piano and guitar timbres as LaBrie glossily and vulnerably wallows in grief. Symphonic swells and off-putting tones add to the morose and surreal sense of calamity and injustice. Although they're not openly linked, the elevated chorus – 'Who would wish this on our people? / And proclaim that his will be done / Scriptures they heed have misled them / All praise their sacrificed sons' – perceptibly ties back into the message of 'In the Name of God'.

Suddenly, Myung and Petrucci mirror a gravelly riff; it abruptly transforms into an entrancing jam that's strangely similar to a segment of 'In the Presence of Enemies- Part I' from the upcoming *Systematic Chaos*. Rudess and Petrucci unleash a few hysterical and catastrophic observations as it continues to alter gloriously. From there, it returns to LaBrie's central flourishes for a thickly dramatic and heart-stopping climax. Overall, it's colossally rousing and admirable.

'Octavarium' (LaBrie, Petrucci, Portnoy)

Like a lot of modern progressive rock, it proudly and overtly self-references amidst imitating older music (Dream Theater even publicise vintage impersonation as the main ploy); in the process – and despite what those who grew up with those 1970s benchmarks might say – they arguably surpass much of it along the way. Hence, 'Octavarium' is not only the standout piece from its namesake collection and one of the band's apex achievements, but it's also a top-tier epic track within the entire genre.

Petrucci's introspective first phase, 'Someone Like Him', finds Rudess using his lap steel guitar and Haken Continuum Fingerboard to tranquilly tip his hat to Pink Floyd's 'Shine On You Crazy Diamond', among other influences. It's slightly drawn-out, I concede, but it does give the full-bodied score more impact once it hits around the four-minute mark. The resultant union of flute and acoustic guitar is lovely and affords a sublime backdrop for LaBrie's seductive and poetic search for meaning. Petrucci's fingerpicking is charmingly inquisitive as he explicitly emulates Steve Hackett's idiosyncrasies in early Genesis. Emblematically – and as Portnoy's percussion and Rudess' piano help magnify the section's muscle – they revise those lyrics to reflect discovery: 'Then all I swore / That I would never be was now / So suddenly / The only thing / I wanted / To become / To be someone just like him'.

Myung funkily propels us into LaBrie's 'Medicate (Awakening)', which was foreshadowed at the end of 'The Root of All Evil' and somewhat duplicates the narrative of the film *Awakenings*. Unmistakably, the topics of self-actualization and mental health harken back to 'A Change of Seasons' and 'Six Degrees of Inner Turbulence', with the protagonist waking up after thirty years of catatonia to pensively ponder his condition with his doctor. It's another habitually sedative sliver of 'Octavarium' – that is, until Rudess' loony decoration seizes the spotlight as his bandmates chaperon him with perfect reservation. It's breathtaking, and the ways in which it fluidly mutates into

Portnoy's more mischievous 'Full Circle' is masterful.

A captivatingly flamboyant fever dream, this is where Dream Theater get to shout out countless artists who drove them to become what they are. As others have pointed out, the core keyboard brashness is reminiscent of Genesis' 'In the Cage', while the opening line – 'Isn't this where we came in?' – is taken from *The Wall*. Its swarm of other musical winks is far too bloated to account for, and some feel a tinge forced and amateurish. Nevertheless, rushed innuendos such as 'Supper's ready / Lucy in the / Sky with diamond / Dave's not here I / Come to save the / Day for Nightmare / Cinema show / Me the way to get back home again' slickly and artfully conjure Genesis, Judas Priest, the Beatles, David Lee Roth, Cheech and Chong, Styx, Spock's Beard, and a handful of historical Dream Theater tidbits in one fell swoop. The call-and-response chorus is also eye-catching, and it leads to a jaw-dropping voiceless labyrinth of irregular and zany descents whose coolest moment is an acoustic guitar callback to Rudess' aforementioned decoration.

Portnoy's fourth faction, 'Intervals', is utterly ingenious since it involves him naming scale degrees as compositional and lyrical gestures to every song on *Octavarium* – including a former fragment of 'Octavarium' –flash by. For instance, it begins with him and LaBrie switching off on the following exclamations: '(Root) / Our deadly sins feel his mortal wrath / Remove all obstacles from our path / (Second) / Asking questions, search for clues / The answer's been right in front of you'. As it advances, so too does the musical tautness, finally exploding as LaBrie screams, 'Trapped inside this Octavarium!' Whereas his voice is typically the exact opposite of ornery, he's startlingly venomous here.

The chronicle ceases with Petrucci's 'Razor's Edge', with strings recalling 'Someone Like Him' on top of Dream Theater's leisurely bedding. Beyond relating to the recurrent nature of the album and track, LaBrie's victorious decree of 'A perfect sphere / Colliding with our fate / This story ends where it began' is allegedly a nod to 'Cygnus X-1 Book II: Hemispheres' by Rush. Petrucci's wah-wah solo, coupled with more classical grandeur, excellently expands upon the initial themes, bolstering the suite as the pièce de résistance of *Octavarium*.

'Systematic Chaos' (2007)

Personnel:
James LaBrie: lead vocals
John Petrucci: guitar, backing vocals
John Myung: bass
Jordan Rudess: keyboards, Haken Continuum Fingerboard
Mike Portnoy: drums, backing vocals, co-lead vocals (3, 4)
Steve Vai: guest spoken words (5)
Corey Taylor: guest spoken words (5)
Chris Jericho: guest spoken words (5)
Jon Anderson: guest spoken words (5)
Steven Wilson: guest spoken words (5)
Mikael Åkerfeldt: guest spoken words (5)
David Ellefson: guest spoken words (5)
Daniel Gildenlöw: guest spoken words (5)
Steve Hogarth: guest spoken words (5)
Joe Satriani: guest spoken words (5)
Neal Morse: guest spoken words (5)
Paul Northfield: engineer, mixing, vocal track co-producer
Chad 'Sir Chadwick' Lupo: assistant engineer
Hugh Syme: art direction, design, illustration
Daragh McDonagh: photography
Produced at Avatar Studios in Manhattan, New York, September 2006 – February 2007 by Mike Portnoy and John Petrucci
UK and US release date: June 2007.
Highest chart places: UK: 25, USA: 19
Running time: 78:41
Current edition: Roadrunner Records 2014 Japanese CD Limited Edition

Strewn flaws notwithstanding, *Octavarium* was a winning way for Dream Theater to simultaneously pay tribute to their progressive rock ancestors and dish out more superbly colourful and unforgettable characteristic landmarks. Likewise, their Radio City Music Hall commemoration was a resounding feat, so the band took a much-needed rest during the summer to mend from the exhaustive past several months and spend time with their families. Always a workaholic, Portnoy used the time to joyously toil away on making sure *Score* was nearly perfect for its August release. When September arrived, though, it was time to hit the ground running and make their next statement, *Systematic Chaos*. Created somewhat off-the-cuff and in the middle of a few behind-the-scenes shakeups, its darker, odder, and partially more commercial vision still spurs palpable puzzlement and indignation from many devotees. While it's hands down Dream Theater's weakest project since *Falling Into Infinity*, it's also a sizably underrated part of their discography that should be more revered.

At this point, their contract with Atlantic Records was done, and although the label may have been interested in sustaining the partnership, Dream Theater were not. Portnoy recounts: 'We said we wanted to do a video for 'I Walk Beside You' and they kind of held us to ransom and said they weren't going to do anything for the album ... unless we committed to them and signed for another three albums'. Instead of waiting to sign with someone else before commencing work on *Systematic Chaos*, they confidently yet riskily chose to finance it themselves and recoup the money whenever they found their new benefactor. Fast-forward to early February 2007 – when they were finishing the LP – and they sealed a deal with the illustrious Roadrunner Records, who provided them not only the same creative freedoms as before, but also the 'substantial marketing muscle' and 'independent spirit' that Atlantic lacked.

Going back to September 2006 for a moment, they returned to Avatar Studios for the first time in a decade and made the comparably staggering decision to replace Doug Oberkircher – Dream Theater's lead engineer since *A Change of Seasons* – with Paul Northfield. With past credits including Porcupine Tree, Rush, Marilyn Manson, Ozzy Osbourne, Gentle Giant and Queensrÿche, he was undoubtedly fit for the job and gave the group the 'fresh ears' they were looking for. Portnoy illuminates: 'I guess it just felt like a new chapter for us, coming off the back of *Score*, having the summer off, and starting with a new label. So really it was just a time for a change.... We'd also been looking for an engineer who could also mix an album'. As we've discussed, Northfield was a contender for engineering *Falling Into Infinity* before Kevin Shirley getting the gig, yet he's glad that that role was delayed until the band were in a more symbiotic state of mind.

Granted, Dream Theater were used to writing and recording a record at once, but *Systematic Chaos* is an anomaly in that they entered the studio without having a concrete course set in stone. Rudess jokes, 'I think it was almost harder for [Portnoy] *not* to think of something ... That was part of the challenge for us, as both Mike and John Petrucci just love to think of these great concepts for each album.' According to Portnoy, he did have a few ideas at first, yet he decided to 'keep [his] mouth shut out of curiosity to see what would happen'. The only caveat the mastermind duo stipulated was that the new material had to have 'balls'; in contrast to his initial struggles fitting into *Train of Thought*, however, Rudess likely found it easier and more exhilarating to find his place within the heavier route.'I would just let them hang out and do the seventh-string metal thing, and I'd wait until it cleared and there was an opening ... I'd turn on my sequencer and lay down something really wacky', he admits.

Indeed, the sequence is like the more up-to-date and fun younger sibling to its superior precursor, and a big reason why is Petrucci's lyrical focus on shadowy fantasy worlds and battles between good and evil. He gloats: '[T]he dark angle is always the most interesting, more metal, and to me, it fits better and is a lot easier to dive into that subject matter'. There are more realistic and autobiographical topics afoot, too, such as Portnoy confronting his OCD via 'Constant Motion' and continuing his 'Twelve-step Suite' via 'Repentance'.

As in the past, Portnoy encouraged some fan involvement in the making of *Systematic Chaos* by inviting them to Avatar Studios on January 26, 2007, to sing chants on 'Prophets of War' and 'In the Presence of Enemies – Part II'. Portnoy specified that anyone who camped out overnight or showed up before the scheduled time would not be allowed in; however, the studio ignored that request due to fears of the place being overcome once doors opened. Hundreds of people turned up – including myself – but only forty-five or so were picked. Afterwards, some of them received *Romavarium*, a 2006 live DVD that shows Dream Theater performing all of *Octavarium* in Rome in 2005. Logically, many followers who were denied entry lashed out about the confusion and double standards regarding Portnoy and Avatar Studios' differing rules that day. The former absolved himself of responsibility.

Portnoy discloses that the title was picked once they 'sat down with all the lyrics, read through them together and wrote down any words or phrases that jumped out,' adding, 'And then we started thinking about how everything about this band musically is controlled chaos.' As for the cover art – once again done by Hugh Syme – little has been divulged regarding its conception and realization. He produced three variations of it: the main one, which finds ants mulling around an unruly highway system; the special edition, 'featuring an embossed cover with the reversed stoplight on a backdrop of clouds'; and the interior one, which is 'a variation of the standard cover with the stoplight present'.

When the public finally heard *Systematic Chaos* in June 2007, they predictably chastised it for a few reasons, with a major one being Portnoy's protruding vocals on 'Constant Motion' and 'The Dark Eternal Night'. Rather than viewing it as self-indulgence – as some listeners did – Portnoy justifies it by saying that LaBrie couldn't 'convincingly' pull off the needed gruffness, so he had to. Humorously, Rudess seems to share the perspective of those hecklers: 'Oh my God! And for me, it was a bit of a shock. I was like, 'What is that? Why?'' As Portnoy loyalists know, his distinctive yet divisive voice would also play a considerable part in his later endeavours outside of Dream Theater, particularly in his work with The Neal Morse Band and Transatlantic.

Another chief concern of spectators was an accustomed one: that Dream Theater were tailoring their sound to harness chic and commercial viability. Spitefully – and despite the fact that *Systematic Chaos* was essentially done *before* they joined the new label –disparagers attacked them for deliberately trying to compete with and/or copy other acts on Roadrunner's roster.'Yeah, it's more contemporary. Not that we're trying to sell out to MTV or whatever, but if you listen to the bands that are out there today, that's the style and what everybody does. We are not trying to be something that we're not, but we do want kids to at least find us *listenable*', Portnoy rebukes.LaBrie backs up that rationale by surrendering, 'That's fine and valid. People are going to say that no matter what Dream Theater puts out. This song is too much in that direction, or that something is a blatant copy of another band. I think that is going to happen when they hear songs that remind them of a band they're also close to'. With his fresh and more objective perspective, Northfield contends that Dream Theater 'just love playing and are serious music fans, and when they like something, they don't mind letting it show ... So they tend to spend most of their time using those [songs] as inspirations, but then spend a lot of time trying a unique twist on a certain style of arrangement or approach'.

Like many artists – chiefly, the Beatles – Dream Theater aren't shy about changing how they look if the mood or occasion strikes; this time, though, their altered appearances proved particularly irksome for a fraction of the audience. Predominantly, LaBrie's lean facial hair was singled out for signifying a mid-life crisis and need to rival his more youthful fellow singers. Laughably, he rejects that reason in favour a simpler and more endearing one: 'It's because I'm a huge *Pirates of the Caribbean* fan. Jack Sparrow at your service. You can't just stay looking the same. You get bored with yourself'. Meanwhile, Rudess had what LaBrie called 'the Tony Levin look', while Petrucci's thicker beard and longer mane 'initially even alarmed his bandmates' before becoming normalized.

Moving onto the professional reactions to *Systematic Chaos*, they were majorly complimentary, which surely helped it be Dream Theater's highest-charting LP thus far in the UK and US. *Classic Rock*, *Metal Hammer* and *Kerrang!* all recommended it, and Jon Eardley of *MetalReview.com* said that it contains 'some of the best riffs Petrucci has brought to the table'. In 2014, *Rhythm* magazine voted it beneath Rush's *Moving Pictures* as the second greatest drumming album in progressive rock history.

True to their word, Roadrunner supported it in many ways, such as by getting Dream Theater 'high-profile interviews in metal and musician magazines', plus 'a substantial advertising campaign, and a 5.1 surround sound version of the album coupled with a 90-minute documentary ['*Chaos in Progress*: the making of *Systematic Chaos*'] on a limited-edition two-disc release'. At the time, Rudess was impressed and grateful yet also a touch uneasy about possibly doing too much too quickly: 'I hope we don't over-saturate and the fans don't get turned off. But it's exciting as we've always wondered what our band could do if we had somebody behind us, as we've become so incredibly self-sufficient until now'.

That summer, the Chaos in Motion tour – which, unsurprisingly, would get its own home video release on September 30, 2008 – kicked off. Spanning thirty-five countries and over one hundred shows, it saw them perform *Images and Words* in full at the 'Gods of Metal' festival in Milan, appear at the Download Festival in Leicestershire, England, and make it to the Wembley Arena. As usual, the press adored these concerts. They also made their live debuts in Australia and China, although the latter occurrence wasn't enjoyable for the band since they 'just didn't have it together in terms of preparation and accommodation'. For Rudess, there was the extra excitement of getting to show-off his Zen Riffer keytar and 'step away from [his] position on stage, come up front and rock out' alongside Petrucci.

In the midst of it all, Dream Theater also issued their first compilation: the tongue-in-cheek titled *Greatest Hit (...And 21 Other Pretty Cool Songs)*. Syme came up with the cover – 'a red armchair... sporting a large white stain which had been created by a passing seagull' – and Portnoy designed the tracklist to both 'be a starting point for new listeners' and guarantee 'that there were enough rare versions and single edits of songs to keep even the most ardent fans satisfied'. Cynically, Portnoy later told *Metal Edge* that it was also meant as 'a mockery of the whole idea of a Greatest Hits package.... Inevitably, when your contract ends with a record company, they're going to take advantage of the back catalogue'.

Around the same time, he launched the now-legendary Progressive Nation festival that began on land and then – in 2014 – set sail on the ocean before fusing with Cruise to the Edge in 2016. Intended to 'celebrate the diversity of progressive rock and metal', it had Opeth, Three, and Between the Buried and Me open for Dream Theater. Over the subsequent decade, many equally wonderful artists – Big Elf, Devin Townsend, Riverside, The Flower Kings, Gazpacho, and Steve Hackett– would stop by. With a 2020 line-up that lists Anathema, Marillion, Moon Safari, Haken, and Flying Colors amongst its arsenal, Portnoy's dream festival remains America's premiere progressive rock event.

With sizeable distance and time having passed since *Systematic Chaos* originally erupted, it's easier to appreciate its station as another semi-experimental and individualized part of Dream Theater's arc. Unfortunately, that doesn't stop it from being generic, lame, and stale at times, coming off as less magical and more perfunctory than its immediate predecessors. However, it's almost never flat-out bad – there's plenty of greatness with the lacklustre rubble – and it does outdo almost everything that came after it, including the tellingly named *Black Clouds & Silver Linings* that lay ahead.

'In the Presence of Enemies - Part I' (Petrucci)

Initially written as a self-contained twenty-five-minute piece, 'In the Presence of Enemies' – formerly known as 'The Pumpkin King' – was split into the bookends of *Systematic Chaos* because – as Portnoy tells it – they couldn't decide if it should open or close the LP. Petrucci suggested that it be 'cut in half' due to his love for Rush's *Hemispheres*, which 'has a side-long suite written as a continuation of a storyline from a song on their previous record, *A Farewell to Kings*'. Furthermore, it's inspired by a Korean Manhwa –comic book – called *Priest* and deals with 'somebody who loses himself and ... struggles with the darkness, symbolized by the Dark Master. And the story ends up really being the darkness within and goes through the different phases where he has to fight demons and things like that'.

The 'Prelude' movement takes up the first half of this first part, and it delivers some of Dream Theater's most vibrantly hypnotic instrumentation ever. Beginning with a grippingly unified collapse from Portnoy, Petrucci, Rudess, and Myung, its typhoon of twisting rhythms and patterns is just about as addictive as anything else they've done. True to his word, Rudess' scattershot sound effects infuse it with droplets of battiness. About ninety seconds in, his

quirky synth theme instantly appeals, leading to malevolent crashes around
Petrucci's frightened shredding. After reprising the opening sonic cave-in,
Petrucci's piercing mixture of jubilation and trepidation guides us toward an
ornamentally stacked segue into the second phase, 'Resurrection'.

LaBrie's disconsolate verses – 'I saw a white light / Shining there before
me / Walking to it / I waited for the end' – and enticing chorus – 'Do you still
wait for your God / And the symbol of your faith?'– are bewitching. They also
establish Petrucci's narrative well, and Rudess' strings and inexplicable tones
are a treat. Near the end, LaBrie's bridge – 'Through a veil of madness / With
a vicious play / One man rises up / Standing in their way' – makes good use of
Petrucci and/or Portnoy's grumpy secondary voices as it sees the protagonist
stepping up to be a saviour. The ensuing solo from Petrucci and ominous gusts
of wind work as a solid cliffhanger as well.

'Forsaken' (Petrucci)
The working title for it was 'Jet Lag', and it was released digitally as an EP –
consisting of studio and live versions, plus a live version of 'Constant Motion'
– and a single on March 21, 2008. There was also an animated music video
spearheaded by Petrucci and directed by Yasufumi Soejima that's set in a sci-
fi future and depicts a man being tricked by a vampiress. The track itself is
surprisingly poppy yet disproportionately ridiculed, with Rudess' piano motif
and LaBrie's charisma, in particular, making it adequately pleasing even if it's
too conventional and cliché, too. Everyone else is unremarkable but totally fine
for what 'Forsaken' is trying to be. It's nothing exceptional, but it's far from
their worst composition.

'Constant Motion' (Portnoy)
More or less, the same can be said for this exploration of Portnoy's OCD, which
he regards as 'the perfect metaphor for what is inside my brain 24 hours a
day'. It was going to be called 'Korma Chameleon', and on April 27, 2007, it
became the first digital-only single from *Systematic Chaos*. The initial attempt
at a music video – their first since 'Hollow Years' – was 'a disaster', as LaBrie
unveils: 'Well, first of all, everything was completely disorganized ... And then
we were confronted with something that looked completely confused and in
complete turmoil'. Luckily, a new director – Andrew Bennett – got the job done
with an average dichotomy of performance footage and manipulated imagery
from the album's cover. It was played a lot on MTV2's *Headbangers Ball*, and
the song was also contained in 2007's *Rock Band* video game.

Apart from the emblematic time signature changes and hostile genetics, it's
honestly run-of-the-mill. Actually, it comes off as a less absorbing and eccentric
take on 'The Test That Stumped Them All'. LaBrie and Portnoy are good
enough as co-lead vocalists, but everything they sing – as well as the music
that surrounds them – is painfully humdrum. The jam two-thirds through is
effectively peculiar and intricate, but then it reverts back to its mundane focal

points. It's unequivocally tolerable, and the naysayers who deem it a lazy and bland attempt at cashing in on the popular music zeitgeist of the late 2000s aren't entirely wrong.

'The Dark Eternal Night' (Petrucci)

Using H.P. Lovecraft's prose poem 'Nyarlathotep' as a stepping off point, its tale of a Pharaoh coming back from the dead and tormenting the living is fairly titillating and assorted outside of its bland borders. It was preliminarily called 'N.A.D.S. ('North American Dream Squad')', and a readers' poll in the October 2010 issue of *Total Guitar Magazine* selected the main riff as the fourth greatest riff of the 2000s. It is a markedly guttural way to start – with Portnoy and Myung summoning their own diabolical manifestations – and Portnoy's distorted cautions in-between LaBrie's verses are purposely unpleasant but conceptually suitable.

Truthfully, the opening and closing segments are mostly obnoxious and boring aside from the latter's keyboard exaggerations, but the instrumental crusade that launches about three-and-a-half minutes in is quite attractive. Customary but alluring at first, Rudess' improvised foibles – reminiscent of his strangest surges on Scenes from a Memory and Octavarium – really give it life. All in all, some of the ugliest and coolest moments of Systematic Chaos are here, so it's truly a mixed bag.

'Repentance' (Portnoy)

Fixating on the eighth and nine steps of Alcoholics Anonymous – which are all about making amends to people you've hurt due to your disease – 'Repentance' is deliberately the most modest episode of Portnoy's multipart framework. 'We needed a breather in there somewhere', he states, and it definitely meets that goal. In fact, there's not much to it other than sinister but mild guitar and bass rounds, refined piano chords, slender drumming, and LaBrie's contemplative confessions after he recalls the 'Hello, mirror' line from 'This Dying Soul'. Cleverly, he ends every other sentence with 'me' – playing into the idea of taking responsibility for your actions – and the chorus is amiable and touching. The angelic supporting harmonies and strings are useful, too.

That method alone would make the track noteworthy, but it's the spoken word revelations at the midpoint that make it weightier. Portnoy invited over a dozen of his industry buddies to briefly suggest their own misdoings and seek forgiveness; while a few declined the chance – such as Geoff Tate, Bruce Dickinson, Megadeth's Dave Mustaine, and Metalica's James Hetfield –many others agreed. Those by Slipknot's Corey Taylor, Opeth's Mikael Åkerfeldt, Fozzy's Chris Jericho, and Neal Morse are the most poignant, whereas Steven Wilson's is the most appropriate since it refers to him publically voicing his dislike for Dream Theater. He later told *progarchives.com*: 'The thing is that they are good friends of mine and they know I'm not really into their music.

They don't mind it, but their fans get more irate about it'. It does go on too long – the almost eleven-minute runtime is a hair self-indulgent and tedious by the end – but it's a novel and powerful tactic all the same.

'Prophets of War' (LaBrie)

LaBrie used Joseph C. Wilson's book *The Politics of Truth* for this condemnation of the Iraq war and how – from a broader POV –the 'powers-that-be in the US government' profit from 'their political agenda[s] and ulterior motives'. He's also lamenting 'the idea that we're still trying to solve issues and differences by gun and warfare'.Considering that serious motivation, the working title – 'Carpet Babies' – is amusingly incongruent.

Rudess' robotic waggles stirringly cradle LaBrie's forlorn investigations; likewise, thumping bass drums, stimulating riffs, and interdependent shouts from other members help the inquisitive hook – 'Can we help them break away? / Are we profiting from war?' – more invigorating. The helping of fan participation – chants of 'Time for change / Find the truth' after the second chorus – is successfully empowering as well, and the sequential duality of singing and speaking more socially conscious judgments works well. Petrucci's momentary acoustic plucks beneath LaBrie's tamer delivery are nice, too, and make the final playbacks more potent by contrast.

'The Ministry of Lost Souls' (Petrucci)

Full of philharmonic spectacle, woeful songwriting, and wild arrangements, Petrucci's chronicle of someone who wants to reconnect with the hero who saved them from downing after 'that person died in the process' is easily a towering addition to *Systematic Chaos*. Prematurely named 'Schindler's Lisp', it begins with theatrical synthesized orchestration over an unassuming metal base. Then, haunting guitar arpeggios and piano chords escort sorrowful reports, prompting a shattering insight – 'Living in a world without you (drowning in the past) / Is living in no world' – and incitement – 'Remember me: I gave you life / You would not take it'. It's one of the most harrowing pockets of the whole album.

Petrucci's self-pitying solo enlarges the sensation. After a self-assured bridge and some crunchy wordless postscripts, it metamorphoses into a feisty jam that's concurrently barbaric due to Petrucci's deadened grunts and ultramodern due to Rudess' futuristic sorcery. As opposed to most of their other virtuosic duels, however, this one is passable yet old hat and longwinded. It's still mind-blowing from a procedural perspective, of course, and the venture back to the key melody is anticipated but refreshing.

'In the Presence of Enemies – Part II' (Petrucci)

Naturally, the aforesaid ominous gusts of wind instigate the lengthier yet cumulatively extraneous and less fulfilling other half of *Systematic Chaos*' larger-than-life yarn. The Western 'Heretic' division maintains that arid environment thanks to its two-note coating – no doubt evoking Pink Floyd's 'Goodbye Cruel World' – and chilling reversed piano tones. LaBrie's lethargic greeting, 'Welcome, tired pilgrim / Into the circle / We have been waiting / Everyone's gathered for your arrival / All the believers', is also purposefully edgy. Here, one can imagine Petrucci looking to the antagonistic setting of Stephen King's *The Stand* as much as he is *Priest*, and his sustained outcries are carefully placed to accentuate LaBrie's unsettling prophecy: 'Angels fall / All for you / Heretic'. Following some melodic forewarning, Myung trudges along authoritatively until the prophecy is intensified– kudos to LaBrie for his range – and then dispersed so that the apocalyptic 'Dark master within / I will fight for you' declaration gets the limelight.

Hearty percussion and cheers signal the start of 'The Slaughter of the Damned'; despite its default tricky hipness and villainous voiceovers, it's possibly Dream Theater's least interesting bit of heaviness up to this point. What's more, its similarities to the 'I need to learn / Teach me how' slice of 'The Glass Prison' is disappointingly – if unintentionally – neglectful. Thankfully, it wraps up with a dashing deviation, 'Servants of the fallen / Fight to pave the way', that goes into one of their most rigid yet deranged and frenetic instrumental trials ever, 'The Reckoning'. As it develops, Petrucci and Rudess augment facets of 'In the Presence of Enemies – Part I' with both superfluous shredding and imaginative new garnishes. The climb toward the finale –'Salvation' – is enlivening, but LaBrie's closing lacks verve as it flies above more invocations of the opening half. Clearly – and like several past inclusions we've discussed – 'In the Presence of Enemies – Part II' would fare better if it were either shorter or did more outstanding things within the time allotted.

Bonuses

The special edition of Systematic Chaos comes with a 5.1 surround sound mix and the 90-minute Chaos in Progress documentary. Its myriad glimpses into the writing and recording procedures – including screw-ups, loveable banter, and a lot of self-reflection and explanation – makes it a must-watch for fans of the record. Also, its home movie quality helps humanize the band, so it truly feels like you're a welcomed fly on the wall during each session.

'Black Clouds & Silver Linings' (2009)

Personnel:
James LaBrie: lead vocals
John Petrucci: guitar, backing vocals
John Myung: bass
Jordan Rudess: keyboards, Haken Continuum Fingerboard (1, 4), lap steel guitar (1), Bebot iPhone app (2)
Mike Portnoy: drums, backing vocals, co-lead vocals (1, 4)
Jerry Goodman: violin (5, 9, 11)
Paul Northfield: engineer, mixing, vocal track co-producer
Dr. Rick Kwan: assistant engineer
Kevin Shirley: mixing (12)
Hugh Syme: art direction, design, illustration
Dan Mandell: photography
Produced at Avatar Studios in Manhattan, New York, October 2008 – March 2009 by Mike Portnoy and John Petrucci
UK and US release date: June 2009.
Highest chart places: UK: 23, USA: 6
Running time: 75:25
Current edition: Roadrunner Records 2014 Japanese CD Limited Edition

Although *Systematic Chaos* has its problems and remains one of the most polarizing Dream Theater collections, it brought them unprecedented prosperity and verified how much further they could go. After all, their new label was donating a breadth of support they'd never had before, they were playing bigger venues across the world, and new fans were hopping on the bandwagon all the time. Therefore, it's no shock that they enthusiastically returned to Avatar Studios in October 2008 – following a few months of recuperation after the last tour – to work on what would become the ultimately bittersweet and prophetically titled *Black Clouds & Silver Linings*. Ditching the fantastical songwriting and mechanical mode of the last record in favour of more personal incentives and expansive qualities, it is quite varied. Sadly – and in opposition to the majority opinion – it's actually too sundry, juxtaposing some of the band's best and worst material yet to end up a significantly inconsistent swan song for the perceived architect of Dream Theater, Mike Portnoy.

Once again, they entered the studio without any singular plan in mind. Rudess attributes this relaxation to them 'having more confidence in allowing the music to grow more organically', as Wilson puts it. Rudess enlightens: 'I think what is happening in some ways is that everybody is getting more easygoing and less controlling about that kind of stuff'. Eventually, they determined that it should look back to what made earlier works 'so distinctively Dream Theater – the mixing up of styles within a track'. Petrucci even admits that his major criticism of *Systematic Chaos* is that its songs 'stay too long in one direction', and Portnoy notes the need to also 'have a little bit more of a non-traditional arrangement' this time around. He also championed filling the disc with fewer but lengthier pieces comparable to 'Rush's *Hemispheres* or Yes' *Close to the Edge*'. On his website, he says that *Black Clouds & Silver Linings* is like having "A Change of Seasons', 'Octavarium', 'Learning to Live', 'Pull Me Under', and 'The Glass Prison' all on one album'. Northfield rightly considers it 'more spontaneous than the last record'.

Despite deciding previously that LaBrie should be more involved in the formation of new material, he was virtually absent here. Officially, the other four guys were already going at it by the time LaBrie was ready to join them, so they felt that it'd be wise to keep that 'chemistry' going and have LaBrie come in when he was needed for recording. Rather than see it as a hypocritical and passive-aggressive move, the typically good-natured and egoless LaBrie understood and took it in stride. That said, he did let Petrucci and Portnoy know that he wanted to be included from the start next time around.

Neither Myung nor Rudess contributed lyrics, either – although they were invited to – so Petrucci and Portnoy are the only songwriters here. Moving away from the outward observations and mythical tales of Systematic Chaos, they drew heavily from their own lives. In addition to finally wrapping up his 'Twelve-step Suite' with 'The Shattered Fortress', Portnoy memorializes his late father, Howard, with 'The Best of Times'.As for Petrucci, he was persuaded by his wife to expose some of the real-life 'colorful stories' he loves telling via 'A Nightmare to Remember', 'The Count of Tuscany', and others. He reveals: 'All these people that seem like really weird characters are actually real people. And when you hear the lyrics you will be like 'What the hell happened here? Who the hell are these people?''

As with its predecessor, they chose the moniker because of how well it reflected the moods of the music. Portnoy thought of it 'when he was driving into the city on a particularly cloudy and gloomy day' and felt that it 'summed up' how 'everything you look at can be either optimistic or pessimistic'. Looking back, it's also a clairvoyant reflection on the mixed emotions and outlooks of Portnoy's exodus the next year. Likewise, Syme was brought back to do the artwork, which visualizes the sentiment of the name in the midst of channelling prior cover art by showcasing references to several lyrics. Portnoy says that that direction came 'naturally' instead of being an intentional nod to their younger days.

Like all artists, Dream Theater had been victim to illegal downloads and leaks in the past; to combat this, Roadrunner hoped to guarantee physical sales by offering a few tempting versions of *Black Clouds & Silver Linings*. They were by far the most extravagant treatments any Dream Theater LP had gotten, with the standard single-disc and double vinyl versions being outdone by two larger packages. The first was a three-disc compendium that included instrumental versions of every selection and covers of songs by Rainbow, Queen, Dixie Dregs, Zebra, King Crimson, and Iron Maiden. There was also a deluxe collector's edition set that came in 'a silver foil embossed black velvet box' and presented all of that plus 'a 180-gram double LP, a DVD with isolated audio tracks for each instrument, a lithograph of the album cover, with only 100 being signed by Hugh Syme, and a mouse pad'. In addition, people who pre-ordered it could download 'a newly recorded cover song each week beginning on May 19 2009, until the album's release'. A fraction of those sets also featured a "silver ticket' entitling the purchaser and one guest to a meet-and-greet with the band'.

Black Clouds & Silver Linings came out just over two years after *Systematic Chaos* – on June 23, 2009 – and topped it in terms of the UK and US charts. Expectedly, the press were generally kind as well, with *Record Collector*, *Metal Hammer*, PROG, and *Consequence of Sound* praising it. On the other hand, Chris Conaton of *PopMatters* only gave it six out of ten stars, surmising, 'Dream Theater seem to be out of new tricks, but at least they know how to play to their own strengths.' Similarly, Vince Neilstein of *Metal Sucks* called it 'stock Dream Theater', gave it two-and-a-half out of five 'horns', and wrote, 'I call upon Dream Theater to push themselves a bit harder, to progress once again. They're certainly capable'.

Ironically – given what would happen in 2010 – Portnoy saw the multitude of successes the LP produced as the zenith validation for Dream Theater so far. In corresponding interviews, he sounds immensely dedicated to and optimistic about their future; while his leave wasn't entirely his fault – we'll get to that soon – its sudden occurrence at the height of their game is minimally tragic and baffling in hindsight. Judged as both Portnoy's last endeavour with Dream Theater and on its own merits, *Black Clouds & Silver Linings* is jagged in general but magnificent every now and then. Good or bad, it's inarguably special for concluding the pinnacle era of the most influential progressive metal band of all time before they'd unknowingly encounter a dramatic turn of events going forward.

'A Nightmare to Remember' (Petrucci)

Originally, it was known as 'Halloween', and it's based on a childhood car accident that Petrucci and his family were involved in as they were driving home from his cousin's wedding reception. He expounds: 'It was at night and I believe it was a drunk driver that hit us.... My father went through the windshield. My brother went flying up, as he was just a baby and my mother was holding him on her lap'. He also says that he wound up with glass in his eye – from which he still has a small scar – and that he embellished some of the tale to make it more bewildering.

With its ceaselessly wide-ranging instrumentation and captivating songwriting, it's more than just the highlight of *Black Clouds & Silver Linings*; it's one of the greatest tracks Dream Theater ever cut. Following sounds of thunder and rainfall, an eerie piano allusion to a future melody gives way to crushing progressive metal enthrallment. Petrucci hungrily aids LaBrie's dismayed recollections with madcap outrage as Rudess adds frightening swirls and the rhythm section barrels along feverishly. The narrative chorus is quite fetching, too, leading to clips of a car crash around LaBrie and Petrucci spitting out more disgusted details. It then glides into the far more soothing and somber middle portion.

Ambulance sirens, hospital machine beeps, and a melancholy ambience fill the spaces between Petrucci's clean fingerpicking.LaBrie uses meek rhymes to talk about 'lying on a table' and having a doctor evaluate him. It's already a compelling and effective vibe, yet it becomes downright irresistible when a heavenly segue of synths and more guitar arpeggios produces perhaps *the* best vocal melody Dream Theater has ever had: 'Hopelessly drifting / Bathing in beautiful agony'. It's overwhelmingly gorgeous sonically and lyrically, especially when it comes back a second time with increased fervour.

From there, Petrucci and Rudess' nutty solos – and resultant synchronization – around the shifting scenery yield an adrenaline-charged conduit for the harsh third and final entity. Portnoy's growls – which he initially wanted to be performed by Åkerfeldt before the band vetoed the idea – are tolerable and apropos, even if the final 'Roar!' is cheesy. His irregular percussive breaks – as well as Petrucci's riffs and Rudess' pan flute detour – during the instrumental transition, are very engaging. It then falls back to the song's first chorus – 'Life was so simple then / We were so innocent' – and supplemental scores with impeccable precision. Overall, 'A Nightmare to Remember' is a renewed, tantalising, and comprehensive overview of everything that makes Dream Theater extraordinary.

'A Rite of Passage' (Petrucci)
Put out as a shorter single in May 2009, this examination of freemasonry is somewhat meant to set the record straight about what the classification entails. 'You watch documentaries on the History Channel or whatever, and it's all shrouded in conspiracy ... I make a reference to a book that was written by an ex-freemason called *The New World Order*', Petrucci makes clear. By the same token, LaBrie rationalises that freemasons were 'free thinkers' who didn't 'want to be told what is acceptable'. Ramon Boutviseth directed the music video – an uncomplicated process by all accounts – which shows the group playing in a dark environment while snow falls and monks in red cloaks gather. In and of itself, the tune is adequately catchy and robust, with intriguing voice samples and a friskily belligerent instrumental jam that evokes *Train of Thought*. At the same time, its everyday melodies and slightly hackneyed lyrics bring about something that's endurable but not essential.

'Wither' (Petrucci)
The September 2009 digital single for 'Wither' – written entirely by Petrucci and concentrating on the difficulties of the creative process –came with a few other renditions: one comprised solely of piano and vocal; a demo with

Petrucci singing; and a demo of 'The Best of Times' with Portnoy singing.
All are worth hearing if you like the main takes, and the bundle is both
Dream Theater's last official release with Portnoy and their only one without
the Majesty symbol. Two months later, its music video – also directed by
Boutviseth– would arrive. Featuring clips of them on and off stage while
on tour, it's a great complementary picturing, and it even shows Åkerfeldt
alongside Portnoy a couple of times. Curiously, even Petrucci concedes
that'Wither' is a shade 'wimpy'; its great performances and fruitfully healing
air notwithstanding, it's too clichéd and mushy for comfort. Like 'A Rite of
Passage', it looks unashamedly designed to grab the mainstream crowd, which
wouldn't be a problem if that didn't require a dumbed downed execution.
Petrucci's Queen-esque solo near the end is nifty, though.

'The Shattered Fortress' (Portnoy)
Rather than retrace every marginally modified reprise, suffice it to say that
it brilliantly finishes Portnoy's saga by spotlessly blending quotations from
the preceding periods into the final three steps: 'Restraint', 'Receive', and
'Responsible'. The fluidity with which the earlier sections are entwined is
incredibly pleasing, and the new content is thoroughly satiating. Granted,
Portnoy's barks during the ruthlessly crotchety foundational verses are
awkward, but it's his right to handle his masterplan in any way he wants. The
mellow music behind the 'St. Francis Prayer' – 'That where there Is hatred /
I may bring love' – during 'Receive' is among the loveliest segments of the
suite; equally, the closing pronouncement – 'I am responsible / When anyone,
anywhere / Reaches out for help' – is mightily inspirational. From start to
finish, 'The Shattered Fortress' gives you goosebumps with its tour-de-force
flashbacks and continuity; when played straight through – as 'a concept album
that just happens to be spread across five releases', as Portnoy thinks of it – it's
unquestionably one of the finest feats in modern progressive music.

'The Best of Times' (Portnoy)
Feasibly *the* most private composition Portnoy ever penned, 'The Best of
Times' is a tender tribute to his biological father, who passed away from cancer
at the very start of 2009. He aimed for it to be uplifting and celebratory instead
of a self-pitying downer, and the music was written before he knew what
words and topic would be attached. Fortunately, he was able to play a demo of
it – with him on vocals – for Howard Portnoy before he died, as well as at the
funeral. He also admits that it was kind of strange and troubling to hand it over
to LaBrie to sing, even if it was the right choice.

It begins beautifully thanks to Rudess' nostalgic piano chords and strings;
Petrucci's acoustic guitar follow-up is heartbreaking, too, and channels the
start of 'Hollow Years'. It is a little drawn-out, though, and with zero disrespect
intended, the ensuing morsels of energized memories lean too far toward
corny arena rock to stomach. Lyrically, it's very on-the-nose and syrupy –

understandably so – and the arrangement (including Petrucci's closing solo) is like a discarded template by Boston, Journey, or Foreigner. To be fair, the midway alteration – a murkier milieu as LaBrie lovingly murmurs a callback to 'A Change of Seasons': 'All the things I should've done / But time just slipped away / Remember seize the day' – is impactful. Nevertheless, its highly relatable and sympathetic subject matter doesn't necessarily equate to a worthwhile experience for outsiders. Frankly, it's one of Dream Theater's most stagnant and uninteresting tracks.

'The Count of Tuscany' (Petrucci)
Broken into three parts, it's about an odd trip Petrucci took with his equipment tech, Mark Snyder, and John Myung in Italy during the *Train of Thought* tour. Long story short, they were taken to a weird castle and its vineyard by an odd Count, who told them that his brother was the basis for pop culture icon Hannibal Lecter. Many fans believe that the siblings are Niccolò and Sebastiano Capponi, although this has never been confirmed. Anyway, Petrucci says that 'many bizarre things' kept happening, such as the brother feigning an English accident while taking them to 'this little chapel' where 'a mummified saint' rested behind glass. He smirks, '[I]t was kind of creepy and funny. You can take it tongue-in-cheek, but it really happened'.

The first chunk moves expertly from stately yet compassionate foreshadowing – via Petrucci's wise acoustic plucks and curving electric squawks, plus driving rhythms and Rudess' playful timbres – to high-octane storytelling. LaBrie's charged descriptions, in conjunction with the coarse and antsy music, do a fine job of conveying what Petrucci and company felt and saw back then. Their menacing multilayered retches – 'Let me introduce / My brother' – counterbalance the empathetic sing-along chorus – 'I / Want to stay alive / Everything about this place /Just doesn't feel right' – splendidly. In-between another set of verses and chorus, they ignite some deliciously topsy-turvy instrumental takes on previous themes and innovative threads.

At the halfway point, Petrucci's sky-high licks and Portnoy's plunging percussion birth a restful interlude that owes *a lot* to the 'Soon' movement of Yes' 'The Gates of Delirium'. It skates into the last movement seamlessly as dejected acoustic guitar strums and piano patterns beckon invigorating drumming. Although rudimentary, LaBrie's melody and words – from the POV of the victims – are rapidly enchanting. Astutely, everything gets amped-up as the Count takes over to tell his side of the story: 'Now wait a minute, man! / That's not how it is / You must be confused / That isn't who I am'. Sensibly, the band then echoes the opening motifs to come full circle and elicit lingering closure. It's a stunning resolution.

Bonuses
The aforementioned instrumental versions of Black Clouds & Silver Linings' material is exactly what you'd imagine. There are no overdubs or solos, so

they're more barebones in spots; however, that clarity makes certain elements come through more, so each warrant at least one listen. As for the half-dozen cover songs, they all implement the cherished Dream Theater tenacity without straying too far from the originals. For instance, Petrucci and Portnoy clearly have fun emulating the harmonies on their Queen medley – a mixture of 'Tenement Funster', 'Flick of the Wrist', and 'Lily of the Valley' from Sheer Heart Attack – which Brian May later called 'amazing' and 'a great compliment'. Predictably, they also nail many of the gradations that make King Crimson's 'Larks Tongues in Aspic, Part Two', Iron Maiden's 'To Tame a Land', Zebra's 'Take Your Fingers from My Hair', Dixie Dregs' 'Odyssey', and Rainbow's 'Stargazer' so resilient.

'A Dramatic Turn of Events' (2011)

Personnel:
James LaBrie: lead vocals
John Petrucci: guitar, backing vocals
John Myung: bass
Jordan Rudess: keyboards, Haken Continuum Fingerboard, Morphwiz iPad app
Mike Mangini: drums, percussion
Paul Northfield: engineer, spoken words (8)
Joe Maniscalco: assistant engineer
Richard Chycki: vocal track engineer
Andy Wallace: mixing
Hugh Syme: cover art
Produced at Cove City Sound Studios in Long Island, New York and Mixland Studio
in Midhurst, Canada (vocals only), January – May 2011 by John Petrucci
UK and US release date: September 2011.
Highest chart places: UK: 17, USA: 8
Running time: 71:01
Current edition: Roadrunner Records 2014 Japanese CD reissue

Black Clouds & Silver Linings will forever be remembered as Dream Theater's
unplanned last hoorah with Mike Portnoy and the culmination of their nearly
twenty-five years together as a musical family. By no means flawless – it's
shockingly uneven, actually – it's a fine farewell in retrospect, especially since
Portnoy got to complete his 'Twelve-step Suite' and say goodbye to his father
before exiting. Consequently, what was supposed to be another year or so of
business-as-usual teamwork to bring their eleventh LP to light instead became
many months of confused feelings and uncertain horizons as they parted ways
and set new plans.

For Portnoy, the 2010s would start with a slew of new projects with Neal
Morse and Adrenaline Mob, among others; for Dream Theater, it would begin
by justifying their choice to carry on with a new drummer, Mike Mangini,
and a new album, the aptly named *A Dramatic Turn of Events*. To the relief
of all concerned, the record is more than just an adequate debut from the
current iteration of Dream Theater. Oozing restoration, determination, and
memorability, it's their steadiest and greatest work since *Octavarium*, if not
Train of Thought.

There has been an immeasurable amount of discussion and debate regarding
Portnoy's departure and Mangini's arrival – much of it is ongoing, for better or
worse – so you're encouraged to peruse outside materials for a fuller scope.
For the sake of brevity and objectivity, we'll keep it quick and easy here. At the
very end of August 2010, Dream Theater got together to talk about the next
steps of their career. Portnoy had been playing with Avenged Sevenfold – who'd
lost their founding drummer, James 'The Rev' Sullivan, at the end of 2009 –
for a few months at this point and he was enjoying the freshness of it all. As a

result, and in addition to other reasons, he told LaBrie, Rudess, Myung, and Petrucci that he wanted Dream Theater to take a breather and reunite once everyone was recharged. Despite the other members' possibly noticing vague signs of weariness from him on the last tour – as well as feeling half-serious paranoia about him wanting to join Avenged Sevenfold permanently – they were caught completely off guard.

Portnoy claims that his choice was unrelated to 'the musical chemistry within the band', adding that he actually still felt very motivated by and proud of what they'd been doing. Rather, it was the 'personal relationships' and background troubles between them that led to his ultimatum: they go on 'an indefinite hiatus' or he quits. Obviously, it was a tough call, and after a lot of deliberation, they realized that Dream Theater needed to exist with or without him. As Petrucci deduces: 'It's part of our identity and our family, and our career and our business and we love it. We had no intentions or reason to stop it, see it end or take a break'.At first, they tried to figure out compromises – such as Portnoy showing up for 'sporadic live shows' while someone else filled in on stage and in the studio – but to no avail. With mixtures of resentment, disappointment, and empathy on both ends, the two parties decided to dissolve their partnership.

On September 8, 2010 – mere hours after their last conference – Portnoy posted an in-depth and genuine resignation statement to his Facebook page. Part of it reads as follows:

> After having had such amazing experiences playing with Hail, Transatlantic and Avenged Sevenfold this past year, I have sadly come to the conclusion that I have recently had more fun and better personal relations with these other projects than I have for a while now in Dream Theater ... Please don't misinterpret me, I love the DT guys dearly and have a long history, friendship and bond that runs incredibly deep with them ... it's just that I think we are in serious need of a little break.

With the decision set in stone and publicized – and tons of legal complications, fan feedback, and more to contend with – the remaining four guys wasted little time searching for a new drummer. Said person needed to be compatible musically and personably, so they drew up a shortlist of about a dozen candidates and held auditions at the start of October, on stage 2 of S.I.R. Studios. Some of them passed on the opportunity, but most showed up; among them were Aquiles Priester, Thomas Lang, Virgil Donati, Derek Roddy, Mike Mangini, Marco Minnemann, and Peter Wildoer. Each person had to run through three Dream Theater staples – 'A Nightmare to Remember', 'The Dance of Eternity', and 'The Spirit Carries On' – before running through some new ideas and then having informal chats with the band to gauge how well their personalities fit. The whole process was documented in a three-episode series called 'The Spirit Carries On', which Roadrunner uploaded to *YouTube* in April 2011.

Eventually, Dream Theater narrowed down the options to just two people: Mike Mangini and Marco Minnemann. Reportedly, Minnemann had never heard of Dream Theater prior to his audition, and he wasn't exactly devastated by not getting the job since it wouldn't have matched with his schedule or goals. Therefore, Mangini – who was an instructor at Berklee at the time – was the clear choice, as Rudess explains: 'It's the fact that he's such a terrific player, a really nice guy and also that he really wanted this position'. Indeed, Mangini felt like his entire life was leading up to this chance – especially since he'd performed on several LaBrie solo albums – so he was reasonably overjoyed when he got the news and could finally tell others. 'I don't want to say that waiting on the DT news was on par with waiting on news when someone close to me is sick, but to me, it was like that as it was a life-changing decision, not just a job change. It was an extension of me fulfilling who I want to be when I've alive', he says.

In an ironic twist of fate, Portnoy tried to re-join in December 2010, after he found out that Avenged Sevenfold never intended him to be a fulltime member. By that point, however, the gears were already turning for the next record and chapter in Dream Theater's story, so it was too late to look back. Since then, both of them have essentially let bygones be bygones, with Petrucci and Portnoy publically re-establishing a friendship. As for Mangini, the announcement of his entrance was expectedly met with a lot of negativity from devotees. True to his humble and jovial nature, though, he completely saw where they were coming from and vowed to honour what Portnoy did while also bringing his own specialities and flavour to the table.

Having now reached the figurative light at the end of the tunnel, it was time for the new Dream Theater to ensure that their studio comeback would be as substantial and reassuring as possible. They returned to Cove City Studios at the start of 2011 with newfound concentration and hopefulness, single-mindedly aiming to prove themselves by incorporating everything their admirers knew and loved about them. For that purpose, they agreed that Mangini shouldn't be a part of the writing process; instead, Petrucci used drum machine drafts on the demos for Mangini to 'interpret in his own style' later. To his credit, Mangini was totally on board with it since he was 'dying to see what they'd come up with without a drummer' and he 'really didn't want to be in the position of being tested in that kind of environment'. Petrucci clarifies: 'I guess we weren't sure how it was going to go with a new person, a new personality and influence. So we thought that we would kind of bring it back to basics'. That's not to say that Mangini didn't affect the ether in other ways. Specifically, his bandmates felt 'a bit of a perspective change' and 'a different sort of energy' – as Petrucci recalls – and the absence of Portnoy actually 'led to a more relaxed atmosphere in which they were able to explore musical ideas and themes at their own pace'.

Although they unavoidably allude to what they'd just gone through on the LP, it doesn't steer in that direction as much as you'd think. Likewise – and as with the name of its predecessor – the title is only coincidentally symbolic of those circumstances. Really, the term *A Dramatic Turn of Events* was picked because the majority of its contents 'had something to do with dramatic events that happened either historically or recently', as Petrucci told the *Voices UK* fanzine. As with *Black Clouds & Silver Linings*, more elaborate versions of the album came out alongside the regular CD one. In particular, the special edition landed with alternate packaging and 'The Spirit Carries On' documentary on a DVD, while the deluxe collector's variation included all of that plus instrumental cuts of all the tracks, a 180-gram double vinyl set in a gatefold jacket, a Dream Theater-branded custom turntable slipmat, and a litho print of the album cover. Plus, fifty 'lucky winners' also found a 'Ticket for Life' randomly placed into the custom box.

By and large – and in the face of many outspoken listeners who disliked Mangini by default – the collection garnered shining reviews from critics and aficionados. Opener 'On the Backs of Angels' even got Dream Theater their first Grammy nomination for Best Hard Rock / Metal Performance; even though they lost to The Foo Fighters' 'White Limo', it was nonetheless quite a rewarding precedent since they'd never really sought out mainstream accolades. Plus, the irony of them achieving it with their first post-Portnoy sequence can't be ignored. Mercifully, the fourteen-month 'A Dramatic Tour of Events' cycle – which was filmed for 2013's *Live at Luna Park* release – saw further acceptance of the new line-up from the majority of concertgoers.

For numerous followers – including yours truly – *A Dramatic Turn of Events* remains Dream Theater's superlative effort with Mangini. Stable, revitalized, and methodically appealing, it merges their strengths as praiseworthy songwriters and virtuosic players without ever succumbing to the off-putting banality that plagued its direct ancestors. On the contrary, it unmistakably sees the band digging themselves out of a rut to reign over the realm of progressive metal once more. Some have even speculated that at least half of the sequence borrows directly from *Images and Words*, but Petrucci denies any deliberateness with those similarities. Given the fact that he was literally following Petrucci's programmed prototypes, Mangini's fairly safe approach is fathomable, too. Hell, even if he isn't as adventurous or idiosyncratic as Portnoy when left to his own devices, he's an excellent drummer who simply doesn't deserve the hate that he gets. Honestly, it's hard to imagine anyone better taking Portnoy's place on the stool, and *A Dramatic Turn of Events* is reason enough that he belongs there.

'On the Backs of Angels' (Petrucci, Rudess, Myung)
Designed to demonstrate their 'signature sound' with deliberate stimuli from Pink Floyd, it was released as a single on June 29, 2011. On September 14, 2011, a music video – directed by Boutviseth – arrived; it depicts them playing in-between shots of buildings, gravestones, gears turning, the White House, and more as rain pours. In keeping with tradition, the track was made available

for download in *Rock Band 3* that November.

Petrucci's introductory arpeggios are threatening and unhappy yet instantly entrancing, and Rudess' faint carnivalesque tapestries bring his usual adventurous vibrancy to the proceedings. It becomes more spellbinding as the peculiarity piles up, with Myung and Mangini teaming up dexterously for inventively erratic rhythms. Before long, LaBrie storms in with steadfast criticisms of political greed and disruption that are fashionably dissimilar to the surrounding chaos. An awesome unified guitar and horns keynote junctures into the very likeable chorus: 'Selfless are the righteous / Burden me, lead me like a lamb to the slaughter'. Around the six-minute mark, Rudess' tasteful improvised piano meditation sets up Petrucci's impassioned and spiralling solo, a return to LaBrie's best hook, and scattered influxes of more windingly breath-taking instrumentation. There's a sublime sense of meticulous and grand initiative to every second of it, making it one of Dream Theater's top album openers and a resoundingly rich display of their rejuvenation.

'Build Me Up, Break Me Down' (Petrucci, Rudess, Myung, LaBrie)

Petrucci states that it was created 'pretty far' into the writing sessions, with a clear agenda of bringing something 'direct and full of attitude' to offset the 'progressive elements' that were occurring elsewhere. On January 26, 2012, Loudwire premiered the somewhat gaudy lyric video. The song itself is temporarily absorbing but ultimately middling and forgettable, with a nü-metal base and mostly dull singing about the intertwining highs and lows of celebrity obsession and the media. Even the intermittent strings and stacked guitar solo in the centre are cool but commonplace. It's not terrible, but it's not really good or noteworthy, either.

'Lost Not Forgotten' (Petrucci, Rudess, Myung, LaBrie)

Spotlighting 'this ancient Persian elite fighting force that kind of died out', 'Lost Not Forgotten' is similarly run-of-the-mill aside from its horde of striving and exciting wordless turns. Rudess' piano chords, alongside sounds of horses galloping in the desert, definitely set the scene well. The full-bodied spiciness that follows – which they named 'The Tickle Section' after how some people from Roadrunner reacted to it – is foreseeable but still thrilling because of its Zappa-esque zany complexity. Luckily, the same can be said for the breakdown that comes later, as it even arouses the feeling of divine destiny from 'Blind Faith' two minutes from the end. Unfortunately, LaBrie's parts are less gripping and more generic; accordingly, the songwriting at the heart of it brings down the whole experience a peg or two.

'This is the Life' (Petrucci, Rudess)

It's one of the band's sturdiest ballads in quite some time, and its title came to Petrucci after seeing the phrase on a pickup truck bumper sticker while driving with his mother and thinking about his sister's pregnancy. The starting decoration is endlessly evocative, and the ensuring timbres and pace are exquisitely gentle and calming. While LaBrie's extended exhales tend to annoy some listeners, he delivers lines like 'Have you ever wished that you were someone else? / Traded places in your mind / It's only a waste of your time' with endearingly dreamy peacefulness in this instant. It reaches peak life-affirming grandeur during its emphatically blissful bridge, 'Feed the illusion you dream about / Cast out the monsters inside', and Petrucci's subsequent showpiece is classily purifying. It may be too sappy for some, but it's hard to wholly reject its idyllic and inspirational message and performance.

'Bridges in the Sky' (Petrucci, Rudess, Myung)

Likely the utmost example of mesmerizing bizarreness in their whole discography, 'Bridge in the Sky' begins with shamanic percussion and throat bellows, as well as dark choral carols, bird chirps, and plucked strings. It's an enormously vivid and disquieting aural locale, and it's no wonder why the working title was 'The Shaman's Trance'. LaBrie comments, 'It's about being in a very dark, soulless period and then trying to go through the healing process'; the blisteringly frenetic build-up in-between that tribal prelude and his foreboding verses expresses that perception fascinatingly.

On that note, LaBrie's verse and pre-chorus chronicles rousingly maintain that vein until finding relief through his hypnotic hook: 'Sun, come shine my way / May healing waters bury all my pain'. When it returns, the extra movement – 'And at last the time has come / To unite again as one /To the power of the Earth I'm calling' –is even more charismatic. The jam afterwards is absolutely magnetic, fusing their trademarks with Middle Eastern flourishes and a touch of early '70s Yes. Instinctively, they go back to those hooks prior to wrapping up with more throat bellows. Like 'On the Backs of Angels', it's an eager encapsulation of all that this latest incarnation of Dream Theater can do.

'Outcry' (Petrucci, Rudess, Myung)

'Outcry' was meant to be the anthem of *A Dramatic Turn of Events*, and its origin goes back to a riff Petrucci made up during the drummer auditions. He also says that it made him 'envision flying through the air in slow motion', which helped shape the lyrical content that deals with 'the uprisings in the Middle East [and] people fighting against oppression'.

Its unsettling airy start conjures the 'Metropolis' stuff, and it's generally successful in capturing a quirky but severe setting simultaneously. At first, LaBrie sings with fervent frankness to complement the group's aggression, but they soon switch to a more transcendental fragment: 'We suffered far too long / We gather now, growing stronger'. Rudess' symphonic synths enhance its serenity, and the chorus is appropriately empowering. Naturally, more hectic timbres assist the next verse, leading to a mouth-wateringly bombastic instrumental disruption with all of the colourful sophistication and bewitching melodies you'd desire. It's like a classical piece run amuck, and Myung's singled-out cycles are surely a highpoint. Its devolution into a mournful mingling of piano notes and rhythmic veneers is masterful, too, allowing LaBrie so offer more solace – 'You can look the other way / Or you can face the light' – before Dream Theater champions the chorus as it concludes with unclear disobedient shouts. All in all, it's an extremely powerful track in multiple ways.

'Far from Heaven' (Petrucci, Rudess, LaBrie)
LaBrie was the driving force behind 'Far from Heaven', which the group also considers 'Part 1' of 'Breaking All Illusions' since the two share themes. It's undoubtedly one of Dream Theater's most gracefully nuanced and unshakeable songs ever, with gut-wrenching strings and piano wondrously catering to LaBrie's every kind-hearted affection. Although its subject matter may relate to 'pushy parents', admittances such as 'Every day I put a brave face on / Serves me well / Feeling helpless / Facing it alone / Hard to tell that I can't change who I am' make it astoundingly universal and pertinent. It's a phenomenal tear-jerker, for sure.

'Breaking All Illusions' (Petrucci, Rudess, Myung)
The watermark of A Dramatic Turn of Events – and of the Mangini era as a whole thus far – it's the first tune Myung wrote lyrics for since 'Fatal Tragedy'. From beginning to end, it's a marvellous epic whirlwind of flamboyant bounciness and tense triumph. It kicks off like the agitated younger brother of 'On the Backs of Angels', as snaky riffs and rhythms cascade with seductive flair as they hint at things to come. Once it moves into its colder and more isolating sensation, its unconventional verse structure – tarcets, or groups of three lines – is as inventive as it is persuasive; likewise, the use of pre-recorded voiceovers in-between LaBrie's thoughts hurriedly reminds you of their earlier LPs. Of course, all of it also makes the healing chorus – 'Live in the moment / Breathe in a new beginning' – more effective.

Then, speedy musical upswings and defiant vocals present a pleasantly abrupt redirection; after the modified chorus comes back, Dream Theater blast-off into one of their greatest instrumental sections of all time. Destructive yet lovably off-the-wall, it invokes the boundless technical merriment of 'Learning to Live'. Shuffling between absurdly precise counterpoints and changes of temperaments and time signatures – plus a multitude of eccentric tones from Petrucci and Rudess – it's all glued together with idiosyncratic ingeniousness. Petrucci's bluesy solo during the lull is first-rate, too, and provides a much-appreciated breather before the awe-inspiring musical madness restarts.

Eventually, LaBrie brings it home by reprising the chorus and then segueing into a meaningful afterthought: 'Embrace the days / Don't turn away / Life's true intent needs patience / Karma starts the signal'. Brilliantly, a main melody from 'Far from Heaven' comes back as Mangini's syncopation wraps it up succinctly. While it's true that – as with the entire collection – he does little more than holding it all together, he's does so flawlessly and deserves applause for it. As such, and in terms of merging top-notch songwriting and daredevil playing, Dream Theater have rarely been better than on 'Breaking All Illusions'.

'Beneath the Surface' (Petrucci)

It was the last track written for the record, and Petrucci demoed it himself before bestowing it on the rest of them. He felt that 'Breaking All Illusions' would be too 'intense' a way to go out, so he was encouraged by his wife, Rena, to scribe this as a 'cool-down' ender. Expectedly, its message is meant to be 'lighter' and 'reach deep into your soul in a very honest way'.

Its opening composite of acoustic guitar fingerpicking, diplomatic orchestration, and water drops instantly accomplishes that objective. LaBrie's serenely moves from self-doubt to self-assertion as he confesses considerate poeticisms like 'Sad to think I never knew / You were searching for the words / For the moment to emerge' with unbroken poise. Rudess' sensitive yet machinelike solo and Petrucci's heart-warmingly lumbering chords commandeer the score toward a commanding multitracked bridge: 'I would scream just to be heard / As if yelling at the stars / I was bleeding just to feel'. Judiciously, LaBrie adds far more elation to his final phrases, insinuating growth and conquest after suffering so much misery and certifying 'Beneath the Surface' as one of their most lingering last statements.

Bonuses

Just like the instrument-only varieties on *Black Clouds & Silver Linings*, the ones on the special editions of *A Dramatic Turn of Events* are most valuable with deep analysis, as each allows you to hear things – clearer guitar riffs, weightier strings, gutsier modifications, etc. – that are somewhat buried by LaBrie on the official takes. As just about every diehard fan knows, the other major bonus – 'The Spirit Carries On' on DVD – is a priceless sixty-minute look into how they found Portnoy's replacement. It's shot and edited very well, with humbling interviews with Dream Theater and the prospective candidates in-between footage of the sessions and outside activities. It's especially intriguing and emotional to view the final stages when the other drummers hear and react to being turned down before Mangini gets that all-important phone call.

'Dream Theater' (2013)

Personnel:
James LaBrie: lead vocals
John Petrucci: guitar, backing vocals
John Myung: bass
Jordan Rudess: keyboards, GeoSynth iPad app, Seaboard
Mike Mangini: drums, percussion
Larisa Vollis: violin
Misha Gutenberg: violin
Yevgeniy Mansurov: violin
Yelena Khaimova: violin
Noah Wallace: viola
Aleksandr Anisimov: viola
Anastasia Golenisheva: cello
Valeriya Sholokhova: cello
Len Sluetsky: double bass
Richard Chycki: engineer, mixing
James 'Jimmy T' Meslin: assistant engineer
Kevin Matela: assistant mixing
Dave Rowland: assistant mixing
Eren Başbuğ: orchestral arrangement, conducting
Hugh Syme: cover and album design
Larry DiMuzio: photography
Produced at Cove City Sound Studios in Long Island, New York, January – May
2013 by John Petrucci
UK and US release date: September 2013.
Highest chart places: UK: 15, USA: 7
Running time: 68:01
Current edition: Roadrunner Records 2014 Japanese CD reissue

Dream Theater entered the 2010s by rebounding fabulously from the loss
of Mike Portnoy. After all, they found a massively suitable – if perpetually
controversial – new drummer in Mike Mangini; created a superb first studio
record together with *A Dramatic Turn of Events*; earned their first Grammy
nomination; and had a tremendously fruitful touring cycle that led to a superb
first live record together, *Live at Luna Park*. Unsurprisingly, hopes were high that
whatever they did next would live up to that quasi debut victory. Unfortunately, it
doesn't; rather, their self-titled twelfth album suffers from a pseudo sophomore
slump of bland sameness and wasteful diversions. It's not out-and-out bad, but
like its title, *Dream Theater* is majorly forgettable and boring. When taken as the
well-produced and well-performed sum of its dependably mediocre parts, it's the
band's worst album since *When Dream and Day Unite*.

They started writing it collectively during A Dramatic Tour of Events, with
Petrucci also working on his own as the foremost creator. Now rightly embedded

into the Dream Theater flock, Mangini contributed as well. As is often the case with self-titled releases, they called it *Dream Theater* to accentuate how this iteration planned to move forward and be treated as legitimately as any that came before it. In an interview with *Guitar World*, Petrucci expounds: 'We wanted to make this album a reference point for fans as far as what Dream Theater is all about. That was the goal and the mission, and it set the tone for the entire project'. Likewise, Rudess told Joe Bosso of *MusicRadar* that 'there was no question that we were a real unit now. With Mike [Mangini] really locked in, the pieces fit together so well ... The affirmation from our fans that the new Dream Theater was something that could move into the future really energized us as we went into the studio again.'

Petrucci also acknowledges the deliberate test of stacking the LP with shorter tracks, as he told *Blabbermouth* in 2014: 'The basic mentality is that every song doesn't have to be 12 minutes long. It's actually hard to do. The challenge is to try to write and keep the style that we write in without straying from the thing that makes us unique'. Never ones to shy away from important topics of the time, the songs concern a number of serious cases, including the April 2013 Boston Marathon bombings, PTSD, and the 2002 Elizabeth Smart kidnapping. They also recruited Berklee student Eren Başbuğ to help with organic string arrangements, as well as wrote their first wholly instrumental tracks since *Train of Thought* ten years prior.

Like its predecessors, *Dream Theater* was available in several forms, including as a limited edition boxset. In addition to the usual 180-gram double vinyl housed in embossed gatefold – as well as the two-disc embossed deluxe CD digipak with a bonus 5.1 surround sound mix – it also packs in exclusive artwork by Syme, a custom 2GB USB stick with the Majesty symbol, a thirty-minute documentary called 'Take This for the Pain (Mike Mangini Audition Improv Jam)', and more.

During the summer of 2013, they uploaded a short but sweet four-part 'In the Studio' video series to *YouTube* to take fans through the creation process. On July 30, they held their first-ever listening party for the press at Germano Studios in New York City. In another move that Portnoy likely never would've gone for, the entire sequence was streamed by *Rolling Stone* on September 16, a full week before it came out. Once it did, it sold more than 34,000 copies in its first week alone, making it their third Top 10 album in a row. It also fared well internationally, landing Top 10 spots in over twenty other countries, such as Canada, Japan, Denmark, Italy, Switzerland, and Norway.

Deservedly, professional reactions were somewhat split. Places like *AllMusic*, *Revolver*, and *Loudwire* were largely positive about it, whereas *PopMatters* and *DPRP* were less enthusiastic. Still, its lead single, 'The Enemy Inside', got them a second Grammy nomination, this time for Best Metal Performance. Sadly, they lost to Black Sabbath's 'God Is Dead?' and haven't been nominated since. The tour that followed included many standout nights, with their March 25, 2014 'homecoming' show at the Boston Opera House being the major one.

Recorded alongside the Berklee Concert Choir and Berklee World Strings, it was put out that September as the *Breaking the Fourth Wall* set.

Dream Theater is quite listenable, but it has very little staying power. Sure, some melodies hit and the playing is always commendable, but it almost always comes across as either maddeningly flavourless or favouring style over substance. While they've always rejected the notion that they diminish their creativity and integrity for commercial gains, it's hard not to feel like that's happening throughout this one. On the other hand, changing things *too* much can be immensely polarizing, as they'll soon verify with a follow-up whose lofty ambitions manifested astonishingly contentious responses.

'False Awakening Suite' (Petrucci, Rudess)

They crafted it specifically to open their concerts, with Petrucci later telling Ultimate-Guitar.com that they 'like to have some sort of ... dramatic piece of music and something cinematic' when they take the stage. He adds, 'We've used the music from Psycho before and Hans Zimmer... It was kinda like, 'Well, let's write our own. We can do this. How hard could it be?'' Truthfully, it is a magnificently imposing way to begin, with an abundance of orchestral heft – courtesy of Başbuğ –perfecting Dream Theater's militaristic fury. Curiously divided into three parts – 'Sleep Paralysis', 'Night Terrors' and 'Lucid Dream' – its various shake-ups keep you invested yet never veer too far off-course, highlighting the group's dynamic prowess without getting in the way of its purpose as an arresting preface. It accomplishes exactly what it should and makes you jolted for whatever comes next.

'The Enemy Inside' (Petrucci)

Regrettably, that exhilaration is subdued by this lacklustre lead single, which – oddly enough – was streamed by USA Today on August 5, 2013. Its unending wrath is befitting considering the topic it covers – the trauma of war – and it's resourcefully juxtaposed by LaBrie's softer singing. Lyrically, there are some potent expressions, too, such as 'I'm a burden and a travesty / I'm a prisoner of regret / Between the flashbacks and the violent dreams / I am hanging on the edge'. That said, and aside from Petrucci and Rudess' typically harmonious syntheses, nothing about it is really notable. Instead, it's like an exceedingly ordinary lost track from Train of Thought, with sizably average melodies, guitar riffs, and overarching frameworks. At least Bill Fishman's music video – which features actual soldiers discussing their PTSD before we follow the fictitious day-in-the-life of a suffering veteran–raised awareness for the Save a Warrior foundation that helps people recover from the tribulations of combat.

'The Looking Glass' (Petrucci)

The first easygoing song on *Dream Theater*, the Rush-esque 'The Looking Glass' was issued as the LP's third and last single on February 4, 2014. Like its predecessor, it's decent at best and equally disposable, plainly shining a spotlight on up-and-comers who get lost in their quest for fame. LaBrie's harmonies are pleasing, as are Petrucci's licks and shredding, but the whole thing reeks too much of stadium rock cheapness that countless other acts could've generated. Boutviseth's music video doesn't do it any favours, either, as its inconsistently saturated portrayal of Dream Theater playing in-between shots of a woman looking into a magic ball is proudly ho-hum and unmemorable.

'Enigma Machine' (Petrucci, Rudess, Myung, Mangini)

Named after a German electro-mechanical cipher device used during WWII, its unfriendly and mysterious anarchy intentionally captures the tension of covert espionage. Rudess' chilling isolated theme is judiciously expanded upon by the other players, with Mangini and Myung not missing a single step in following his and Petrucci's shape-shifting hostility. In a way, its evolution around the main idea evokes 'The Ytse Jam' while also seeming more futuristic and decisively merciless. About three-and-a-half minutes in, Petrucci's lead resembles part of 'A Nightmare to Remember' too closely – unless it's a calculated reference – and the rest of it sticks to the set plan. By the end, its relative simplicity and repetitiveness wears thin but doesn't prevent it from being more enjoyable than not.

In perhaps the most delightfully incongruous Dream Theater music video to date, director Katia Spivakova and choreographer Laura Kowalewski collaborated on having the New York-based Ballet Deviare enact a routine based on 'Enigma Machine'. There is also Tool-like macabre imagery interspersed throughout it – such as fiery distortions, slow-motion purple sequences, and cryptic medical situations –so it's definitely worth a watch.

'The Bigger Picture' (Petrucci)

This track – which began as a segment of 'The Enemy Inside' before being extracted and developed – relates to 'being able to step back and really see what you're trying to do from the beginning' regarding accomplishing a goal. For Petrucci, that links to his role as a producer, but the message can apply to any endeavour. There's an overt sentimentality to just about everything at the beginning, yet there's also a relatable sincerity to LaBrie's singing, Rudess' piano work, and Petrucci's acoustic guitar work that makes it strengthening and cosy.

Admittedly, the chorus – 'Shed your light on me / Be my eyes when I can't see / Shed your light on me / Be my guide so I can see' – is cheesy and cliché; however, the enticingly heated bypass it takes immediately afterwards is a saving grace, even if it does borrow melodically from Queensrÿche's 'Suite Sister Mary'. Petrucci's bluesy dual-layered solo halfway in finds its place without much effort, and the remaining minutes blossom into derivative encouragements. It's the best non-instrumental entry thus far, but not by much.

'Behind the Veil' (Petrucci)

Rudess made the 'cinematic' and 'otherworldly' – as he calls it – sound collage at the start through a program called Alchemy, and it gorgeously establishes a sense of spiritual injustice and misfortune. That vibe is pertinent because the tune deals with how, as Petrucci claims, 'there's people in the world that really do very horrific things [and] unspeakable things and somehow justify that behaviour', such as kidnappers. In this instance, Dream Theater are motivated by how Elizabeth Smart would accompany her captors in public without anyone noticing because she was wearing a veil over her face. Logically, 'Behind the Veil' is also meant to honour the 'bravery' of captives who manage to escape.

The piece inarguably parallels the heroic heaviness of classic Iron Maiden when the rest of the music kicks in, and Mangini serves up stellar syncopation and fills in the process. The effects on LaBrie's timbre make him sound just as malevolent as he poses rhetorical questions like 'What kind of monster would come to feast / When the devil shows his face?' In great contrast, the pre-chorus is fragile and longing; thus, he places the evilness of the perpetrator and the hopefulness of the victim side by side. Observably, the chorus – 'Someone save me / Look behind the veil / Please don't walk away' – is colossally touching since he's literally speaking for Smart and anyone else who's been in her situation. Myung's quick transition into the second half is cool, and the slight retooling of prior parts is novel. The instrumental break afterwards manages a faultless balance of technique and thematic resonance, too, so it's impressive and impactful at once. In general, it's a forceful and penetrating track that stands out amongst the rest of *Dream Theater*.

'Surrender to Reason' (Myung)

The first thing they composed for the LP, it bursts out of the gate with the same kind of upliftingly uproarious commerciality that dominated previous selections. Petrucci recalls the final third of 'The Count of Tuscany' with his browbeaten acoustic strums, and LaBrie's yearning verse matches that tone well. The arrangement then takes off into a twisty tunnel of admirable asymmetrically as instruments battle around LaBrie's shadowy proclamations. His chorus mirrors that of 'Breaking All Illusions', and the tricky bits that follows are more obligatory than outstanding. Gratefully, Petrucci's purposefully 'obnoxious and dry and right in your face' second solo – abetted by Myung's sludgy slogs – is an interesting change of pace. Beyond that, 'Surrender to Reason' is sufficient but not special.

'Along for the Ride' (Petrucci)

September 9 2013, saw this one arrive as the album's second single, and Petrucci views it as a 'breather before the grand finale' and 'a point of reflection'. He penned the words before the music and drew from the horrors of the Boston Marathon bombings to express how 'there are so many situations that are out of our control, and this is one of them ... but it shouldn't break down our spirit – not as a country, not as a people. It shouldn't break down our belief in the good of people'. Musically, he 'wanted something that people could sing along to, waiving their phones and lighters in the air'.

Its initial noises of nature are pacifying, as are Petrucci's morose arpeggios. Rudess' piano chords and the soaring strings enrich that environment as LaBrie's earnest chorus radiates communal fortitude and closeness. The subsequent passages work fine within their more macho handling, although they're slightly staler as well. Rudess' Emerson-esque off-the-cuff solo is familiar but stirring, elevating the song to an above-average ballad and a crowd-pleasing anthem.

'Illumination Theory' (Petrucci)

On Record Store Day 2014, it was given an exclusive 12' picture disc treatment with a main image of a shattered lightbulb against a white background. They 'storyboarded' it ahead of time and knew how it would start and end before 'working on the curve' in the middle. Conceptually, it ponders the things in life that people are willing to live, die, and/or kill for. The brief first chapter, 'Paradoxe de la Lumière Noire' (or 'Paradox of Black Light'), is characteristically heavenly, measured, and explosive. Drums and electric guitar riffs collide around slow symphonic urgency, all of which drains into a rugged continuation aptly named 'Live, Die, Kill'.

Like much of the voyage – and *Dream Theater* in total – it's a serviceable sequence that'd have more longevity if it wasn't so recognizable. In other words, it's just Dream Theater going through the viciously intricate motions without doing anything remarkable or fresh. The computerized components are somewhat engaging, and Mangini'splaying – love it or hate it – is at least distinctive, but there's not much else here to care about. Even LaBrie'smelodies are too dull and accustomed. Thankfully, its devolution into the third phase – 'The Embracing Circle' – is productively sinister and moody, if also overly elongated. Once Başbuğ and his crew pick up from those ethereal oscillations, the centrepiece swells with unassuming classical grace that's lovely and dramatic yet too dragged out. It is a nice reimagining of the opening theme, though.

Rush's 'YYZ' irrefutably comes to mind as Myung and Mangini's wooden taps segue into the irritatingly quarrelsome 'The Pursuit of Truth'. As with 'Live, Die, Kill' – and despite all of its intimidatingly showy musicianship and wild mutations – it's mundane more than it is magnetic since Dream Theater have done virtually all of this already. As for the last part, 'Surrender, Trust & Passion', it reprises the central motif smoothly before building to a sugary outro ode that's no less manufactured and trite. Rudess and Petrucci's epilogue duet is unexpectedly wholesome and jazzy, so it's a shame that it's treated as a tacked-on secret instead of being grown within 'Illumination Theory'proper.

Bonuses

The Japanese editions come with an instrumental take of 'The Enemy Inside' that's not especially worthwhile since there's almost nothing new to discover about the arrangement. The 'Take This for the Pain' documentary – stored on the aforementioned USB stick – presents additional footage and insight into Mangini auditioning for, joining, and now spending some time in Dream Theater. It's an essential sibling to 'The Spirit Carries On' from the *A Dramatic Turn of Events* extras. The USB stick also houses the several 'stems' – isolated tracks – for 'Behind the Veil', so you can hear the guitar, bass, drums, vocals, and solos on their own and then rework them as you please.

'The Astonishing' (2016)

Personnel:
James LaBrie: lead vocals
John Petrucci: guitars, story and concept
John Myung: bass
Jordan Rudess: keyboards, synthesizer, arrangement, creative direction
Mike Mangini: drums, percussion
Eric Rigler: bagpipes (18)
Pueri Cantores: boys' choir
Fred Martin and The Levite Camp: gospel choir
FILMharmonic Orchestra Prague: orchestration
The Millennium Choir: classical choir
Richard Chycki: engineer, mixing, spoken voice of Nafaryus
Mike Schuppan: engineering
Travis Warner: engineering
Gary Chester: engineering
James 'Jimmy T' Meslin: assistant engineer
Dave Rowland: assistant mixer
Jason Stanniulis: assistant mixer
Brandon Williams: music editing and coordination
David Campbell: orchestral and choir arrangements
Richard Flocca: conducting
Petr Pycha: contractor (Prague)
Susan Youngblood: conductor (The Millennium Choir)
Jie Ma: cover art
Sean Mosher-Smith: cover art direction
Produced at Cove City Sound Studios in Long Island, New York, The Samurai Hotel in Astoria, New Jersey, Street of Dreams in Ontario, Canada, and CNSO Studios in Prague, January – September 2015 by John Petrucci
UK and US release date: January 2016.
Highest chart places: UK: 11, USA: 11
Running time: 130: 23
Current edition: Roadrunner Records 2016 USLimited Edition Deluxe Box Set

At last, we've come to not only Dream Theater's most polarizing album by a mile but possibly one of the most divisive releases in all of progressive music: *The Astonishing*. While not terrible, *Dream Theater* was far less multifaceted, individualized, and endurable than *A Dramatic Turn of Events*. It was as if the group were simply resting on their laurels, satisfied with cooking up excessively habitual content instead of taking risks and wanting more. Rationally, an attempt to do precisely that on the next venture should've yielded gargantuan artistic prosperity and vast ovation from listeners, right? Well, not exactly; in fact, *The Astonishing*– a sprawling and self-indulgent sci-fi rock opera with lavish cross-platform lore – is among the most maligned

115

records of the millennium. It has its supporters and apologists, but most fans treat it as the primary embarrassment of Dream Theater's catalogue, which is truly a disservice to everything that the two-hour opus gets right. For all of its flaws– corniness, pretentiousness, tedium, and verbosity, to name a handful –*The Astonishing* possesses enough conceptual ingenuity and strikingly wide-ranging tactics to make it a markedly underrated and laudable realization.

Petrucci's deep appreciation for fantasy, science fiction, and the like was showcased on *Systematic Chaos*– and elsewhere – so his choice to completely commit to a futuristic dystopian narrative about ill-fated love, technology, war, and oppressive totalitarianism isn't too startling. Openly influenced by *Game of Thrones* and *Star Wars*–and with clear connections to Rush's *2112* and Shakespeare's *Romeo & Juliet*– the tale 'follows the Ravenskill Rebel Militia in their efforts to defy the Great Northern Empire of the Americas using the magical power of music'. Furthermore, Petrucci's 'observations on the ubiquity of technological automation in modern-day society' is an underlying thread.

In terms of bringing it all to life, Petrucci and Rudess would get together daily to go over ideas and compose; they'd then bring those drafts to Myung, Mangini, and LaBrie to get their feedback and see what they could do with the material. They also sought out composer David Campbell to handle real string arrangements, choirs, and miscellaneous sounds – as well as encourage LaBrie to interpret the voices of characters in different ways – to make it sound like a theatrical production. They even worked in several studios, so it's fair to say that *The Astonishing* is easily their most grandiose and strategically complicated endeavour ever. Fortuitously, all of that time and energy paid off for the most part.

Although some singles came out, Dream Theater always intended the LP to be treated as a singular immersive experience. To help the audience follow along, a dedicated website – *TheAstonishingFanGuide.com* – was planned with 'lyrics written in screenplay form, character illustrations and a map'. They even asked devotees to choose a side by subscribing to either the Great Northern Empire mailing list or the Ravenskill Rebel Militia mailing list. Also, Petrucci and Rudess recorded the 'Inside *The Astonishing*' video trilogy that totals about sixty minutes and offers comprehensive yet accessible explanations of their methodology. Of course, the limited-edition deluxe box set boosted fans absorption with 'a collectible 3D NOMAC replica, a lyric book, a 20' x 30' collectible poster, a double-sided 18' x 24' map of The Great Northern Empire of the Americas, and a set of trading cards'.

In January of 2016, Petrucci told *Billboard* that 'because the story is very rich as far as the characters and plot', it might require multiple mediums – video games, novels, movies, 'or even a musical' – to encapsulate the entire project. He wasn't lying, either, as February 2017 saw Turbo Top Games' *The Astonishing Game*– 'a turn-based tactical board-game' – become available on PC and smartphones. In March 2018, Vault Books published a novelization of *The Astonishing*– penned by Petrucci and Peter Orullian – that 'adds new plot lines and intrigue, additional characters and motivations, as well as explanations and ideas not explored' on the record. Its limited edition also included an introduction from Petrucci, interviews with each member of Dream Theater, early demos, 'never-before-seen handwritten notes, early art renderings, [and] photographs', full-colour artwork, and more.

Despite the negativity now associated with it, *The Astonishing* was primarily met with a lot of positivity. It landed top ten spots in Sweden, Portugal, the Netherlands, Italy, Norway, and elsewhere while also earning Dream Theater their first #1 debut on the *Billboard* Rock Chart. Publications like *Rolling Stone, Kerrang!, Blabbermouth*, and *Metal Hammer* were also majorly supportive, and that August, *Classic Rock* even ranked it behind *Scenes from a Memory* and *Images and Words* as Dream Theater's third-best album. In contrast, *Loudwire* concluded that it's their third-worst album – behind *When Dream and Day Unite* and *Falling Into Infinity*– and *Prog Sphere* actually felt that it's the poorest of them all.

Fittingly, they played the whole thing during the Astonishing Live undertaking – with an intermission between the two acts – and occasionally played older tracks, too. They hired a production company to provide a visual representation of the tale on a few screens. The tour started in North America in April 2016, went to South America, and ended back in North America that December. Comparable to the fanaticism of *The Rocky Horror Picture Show*, some devout members of the audience would even dress up as the characters.

The Astonishing is far from being Dream Theater's greatest work, yet it's also far from being an abomination. At over 130 minutes in length, it's unquestionably drawn-out, monotonous, and hackneyed at times. However, it's also filled with some of the most appealing and renewed instrumentation and songwriting of the Mangini era, so it'd be damn near great if its excesses were trimmed down for a single-disc journey. Above all else, the band should be applauded for going all-in on something so extravagant and experimental. Cumulatively, *The Astonishing* is the antithesis of the self-titled LP and a testament to Dream Theater's willingness to reach beyond their traditional grasp multiple decades into their career. Far too few of their contemporaries can say the same.

'Descent of the NOMACS (NOMACS instrumental)' (Petrucci, Rudess)

In 2285, part of the US is governed by the tyrannical Great Northern Empire of the Americas, and the only 'music' residents are allowed to hear is provided by NOMACS or Noise Machines. Thus, the story starts with the first of five robotic patchworks meant to convey what those NOMACS play. Appropriately, it's unruly and unsettling, with sounds of drilling, digital operations, and alarms instilling soulless panic in the listener. It definitely sucks you into the fictional world.

'Dystopian Overture' (Petrucci, Rudess)

The use of choir and classical elements – strings, horns, etc. – really makes it a powerfully cinematic overview of the major themes of *The Astonishing*. It changes course often enough to remain consistently fascinating and get you psyched for what's to come. Honestly, it's one of Dream Theater's most aspiring and many-sided instrumentals, and it kind of works as a film score, too.

'The Gift of Music' (Petrucci)

It's a catchy and upbeat tune about how the protagonist, Gabriel, is naturally musical and 'the one to save' the village of Ravenskill. LaBrie sings passionately and the biting arrangement is straightforward yet cultured and expressive, with a solid solo from Petrucci and a few difficult bits thrown in for good measure. It's easy to hear why it became the album's first single – on December 3, 2015 – with a music video directed by Wes Teshome that blends Dream Theater performance with digital animation that ties into the plot.

'The Answer' (Petrucci)

A quick acoustic ditty reminiscent of 'Beneath the Surface', 'The Answer' finds LaBrie using simple rhymes and slightly exaggerated exhales – one of his most argumentative traits, and it *really* permeates *The Astonishing*– to acknowledge his self-doubt about being the saviour of his community. Rudess' piano work is charming, as are the strings and percussion. It's an agreeable listen and a subtle but successful way to get inside of Gabriel's head. The marching footsteps into 'A Better Life' help it feel fluidly theatrical, too.

'A Better Life' (Petrucci)

Here, the narrative turns to Gabriel's older brother, Arhys, who's the commander of the Ravenskill Rebel Militia. It's a woeful yet warlike account of why Arhys does what he does and believes in his sibling's purpose: 'Still the fires of revolution burn within my eyes / On this perilous road to freedom / He's our one and only guide'. His melodies are gripping, particularly when his vocals are layered as he alludes to his late wife and their son, Xander: 'Evangeline / You lived a life of misery and pain'.His emotive fluctuations are echoed well by the malleable instrumentation, too, so it's a consuming composition in every way.

'Lord Nafaryus' (Petrucci)

One of the biggest problems with the record is its amateurishly on-the-nose symbolism, so yes, naming the antagonist 'Lord Nafaryus' – and the love interest 'Faythe' – is painfully laughable. Nevertheless, this track about the head of the Great Northern Empire of the Americas traveling to Ravenskill to see Gabriel's talent for himself is temptingly stagey and tense. Alternating between being the omniscient narrator and the villainous Nafaryus, LaBrie's acting is passably playful, to say the least; similarly, the music is capably melodramatic, concluding with sweeping orchestration that augments to the believability of the gimmick. Naysayers notwithstanding, those who buy into The Astonishing as a rock opera undoubtedly adore moments like this.

'A Savior in the Square' (Petrucci)

In public, Gabriel plays for Nafaryus and sets his sights on his daughter, Faythe. Its prolonged wordless set-up – piano and acoustic guitar bases beneath faint percussion and electric guitar shrieks – is a tad gushy, but it's pertinent for the emotional connection of the two characters. The regal horns, footsteps and the like add realism to it, too, and LaBrie's tackling of multiple characters over the more aggressive music is attention-grabbing. The ending – Rudess' piano alongside the strings and LaBrie's delicate utterance of 'I'm taken by surprise / An angel just appeared before my eyes' – is banal but heartfelt.

'When Your Time Has Come' (Petrucci)

Picking up where the last one left off, it's a cheerful first meeting for Gabriel and Faythe as the audience applauds around them. Lyrics like 'So let your heart be free / Keep your spirit burning bright / Set down the stones you carry / Take the weight off your mind' are worthy of eye-rolling, but as usual, LaBrie's raw talent and conviction make it an inoffensive moment. He's backed by flowery gusto and a heavy-duty guitar solo until Faythe confesses her affection for Gabriel as the arrangement swells. Although mushy stuff like this is what many fans dislike about the LP – and defensibly so – it's hard to deny that Dream Theater pull off what they're going for.

'Act of Faythe' (Petrucci)

Its glum symphonic start is suitable for Faythe to contemplate a music player she had as a child and the impoverished lives of her subjects. Its instrumentation is sparser yet quite similar to the prior two tracks – another common complaint of the album – so there's not much to say about its piano/power ballad essence. LaBrie retains his compassionate bellows around odd childlike laughter, captivatingly declaring, 'My music player / My private paradise / My music player / A refuge I must hide'. An orchestrated and expanded callback – with angelic croons – to 'A Savior in the Square' then closes it.

'Three Days' (Petrucci)

Despite enjoying Gabriel's recital, Nafaryus sees him as a threat and gives the people of Ravenskill an ultimatum: surrender Gabriel within the next three days or be destroyed. Unsurprisingly, LaBrie adopts a raspy and inflated malice as he speaks for Nafaryus and his guards, and the rest of the band reinstitutes a fetching progressive metal context. Mangini plays with rigged precision as the quirky complexities pour out, and the piece wavers peculiarly and regularly to stay appealing. The raucous swing climax is a great example of Dream Theater trying new things on *The Astonishing*, too.

'The Hovering Sojourn (NOMACS instrumental)' (Petrucci, Rudess)
The second NOMACS interruption is more of a thematic tool than a listenable selection. Still, its metallic and electronic dissonance isn't unbearable since it only lasts thirty seconds, and the inclusion of these snippets makes the fictionalized world and circumstances feel more authentic. It is less involving and vibrant than the previous one, though.

'Brother, Can You Hear Me?' (Petrucci)
Over sounds of commotion, marching, and militaristic music, Arhys vows to stand by Gabriel and defend him. The very structure of its first-half – one character announcing something to another – is pure theatre, so while it's rather generic melodically and musically, it nonetheless adds another drop of genuineness and drama to the rock opera. More strings serve as a segue, after which the second half commences with Gabriel's airy avowals over more piano chords. He triumphantly promises not to let Arhys down as the instruments exude gruff confidence.

'A Life Left Behind' (Petrucci)
The plot thickens as Faythe plans to disguise herself to visit Gabriel in Ravenskill again; aware of her daughter's decision, her mother, Arabelle, sends her son, Daryus, to shadow her. He also sets out with his own self-serving goal. It kicks off hypnotically askew, with Yes-like acoustic guitar and piano patterns, synths, and syncopation luring you in. It's easily among the best passages in all of the current Dream Theater iteration, and fortunately, its conversion into a mellow supplement alongside LaBrie's endearing verses and chorus – which arouse the end of 'Six Degrees of Inner Turbulence' – is pretty as well. Once Arabelle instructs Daryus to follow his sister, and he agrees while also alluding to his 'honest intentions', the piece becomes more evil yet upholds its breezy nature. All in all, it's a very pleasing song.

'Ravenskill' (Petrucci)
Birds squawk and water runs as Rudess' tragic piano notes join Faythe's breathless search for Gabrielle. The tune gets more suspenseful and destructive when she finds Xavier, who takes her to see Arhys. LaBrie's melodies are more compelling at this point, as Arhys and Faythe go back and forth about whether or not she can be trusted. There's an impeccable use of effects and dynamics to make it all as absorbingly over-the-top as possible. The ways in which it transforms into a gentle ode once she and Gabrielle meet and align is clichéd

but wholehearted, with his final lines – 'With music and love on our side / We can't lose this fight / Tomorrow, our dreams come alive' – warranting mockery.

'Chosen' (Petrucci)
Gabriel surmises that if Faythe's parents let them present his music at their home, they'll change their ways and bring peace to the land. Yet again, Dream Theater embody this development as a tender piano and acoustic guitar testimony that turns into a sappily vigorous sing-along. It's engaging to a degree, with a chorus that'll get stuck in your head, yet its sheer familiarity exemplifies why *The Astonishing* is too samey and elongated in spots.

'A Tempting Offer' (Petrucci)
Appreciatively, this vindictive snapshot of Daryus kidnaping Xavier and demanding that Arhys surrender Gabrielle in exchange – in an attempt to impress Nafaryus – is a sufficient breath of fresh air. Its sound effects enhance the believability, and the fact that Dream Theater produce a marginally different style for each character's segments is praiseworthy. It tantalisingly balances spiteful candour and silky pleading as Daryus and Arhys argue, with an ever-changing score that basically samples everything Dream Theater is doing in the sequence.

'Digital Discord (NOMACS instrumental)' (Petrucci, Rudess)
Emptier and less frantic than 'The Hovering Sojourn', its lower register and easy digestibility make it more of a sibling to 'Descent of the NOMACS'. Outside of that, there's nothing to dissect about its whirling computerized processing. However, the last machinery uproar is calming but ominous, so it absolutely insinuates that trouble is afoot.

'The X Aspect' (Petrucci)
Although conflicted, Arhys agrees to give up Gabrielle after remembering the promise he made to Evangeline about Xavier. Rudess' piano work is typically classy, and the choral murmurs that navigate him are overwrought but timely. They fade away so that organ, acoustic guitar strums, and eventually weightier elements can steer LaBrie'sbrief but desirable ponderings. The closing bagpipes are a nice touch, too, and reinterpret a recurring theme.

'A New Beginning' (Petrucci)
It has one of the most riveting introductions of the whole journey, with a grand sense of destiny and upheaval embedded in every tricky timbre. Faythe encourages Nafaryus – who once owned her music player –to give her and Gabriel 'a chance' to hopefully spark 'a new beginning'. Her optimism is immediately shut down by her father's cynicism, and as usual, Dream Theater

revise their approach as they go to keep the struggle ordered but consistently changing. The addition of horns and harpsichord prior to Petrucci's solo is neat, too, and Arabelle's caring recap of her husband's former humanity is an impactful aside. Luckily, he agrees to 'grant the chance' for Faythe and Gabrielle to change his ways. Afterwards, the virtuosic jam reminds listeners that the Dream Theater they've always loved still lives within all of the divisive rock opera newness. Therefore, 'A New Beginning' offers a glimpse into the group's past as it culminates the present methodology.

'The Road to Revolution' (Petrucci)

'Act I' wraps up with a traditional trope of theatre: each main figure reflecting on their situation as Nafaryus heads to Heaven's Cove – an empty amphitheatre – to witness Gabriel and Faythe's performance. Sonically, it's a modest yet fondly decorated orchestral rocker. Its sudden twist as the focus shifts from the couple's positivity to Daryus' sneering impatience is incompatibly – but calculatedly – uncomfortable, as is Nafaryus' retort to Arhy's steadfast self-evaluation. Cleverly, 'The Road to Revolution' also conjures 'Brother, Can You Hear Me?' as it leaves the listener eager to experience the second part of *The Astonishing*.

'2285 Entr'acte' (Petrucci, Rudess)

In keeping with concept album conventions, 'Act II'commences with another instrumental overview. Compared to 'Dystopian Overture', this one is more festive and romantic, with a mostly light-hearted persona and various accentuations– tweeting bells, flamboyant orchestration, etc – imparting luscious assurance. There's a fair amount of hectic doubt as well, so it succeeds in signifying the characters' cognitive dissonance and reminding you of major motifs as the story continues. Its droning descent into 'Moment of Betrayal' is an effective way to glue the two pieces together, too.

'Moment of Betrayal' (Petrucci)

Premiered by *Billboard* on January 22, 2016 – as the album's second single – it finds Gabriel thinking that Arhys is acting bizarrely because of how risky the plan with Nafaryus is; instead, Arhys feels guilty and nervous because he told Daryus about the performance at Heaven's Cove. This dual reasoning for his behaviour alone makes 'Moment of Betrayal' rousing, and the initial combination of downtrodden strings and piano chords effectively conveys the distress of his decision. What's also enthralling is how Gabrielle moves from frank assertions to riotous uncertainty – 'You are acting very strange / Nervous and on edge' – before Arhy's spellbinding chorus. All along, LaBrie's backing vocals commendably push his range, and the rest of the group follows suit with a wealth of zany progressive metal flourishes. Whereas most of the LP works best in the context of the whole picture, this one is complete and catchy enough to be a self-contained gem.

'Heaven's Cove' (Petrucci)

A foreboding build-up of choir and natural sounds leads to sophisticated and sinister acoustic guitar arpeggios evocative of 'On the Backs of Angels'. Once Rudess' keyboard comes in, Dream Theater channel the starry splendour of mid-1970s Camel; from there, the music becomes aggravated as the narrator snippily delves into how the place 'was a wondrous site' before it became 'an empty shell like a memory that time erased'. By the end, it's very robust and dazzling, with a lavish piano coda heightening the unnerving gloom.

'Begin Again' (Petrucci)

It's a syrupy ballad in which Faythe affirms that she wants to be with Gabriel and use her royal status for the betterment of the world. Kindly piano chords and soaring guitar notes glide into introspective strings, increasing the Disney-esque dreaminess. It's warm and charismatic throughout, and the merry upsurge near the end is invigorating, but it's simultaneously a bit worn-out and easy to cast-off. After all, Faythe's sentiments have already been implied, and their aural depiction is majorly humdrum. In other words, it's among the most throwaway entries in the set.

'The Path That Divides' (Petrucci)

Narratively, it's one of the most important and affecting tunes since it's about Arhys changing his mind, confronting Daryus at Heaven's Cove, and ultimately being killed in front of Xavier. It begins almost identically to 'Heaven's Cove' – a crafty detail – before digital noises mix with symphonic fright. Petrucci's piercing plucks and Mangini's irregular hits melodramatically accompany LaBrie's enlightenments. As Arhys states that he won't 'betray' Gabriel, the track gets feistier, resulting in Daryus and him arguing with abrasive stiltedness that recalls the harshness of earlier Dream Theater selections. The arrangement gets more penetratingly crucial and colourful as the two men fight – with grunts and sword clashes bringing their battle to life –until imperial classical traces indicate that 'Arhys' fight for hope / Cost him his very life', as the narrator concludes. The plot point is predictable, but as with many clichés on the LP, it's executed admirably.

'Machine Chatter (NOMACS instrumental)' (Petrucci, Rudess)

The second to last NOMACS instrumental, 'Machine Chatter' is the most mysterious and tolerable one yet. In fact, it's arguably a bit musical, too, since there are hip-hop beats and note intervals rooted beneath the robotic whirring. It also seems like the machines are starting to get worried about being overthrown if Gabriel and Faythe prosper

'The Walking Shadow' (Petrucci)

As Xavier grieves for his father and Daryus prepares to kill him as well, a cloaked figure appears. Assuming it's Gabriel, Daryus rushes to stab him, only to realize that it's actually Faythe. Musically, it's eerie and belligerent, complementing well Xavier's angry accusations of Daryus being a murderer. After more instrumental zig-zags, LaBrie is calmer in suggesting that Xavier will join his father imminently; just then, 'The Chosen One' – Gabriel – steps forward and Rudess' organ grants a gothic overtone to the ensuing instrumental freak-out. Two-thirds in, a lone female voice reprises the central melody of 'Act of Faythe' as footsteps traverse gravel. Next, the narrator slowly – and weirdly – reveals that Faythe was the victim as an ascending metal structure gives way to sounds of Faythe dying. Aside from the storyline development, 'The Walking Shadow' is sufficient but also kind of dull.

'My Last Farewell' (Petrucci)

Arriving moments after Arhys and Faythe are attacked, Gabriel covers Xavier's ears as he lets out a scream that deafens Daryus. Fortunately, Faythe is protected by her earphones. As you'd expect, LaBrie personifies Gabriel's grief with leisurely, wistful lamentations as strings and piano escort him. The lyric 'Now I've found my home in you / Only I'm too late' is a nice nod to Faythe's epiphany in 'When Your Time Has Come', and the initially bland beginning is fixed by transfixing melodies and engrossingly elaborate playing as Gabriel addresses Daryus. Rudess' wacky solo is a treat, too, and in general, 'My Last Farewell' achieves the satisfying mixture of anger and anguish that it goes for.

'Losing Faythe' (Petrucci)

The pun of the title – like the pun of her name – either works for you or it doesn't, but it's hard not to be at least somewhat moved by 'Losing Faythe'. The cries and regrets of her parents open it, and while the combination of acoustic guitar fingerpicking and wistful singing is old hat at this point, it's nonetheless significantly touching. As it goes, Mangini and Rudess add sublime trimmings, and LaBrie's harmonies are lovely. In the end, Nafaryus'acceptance of Gabriel – and request that he use his gift to resurrect her – is anticipated but logical, of course.

'Whispers on the Wind' (Petrucci)

For all of its strengths, as it progresses, *The Astonishing* remains stretched out in terms of plot, as it uses multiple tracks to unearth what could've been covered in one. Case in point: 'Whispers of the Wind', a short but overly acquainted monologue in which Gabriel determines that his 'gift is gone' because of the scream and that Faythe will stay dead. It's a compelling twist for the tale, but it's also a minor one, and without anything fresh in the music department, it would've been better at the tail end of 'Losing Faythe'.

'Hymn of a Thousand Voices' (Petrucci)

Drawn to the scene by Gabriel's scream, the townspeople show up and give him the hope and vocal support he needs to bring Faythe back to life. Its bubbly core is inspirational, smoothly succulent, and thematically deserved; but, it's not especially fetching, and the gospel ending is awkwardly over-the-top and obvious. Suffice it to say that Dream Theater's comparable style on 'The Spirit Carries On' from *Scenes from a Memory* is exponentially superior in every way.

'Our New World' (Petrucci)
Committing to his change of heart, Nafaryus decides to shut down the NOMACS forever; at the same time, Daryus is forgiven and Xavier joins Faythe and Gabriel as a happy family devoted to making life better for all citizens. The enriching radio rock celebration – while a tinge unimaginative and wearisome – is an apropos attitude for how the story wraps up, and even Petrucci's solo seems designed to elicit participation from the crowd in concert.

On that note, it's no wonder why a music video for 'Our New World' was released on May 7, 2016. Filmed during shows in Milan, Italy, its shots of them playing intercut with shots of the audience reacting certainly creates an air of communal celebration between Dream Theater and their fans. That September, an alternate version of 'Our New World' was released as a single. Nearly a minute shorter than the studio cut, the main draw is Halestorm frontwoman Lzzy Hale putting her spin on Faythe's part. Obviously, her voice takes some time to get used to, but it's a welcome change that gives the song and concept more diversity and plausibility.

'Power Down (NOMACS instrumental)' (Petrucci, Rudess)
As the title implies, Nafaryus' guards have indeed turned off the NOMACs, and there's a real sense of dread and creepiness to this industrial collage, in particular. It even comes full circle by reprising the alarms from 'Descent of the NOMACS', and interestingly enough, its scattered tones also evoke the textural craziness at the end of 'Misunderstood' from Six Degrees of Inner Turbulence.

'Astonishing' (Petrucci)
This is really a continuation of 'Our New World' since it has the same purpose: a happy ending for all involved. Specifically, Nafaryus and Arabelle vow to give their people freedom and support, and Daryus is absolved of his crimes and accepted again into the now-united family. Each major character has something to say once the primary theme of 'Act of Faythe' gets a symphonic rock rebirth, with Arhy's spirit revising 'Brother, Can You Hear Me?' before Gabriel and Nafaryus do the same with 'The Answer' and 'The Road to Revolution', respectively. The latter is even fleshed out with colonial instrumentation, and their integrated last message to everyone else – 'We will build our world on common ground / And we'll live once more / Eternally / In harmony / Our lives will be / Astonishing again' – is stately and joyous, if also mildly corny. It's a fulfilling exit for an imperfect yet grossly underrated record.

Bonuses

The boxset doesn't house any new audio, so all that's left to talk about are the physical supplements. All of them are very cool and informative collector's items, with each vinyl sleeve displaying a portrait of a major character. The map of the Great Northern Empire of the Americas is neat, too, as is another poster that resembles a movie advertisement. The 3D NOMAC replica is very detailed and well made. Naturally, the lyrics book is priceless for those who want the most out of *The Astonishing*, and the trading cards are a fun novelty. Together, these items truly make the fantasy world come alive.

'Distance Over Time' (2019)

Personnel:
James LaBrie: lead vocals
John Petrucci: guitars
John Myung: bass
Jordan Rudess: keyboards
Mike Mangini: drums
Richard Chycki: vocal recording, additional vocal production
James 'Jimmy T' Meslin: engineer
Ben Grosse: mixing
Paul Pavao: mixing, assistant engineer
Hugh Syme: art direction, illustration, design
Mark Maryanovich: photography
Matthew 'Maddi' Schieferstein: photography
Produced at Yonderbarn Studios in Monticello, New York, and Mixland Studio in
Midhurst, Canada (vocals only), June– September 2018 by John Petrucci
UK and US release date: February 2019.
Highest chart places: UK: 12, USA: 24
Running time: 56:57
Current edition: InsideOut Music 2019 US Limited Edition Deluxe Box Set

There's not a whole lot to say in setting up Dream Theater's latest album, *Distance Over Time*, outside of pointing out that it's a return to form after the avidly ambitious and experimental – yet immensely combative –*The Astonishing*. As the official website states, it's meant to harness 'a newfound creativity for Dream Theater while maintaining the elements that have garnered them devoted fans around the globe'. Really, it's like 2013's *Dream Theater* in that it's almost completely benign and foreseeable, checking off every by-the-numbers Dream Theater box with faceless, machine-like diligence. There's very little here that's exciting or endeavouring; instead, it's Dream Theater blatantly attempting to reclaim the followers who resented what they did with *The Astonishing*. Whereas that record at least saw them doing new things – even if it wasn't always valuable – *Distance Over Time* sees them merely doing things they did better and earlier in their career.

After spending some of 2017 celebrating the 25th anniversary of their sophomore sequence via the Images, Words & Beyond tour, they reconvened in June 2018 and began working at Yonderbarn Studios while living at its 'adjacent residence'. Of that decision, and in the record's official press release, Petrucci explains how in the past, they'd 'traditionally move into a studio to track the record ... [and] everybody either commutes or stays in a hotel'. Doing it differently here allowed them to be distraction-free and 'just focus on being creative, spending twelve-to-fourteen hours a day working while also having fun in between the writing sessions'. He continues: 'We'd take turns cooking for each other like brothers in a firehouse and since it was summertime, the upstate New York weather was beautiful'.

It was originally called *Velocity*, but they ultimately wanted something more 'poetic', so they replaced it with 'the formula [for] velocity'. In an interview with *Sonic Perspectives*' Rodrigo Altaf, LaBrie mentions that it took them a mere eighteen days to write it. As for its topics, the LP explores the juxtaposition of fear and motivation, the 'aftermath of abuse' for women, an 'intimate slice of small-town lore', and the philosophical need to respect and cherish Earth. At just under an hour in length – not including the bonus track, 'Viper King' – *Distance Over Time* is their shortest album since *When Dream and Day Unite* and the first to include lyrics by Mangini. It's also their debut on InsideOut Music, and to help build hype for it, they launched an online scavenger hunt that led to a site where the title, cover art, release date, and subsequent tour plans were revealed. As it turns out, Dream Theater spent most of 2019 traveling North America, South America, and Europe in a joint celebration of the new record and the 20th anniversary of *Scenes from a Memory*.

Unsurprisingly, *Distance Over Time* was presented in several formats, with the most grandiose being the jam-packed boxset. Kept in a sturdy box with a lenticular cover, it contains a hand-numbered certificate of authenticity, a red 'DT 137' patch, an exclusive 7' picture disc, a pin badge, a 60 x 60 cm poster of the cover, two white vinyl LPs, ten art cords, a slipmat, and an artbook with two CDs, a DVD, and a Blu-ray disc. Musically, you get the album with the 'Viper King' bonus track – of course – as well as instrumental, 5.1 surround sound, and high res versions of all ten songs.

Critically, the collection did very well, with publications such as *Consequence of Sound*, *Metal Hammer*, *Kerrang!*, *Classic Rock*, and *Exclaim!* showering it with acclaim. While it's understandable that so many admirers longed for Dream Theater to fall back on their tried-and-true DNA, it's just as reasonable to dismiss *Distance Over Time* as an unabashed placation for those outraged by their previous double album overindulgence. Admittedly, it may seem like they're now in a lose-lose situation since the Mangini-era has been chastised for being both too different with *The Astonishing* and too similar with *Dream Theater* and *Distance Over Time*. Perhaps a finer compromise between both extremes would make everyone happy next time around, but as it stands, *Distance Over Time* is an uneventful way to end the studio album saga for the time being.

'Untethered Angel' (Petrucci)

The single and music video – a multi-shot supercut of the band in the recording studio – for this opener came out on December 7, 2018. It was originally called 'Song 4' because it was the fourth one they wrote, and Petrucci penned it around the idea that 'fear' can be 'debilitating' and 'prevent us from realizing our true potential'. Thus, it's essential that you untether yourself from such dread to reach your potential and embrace 'the future's countless possibilities'.

It's definitely a stimulating way to begin the album, with demoralised guitar notes and a saintly synth background introducing an explosion of thick chords and rhythms that arouse Portnoy-era gems like 'Honor Thy Father'. LaBrie sings with his emblematic suave fervour, too, resulting in some life-affirming hooks: 'Fear can live inside you / Push you to the edge / Face the fear within you / Wake up from the dead'. As with practically all of the sequence, though, it oscillates between standard metal flavours and well-worn Dream Theater theatrics. The dual solo is a cool touch, but everything else is obligatorily standard.

'Paralyzed' (Petrucci)
Petrucci notes that this second track 'is an introspective reflection on the negative impact that being obstinate or single-minded can have on important relationships'. Wayne Joyner's music video – which premiered on February 8, 2019 – visualizes this message through a futuristic depiction of sentient robotics that feels like a synthesis of the films *Blade Runner, The Terminator* and *Dark City*. It'd be engaging on its own, but the fact that it also helps distract from the blasé blandness of 'Paralyzed' itself is a bonus. The tune isn't flat-out bad, but it is wholly unaspiring, ticking off radio-friendly boxes without anything renewed or intriguing about it. It's enjoyable yet paltry as if Dream Theater are doing the bare minimum at every turn.

'Fall Into the Light' (Myung, Petrucci)
This third entry was the second single put out – on January 11, 2019 – and according to Myung, it's 'about the quest towards enlightenment... [and] looking inside to find your individual happiness'. In contrast to Joyner's footage, the official animated video for 'Fall Into the Light' blends an abstract sci-fi sheen with first-person POV movements around mountains at different locales. It's the most striving piece yet since its initially formulaic aggression transforms into a pleasant acoustic detour halfway in. True, this part is more than a little similar to Metallica classics like 'Master of Puppets' and 'The Unforgiven', but at least it brings some soul and novelty to the composition. Likewise, Mangini's alarmed conduit for Rudess' entrancing solo is electrifying.

'Barstool Warrior' (Petrucci)
Similar to what Haken did on 2016's *Affinity*, 'Barstool Warrior' stands out because of its lively throwback to glitzy 1980s synth-rock. This is expressly evident in Rudess, Petrucci, and Mangini's styles and timbres, all of which resolutely aid LaBrie's thoughtful Billy Joel-esque slice-of-life account of – as Petrucci explained to *Blabbermouth* – 'two characters, unrelated but connected in their lament over being stuck in dead-end situations'. His chorus is particularly alluring, and Petrucci continuously peppers the song with gratifying licks. Despite sticking too closely to 'Losing Time', the piano break in the middle is an elegant diversion prior to the fiery catchiness continuing.

As for the animated supplement that arrived on August 21, 2019, it displays spacey computerized imagery alongside pictures of various boats. There are also drawn shots of the fictional duo – an 'alcoholic who never escaped the humdrum of his sleepy, maritime village [and] a woman trapped in an abusive relationship trying to survive from day to day' – to bring Petrucci's narrative to life. It's easily the best video *Distance Over Time* received.

'Room 137' (Mangini)

Mangini's lone songwriting credit thus far, he based the title on both the tempo of the track and on a physicist named Wolfgang Pauli. As Mangini tells it, Pauli was admitted to a hospital room and 'knew that he was going to die ... because it turns out that he'd spent his life trying to figure out what the answer to 1/137 is. It's supposed to be the quantum key to all different dimensions'. Petrucci compares it to King's X tonally and The Beatles rhythmically; although he's not wrong about that, he gives it too much credit as an atypical Dream Theater tune. The biggest reason why is its parallels to 'The Dark Eternal Night' and *Systematic Chaos* as a whole. Plus, it's rather stale and single-minded, even with Petrucci's commendably uncharacteristic solo, so there's not much to discover with it.

'S2N' (Myung, Petrucci)

Petrucci reveals that 'S2N' – or 'signal-to-noise', referring to the quality of a transmission – is 'a very spiritual John Myung observation. The signal represents yourself and your clarity and how you resonate in a way that is pure, and the noise represents all of the negativity in the world'. Myung's prevailing bass line was the first part written for the record, and his contributions remain the most riveting as the track progresses. The influx of wickedness is also a delight – harkening back to some of Portnoy's past interjections – and the spurts of instrumental wizardry are inherently likeable, however familiar. Disappointingly, the chorus is nearly a dead ringer for that of 'The Looking Glass,' making it perhaps the strongest proof yet that *Distance Over Time* spends most of its duration looking backwards instead of forward. Humorously, the band also denies that the 'Wow!' heard two-thirds of the way through is an Owen Wilson soundbite. Only time will tell, I guess.

'At Wit's End' (LaBrie)

It was the first song written for the album, and in a chat with *Songfacts.com*, LaBrie disclosed that it concerns the 'after-effect of a very traumatic and horrific experience, which is being the victim of rape'. More precisely, it's about a man 'telling his wife that no matter what has happened, she has to remember that he still loves her as he always has, nothing has been lost, and that she needs to see that he is still the man she fell in love with'.

Its frenetic commencement – hyperactive guitar playing amidst heavy bass lines, mournful piano chords and frightened percussion – undeniably bears the horrors of such an incident. LaBrie's key outcry, 'Don't leave me now / Don't leave me now / I know that it's tearing you apart', is poignant as well. Rudess and Petrucci once again make for an invaluable pair during their flashy trade-offs at the midpoint, and the former's dejected piano work afterwards is stirring. The power ballad decadence that follows is a bit much, but cumulatively, 'At Wit's End' is elevated by its subject matter and multi-sectional grit. The echoey concert hall outro is an inventive choice, too.

'Out of Reach' (LaBrie)
LaBrie 'wanted to write a song about how people are affected when they lose a loved one', so he scribed this story of a man who watches a seemingly well-off woman in a coffee shop. '[A]s he sees her from day to day, sitting at her table, he realizes there is a sadness to her' because of a loss, and he wants to 'communicate to her to rediscover love', he clarifies. Rudess says that it was constructed quickly because he and Petrucci had 'one of those magical moments together where things just kind of gel'. For sure, their unified sorrow at the start is gorgeous and lingering, and LaBrie's verses – infused with his trademark exaggerated exhalations – are laudably graceful yet soppy. Sadly, it becomes less moving and more wishy-washy as it gets heftier, leaving little of the haunting impression that similarly subtle odes of the past attained.

'Pale Blue Dot' (Petrucci)
This final stop on the *Distance Over Time* train is inspired by a 1990 photo of Earth taken by the Voyager 1 space probe, as well as astrophysicist Carl Sagan's famous 1994 text on our world and interstellar exploration: *Pale Blue Dot: A Vision of the Human Future in Space*. Also, Dream Theater were stimulated by composers like John Williams and Béla Bartók, as well as finishing the album with something 'epic', 'ominous', and even 'confusing' at times.

Expectedly, it sets a prophetic mood with sounds of space and NASA communications as Mangini jump-starts a symphonically guttural prelude of topsy-turvy instrumentation. It effectively embodies the transcendental terror of galactic probing, which is predominantly essential since the lyrics are a tad forced and elementary. Likewise, LaBrie's melodies are too reminiscent of the drabbest moments in 'In the Presence of Enemies – Part II'. The group's cosmic jackhammer approach wears thin before long, though, and the winding instrumental expedition ahead of the climax is at once innately impressive and mandatorily meandering. As such, 'Pale Blue Dot' caps off the record's penchant for possessing tactics that would be much more exemplary if Dream Theater hadn't done them so many times previously.

Bonuses
LaBrie looked to Deep Purple's 'Highway Star', Rush's 'Red Barchetta', and Van Halen in a broader sense to assemble 'Viper King', his tribute to Dodge Vipers and the larger thrills of 'driving down the road and letting your spirit free'. It

indubitably seizes the kitschy exuberance of those artists from the get-go, with Rudess' gaudy lead guiding Dream Theater as they soak up the 'sex, drugs, and rock and roll' vibe of yesteryear. For better or worse, it never loses that old school, adrenaline-charged buoyancy, so much so that its all-embracing retro rambunctiousness – complete with vintage style keyboard and guitar solos –makes it seem like a discarded cover song from *A Change of Seasons*. It's obvious why they didn't want to include it as an official part of the collection, but there's some fun to be had with its dumbed down and disorderly sonic party.

Like the last few special editions, *Distance Over Time*'s aforementioned extras are fairly meaningful for major fans. The outer box is visually and physically striking, with each knickknack – especially the artbook and art cards – serving as cool swag. The superior audio renditions are crucial for deep admirers, too, with the instrumental versions of virtually all tunes exposing timbres that are somewhat buried in the primary takes. Hence, a truly deep listening of them is required to fully comprehend how, even at its most unremarkable moments, the LP is meticulously organized.

Roundup – Live/Video, Compilation, Extra Tracks, and Official Bootlegs

Live/Video

Dream Theater haven't been as prolific with their official live output as they have with their studio creations, but everything we've gotten has been gold. The obvious starting points are *Live at the Marquee* and *Images and Words: Live in Tokyo*, both of which came out at the end of 1993 (on September 4 and November 16, respectively). The former is Dream Theater's debut live album; it was recorded at London's Marquee Club and has a cover inspired by the Most Sacred Heart of Jesus Catholic devotion practice. Although it's a fairly brief collection – there are only six selections – it does a good job of representing the standouts of *When Dream and Day Unite* and *Images and Words*. In particular, it kicks off with a commendably faithful rendition of 'Metropolis—Part I'. LaBrie's singing isn't as authentic, but aside from that, nearly every nuance of the original is here. Of course, the same can be said for 'Pull Me Under' and 'Surrounded'. Expectedly, LaBrie easily makes 'A Fortune in Lies' his own via a richer and more subdued performance compared to what Dominici offered; afterwards, 'The Killing Hand' is preceded by an instrumental prelude called 'Another Hand' that effectively builds up to the charismatic intensity of the track itself. There's also 'Bombay Vindaloo', an improvisational tune rarely performed and obviously never put on a proper album. It evolves patiently into a hectic jam, with Petrucci's shredding and drawn-out notes leading mildly Middle Eastern ambiance. The crowd is quite respectful throughout it, too, so it's a great initial document of extremely early Dream Theater.

Likewise, *Images and Words: Live in Tokyo* is the band's first home video release. It was shot in August 1993 at Nakano Sun Plaza and features many of the same tunes, such as 'Pull Me Under' and 'A Fortune in Lies'. Of the others, opener 'Under a Glass Moon' is particularly punchy, 'Wait for Sleep' is bit slower and barer – yet arguably even more transcendental – than its studio counterpart, and 'Ytse Jam' is perhaps a tad heftier but virtually identical to the classic take. They also deliver 'To Live Forever', a timid ballad that was devised during the *When Dream and Day Unite* sessions and found a home on multiple assortments later. The opening of 'The Mirror' – called 'Puppies on Acid' here – is also hinted at before 'Take the Time'. Visually, it's your standard multi-angle affair with modest coloured lighting shifts and many close-ups; honestly, it's nothing super exciting on that front, but it's undeniably cool and endearing to see them all so young, especially with Moore there.

In-between the live footage are a few music videos, as well as clips of Dream Theater interacting with fans, discussing the making of *Images and Words*, shopping for clothes and condoms in Tokyo, visiting Abbey Road Studios in London, and much more. In 2004, *Images and Words: Live in Tokyo* was released alongside 1998's *5 Years in a LIVEtime* as a 'Double Feature', and a humble yet insightful band commentary was added. It's quite interesting to hear what Rudess thinks of it all since he wasn't there, and Portnoy's feedback shines most due to his representative sense of humour and meticulous attention to detail. It's an indispensable way to watch the show all over again.

Speaking of *5 Years in a LIVEtime*, it arrived in October 1998, has a cover designed by Storm Thorgerson, and fundamentally applies the *Images and Words: Live in Tokyo* treatment to the *Awake* and *Falling Into Infinity* periods. Even the DVD menus are almost indistinguishable, and the bonuses follow a similar gimmick. For instance, there's a behind-the-scenes film from the 'Waking Up the World' and 'Touring Into Infinity' tours, glimpses into them creating their third and fourth albums, and music videos for 'Lie', 'Hollow Years', and 'The Silent Man'. Arguably the most enthralling addition is the unplugged footage from both Ronnie Scott's Jazz Club in London and another fan show in Holland. The highlight there is easily 'Starship Trooper' alongside Steve Howe. Of course, there's also another band commentary over the live clips that's just as worthwhile as before.

While the spectacle of both home videos is comparable – once again, there are just moving camera angles and colored lights – the visual and audio *quality* of the concert footage is a noticeable improvement. Specifically, the sound is crisper and the images are in high definition, so the sense of immersion is definitely enhanced. Comprised of multiple nights – since it covers two tours – the expansive set contains many timely classics, such as '6:00', 'Voices,' and 'Peruvian Skies', as well as surprises like the sublime medley 'Learning to Live/A Change of Seasons Pt. VII: The Crimson Sunset'.They pull it all off faultlessly, and the fact that it's the only video document of the Sherinian era makes it a must-have release.

Correspondingly, *Once in a LIVEtime* came out on the same day and matches that aural excellence. Recorded by Kevin Shirley at the Le Bataclan in Paris, its two-and-a-half-hour marathon cleverly kicks off with 'The Crimson Sunrise' and ends with 'The Crimson Sunset'.They also spread other sections of the suite throughout the sequence, and intermediately, they more or less give equal attention to *Images and Words*, *Awake*, and *Falling Into Infinity* via fundamentals like 'Scarred', 'Take the Time', 'Trial of Tears', and 'Metropolis—Part I'. 'Puppies on Acid' also appears, as do 'The Ytse Jam' and isolated solos from Portnoy, Petrucci, and Sherinian. In typical Dream Theater fashion, they throw in nods to John Williams, Led Zeppelin, Rush, Pink Floyd, Lynyrd Skynyrd, and even Liquid Tension Experiment along the way.

Rudess makes his live debut on *Metropolis 2000: Scenes from New York* and its audio-only sibling, *Live Scenes from New York*. Recorded on August 30 2000, at Roseland Ballroom, both were released roughly a year later and – as alluded to earlier – the latter came with some controversy. You see, *Live Scenes from New York* was issued on 9/11, and its original cover depicted the World Trade Center in flames; therefore, it had to be recalled and redistributed later, with its revised front instead showing the Majesty symbol. Furthermore. Portnoy collapsed after the performance due to 'over-exhaustion, dehydration, stress, too little food and nutrition, too many Red Bulls, etc', as he explained on his forum.

Those hiccups aside, the set itself is arguably Dream Theater's best to date because of the songs included. Clearly, they do all of *Scenes from a Memory* – impeccably, I might add – with an extended prelude to 'Through Her Eyes' called 'John & Theresa Solo Spot'. Beyond that, the three-hour show features the entire 'A Mind Beside Itself' trilogy, 'A Change of Seasons', Liquid Tension Experiment's 'Acid Rain', 'Jordan Rudess Keyboard Solo', and much more. The third disc includes a video for 'Another Day', too, so it's jam-packed with necessities.

Obviously, *Metropolis 2000: Scenes from New York* is just the visual equivalent, albeit with a much shorter set of non-*Scenes from Memory* encores. It's directed better than the prior concerts, with plenty of close-ups at the perfect moments. Actor Kent Broadhurst does a fine job as the Hypnotherapist, and the interspersed conceptual footage – including a film for the dramatic end of 'Finally Free' – psychedelic imagery, and the like really makes it feel like more of a cinematic experience than a standard show. The opening even features credits for each member, as if they're actors. Another full-length commentary, as well as a tour photo gallery and a fascinating behind-the-scenes documentary, make the DVD even more priceless.

Next is October 2004's *Live at Budokan*, which was filmed the previous April at Nippon Budokan Hall in Tokyo. It's almost as lengthy as *Live Scenes from New York*, and the presentation is similarly top-notch, with three screens showing various angles and pre-recorded visuals to complement the band. Rudess reportedly had to fake his playing during the first few minutes due to his equipment malfunctioning, but you'd never be able to tell. In contrast to the previous live compilations, the CD, DVD, and Blu-ray versions contain identical setlists. Aside from 'Honor Thy Father' and 'Vacant', all of *Train of Thought* is recreated; in addition, Dream Theater pay homage to nearly every preceding record, with 'War Inside My Head', 'The Test That Stumped Them All', an extended version of 'Beyond This Life', and the now-legendary 'Instrumedley' – a composite of thirteen different song excerpts – reigning supreme. The bonuses include the half-hour 'Riding the Train of Thought' Japanese tour documentary, multi-angle footage of 'Instrumedley', a fan-participation Portnoy drum solo, the 'Dream Theater Chronicles' tour opening video, and Petrucci and Rudess going over their stage set-ups. It's fantastic.

Fans were able to score the magnificent *Score* at the end of August 2006, roughly five months after it was recorded at Radio City Music Hall in New York City. Naturally, it's an exceptional celebration of Dream Theater's first twenty years, with Jamshied Sharifi's 'Octavarium Orchestra' helping make the second set and encore – which includes an extended version of 'Octavarium' and the entirety of 'Six Degrees of Inner Turbulence' – as phenomenal as possible. Prior to that, Dream Theater work alone in immaculately replicating requisites such as 'The Spirit Carries On', 'The Root of All Evil', and even two unofficial tracks:

'Another Won' from *The Majesty Demos* and 'Raise the Knife' from the *Falling Into Infinity* sessions. Truthfully, both are kind of generic and dismissible, but the band plays them as well as anything else. It's a relatively extravagant production, too, as it takes place on a large stage with tons of flashing lights and three suspended screens. It also has some of the most dynamic and carefully chosen camera movements of any Dream Theater video release thus far.

As for extras, you get three bonus songs – 'Another Day', 'The Great Debate', and 'Honor Thy Father' – from earlier concerts. In addition, there's the priceless, nearly hour-long 'The Score So Far…' 20th-anniversary documentary that, well, pretty much contains what you'd want: fan reactions, band reflections, old footage and photographs, etc. It's quite in-depth and revealing. Lastly, there's the 'Octavarium Animation', which sees Dream Theater transformed into cartoon characters to depict LaBrie running from a spider as the other four guys play the instrumental break that comes between 'Full Circle' and 'Intervals'. Sure, there could be more to it, but everything that's here is valuable.

In September 2008, *Chaos in Motion 2007— 2008* landed to give devotees the official chronicle of their recent world tour in support of *Systematic Chaos*. Two versions were available: a standard two-disc DVD set and a five-disc set that added audio across three CDs. Obviously, the three-hour film is compiled from many locations, such as Vancouver, Buenos Aires, Toronto, Boston and Rotterdam. A collage of prior live clips and audience shots is paired with their trademark live prelude, 'Intro/Also Sprach Zarathustra', at the start. From there, they bring out 'Constant Motion', 'Forsaken', all of 'In the Presence of Enemies', and 'The Dark Eternal Night' from that latest LP. Other standards – 'Surrounded' and 'Take the Time' – appear as well, and they close with the aptly named 'Schmedley Wilcox', a brilliantly arranged epic composite of 'Trial of Tears', 'Finally Free', ' Learning to Live', 'In the Name of God', and the 'Razor's Edge' portion of 'Octavarium'. In-between songs are informal and endearing documentary snippets, allowing the viewer to feel like they're actually on the road with the group. Although all of the music is executed methodically and the concert clips are taken from several places, the inconsistent video quality is nonetheless a bit jarring and disappointing.

This time, the supplements are comprised of the ninety-minute 'Behind the Chaos on the Road' feature, promo videos for 'Constant Motion', 'The Dark Eternal Night', and 'Forsaken', some live screen projection films, a sprawling photo gallery – that seems to include them bowing in front of the crowd after *every* show – and Portnoy offering quick stage and backstage tours. As usual, he conveys a childlike sense of excitement, frankness, and humility, humanizing himself in the process of showing everything. All in all, it's a stacked and comprehensive account of what Dream Theater were up to between June 2007 and June 2008.

The next live document, *Live at Luna Park*, didn't come until November 2013. Directed by Mike Leonard and featuring a string quartet, it was shot on August 19 and 20 at Luna Park Stadium in Buenos Aires and is likely the most jam-packed set so far. Expectedly, it was available in multiple formats: a two-disc DVD, a two-DVD/three-CD pack, a single Blu-ray, a Blu-ray/three-CD bundle, an audio/video digital download, and even a deluxe edition box set with all three formats at a lengthy book. Most importantly, it marks the official concert debut of Mangini-era Dream Theater.

The chief attraction consists of about twenty tracks, and none are duds. Rather, the requisite cinematic intro leads us into an expected prioritization of *A Dramatic Turn of Events*, starting with 'Bridges in the Sky' and continuing with 'This is the Life', 'Lost Not Forgotten', 'Beneath the Surface', and 'Breaking All Illusions', among others. Breaking up those tunes are fundamentals like 'The Root of All Evil', 'The Silent Man', 'Surrounded', 'The Spirit Carries On', and 'Metropolis Part I'. There are also some solos, of course, with Mangini's appearing early and instantly validating why he deserves to take a stab at anything that Portnoy originally drummed on. By this point, they've mastered how to record their shows, so the entire thing looks and sounds immaculate; true, the absence of a video wall is slightly disappointing, but on the other hand, it means that the viewer never loses sight of the band, so it feels more intimate than some of the previous ones.

Whatever compositions from *A Dramatic Turn of Events* are missing from the main performance are comprised in the extra footage, as well as 'These Walls', 'Wait for Sleep', 'Pull Me Under', and 'Caught In a Web'. In addition, there's a brief documentary – focusing on Mangini's inclusion and some backstage antics – plus a cartoon intro, a trailer, and a quick behind-the-scenes featurette. Undeniably, *Live at Luna Park* is light in terms of bonus fun, but it surely makes up for it with over three hours of concert goodness.

As of now, the most recent live takeaway is September 2014's *Breaking the Fourth Wall*, which was recorded on March 25th as a 'homecoming' show at the Boston Opera House. As mentioned earlier, it sees Dream Theater partially playing alongside the Berklee Concert Choir and Berklee World Strings, and it was filmed by Rush concert film regulars, Pierre and François Lamoureux, who also did *Chaos in Motion 2007— 2008*. The multiformat release – two-DVD, digital MP3, Blu-ray, Blu-ray/three-CD, and the latter with a poster – gave fans plenty of ownership options.

This time, the band promotes *Dream Theater* via opener 'The Enemy Inside', 'The Looking Glass', 'Enigma Machine', and 'Illumination Theory'. Outside of that, the highlights are 'The Shattered Fortress', 'Trial of Tears', the first-ever live recreation of 'Space-Dye Vest', and four pieces from *Scenes from a Memory* (in honour of its fifteenth anniversary). Compared to *Live at Luna Park*, it's a more elaborate production, too, with lots of lightening trickery, multiple camera angles, and a massive video wall making for quite the hyperactive spectacle. The audience seems particularly overjoyed as the band concludes with 'Finally Free' and takes a shared bow.

The home menu of the DVD and Blu-ray is especially quirky – in their trademark tongue-in-cheek way – since it acts as a drawn version of a late-night talk show – *The Bad Larry Show* – featuring Arnold Schwarzenegger, Jim Backus, and Dream Theater. Unfortunately, the only supplementals are a photo gallery and visuals for 'Enigma Machine' and 'Illumination Theory'. They're cool enough, but the absence of anything substantial and significant is irksome since many of its predecessors offered much more.

Compilations, Extra Tracks, and Official Bootlegs

2008's *Greatest Hit (...And 21 Other Pretty Cool Songs)* is divided into two halves: 'The Dark Side' for heavy songs and 'The Light Side' for soft songs. While it does contain some interesting 2007 remixes of 'Pull Me Under' and 'Take the Time' – as well as a few single edits and 'To Live Forever' – it's virtually unnecessary for anyone who already has the studio albums. At least the joke on the cover – the 's' in 'Greatest' and all of 'hit' are shaded red to spell 'shit' – is lovably indicative of Portnoy's sense of humour and spite.

Moving forward, it's worth mentioning two non-catalogue Dream Theater creations. The first is 'Raw Dog', an instrumental track written for the video game *God of War III*'s EP, *Blood & Metal*. It's actually the last arrangement Portnoy contributed to, and it sits comfortably next to selections from Killswitch Engage, Trivium, Opeth, Mutiny Within, and Taking Dawn as an enormously gruff and relentless dive into complex brutality. There's also their cover of Rush's 'Xanadu' that appeared on the fortieth-anniversary edition of *A Farewell to Kings*. It's as fine a balance of faithful recreation and original innovation as any cover on *A Change of Seasons*, which isn't surprising.

Any diehard enthusiast is sure to champion the nearly two dozen entries in Dream Theater's official bootlegs compendium. A mixture of live, cover, demo, and studio series, only a handful make up the cream of the crop. The initial one is 2003's expanded *The Majesty Demos 1985 – 1986*, which includes seventeen new tracks before the original six. Most of them are extremely short soundbites, but the array of more developed originals and covers – 'Your Majesty', 'A Vision', 'March of the Tyrant', Rush's 'YYZ', and Talas' 'The Farandole' among them – means it's very worthwhile. To varying extents, the same can be said for *The Making of Scenes from a Memory*, *When Dream and Day Unite Demos 1987 – 1989*, *Images and Words Demos 1989 – 1991*, *Awake Demos 1994*, *Falling into Infinity Demos 1996 – 1997*, *The Making of Falling into Infinity*, and *Train of Thought Instrumental Demos 2003*, all of which appeared between 2003 and 2009.

Finally, their four recreations of other artists' albums – in order of release: Metallica's *Master of Puppets*, Iron Maiden's *The Number of the Beast*, Pink Floyd's *The Dark Side of the Moon*, and Deep Purple's *Made in Japan* – attest to how precisely and lovingly Dream Theater pay tribute to their idols. To be honest, *The Number of the Beast* sounds bad in spots, but other than that, all four are done very well. Most importantly, it's just a joy to hear how happy they and their audience are, as they bask in mutual admiration of the material.

Bibliography

'The Astonishing Novel.' *Dream Theater*, dreamtheater.net/discography/the-astonishing/novel/.

'The Astonishing.' *The Dream Theater World*, 8 Mar 2017, dreamtheater.club/discography/studio-albums/the-astonishing/.

Avin, Roie. *Essential Modern Progressive Rock Albums: Images And Words Behind Progs Most Celebrated Albums 1990-2016*. Royal Avenue Media, 2018.

Baird, Dave, and Basil Francis. 'Issue 2013-064: Dream Theater - Dream Theater - Duo Review.' *CD & DVD Reviews • DPRP.net*, 15 Oct 2013.

Blabbermouth. 'DREAM THEATER Releases Animated Video For 'Barstool Warrior' Song.' *BLABBERMOUTH.NET*, 21 Aug 2019.

Blabbermouth. 'DREAM THEATER: Unboxing Video Of Limited-Edition Box-Set Version Of New Album.' *BLABBERMOUTH.NET*, 27 Sept 2013.

Blabbermouth. 'DREAM THEATER's 'Enigma Machine' Gets BALLET DEVIARE Treatment.' *BLABBERMOUTH.NET*, 21 Mar 2014.

Blabbermouth. 'DREAM THEATER's JOHN PETRUCCI: 'It's Really Hard' To Write Short Songs.' *BLABBERMOUTH.NET*, 28 Oct 2014.

Blabbermouth. 'DREAM THEATER's New Album Cracks U.S. Top 10.' *BLABBERMOUTH.NET*, 2 Oct 2013,

Blabbermouth. 'MIKE PORTNOY Impersonator Is Back!' *BLABBERMOUTH.NET*, 27 June 2006.

Blabbermouth. 'MIKE PORTNOY Imposter Gets Busted After Stealing Spree.' *BLABBERMOUTH.NET*, 3 Apr 2003.

Blabbermouth. 'Video Premiere: DREAM THEATER's 'The Looking Glass'.' *BLABBERMOUTH.NET*, 3 Feb 2014.

Bosso, Joe. 'Dream Theater's A Dramatic Turn Of Events: Full Album Preview.' *MusicRadar*, MusicRadar, 17 Aug 2011,

Bosso, Joe. 'Jordan Rudess Talks Dream Theater's Self-Titled New Album Track-by-Track.' *MusicRadar*, MusicRadar, 18 Sept 2013

Bravewords.com. 'DREAM THEATER Guitarist John Petrucci Responds To Allegations Band 'Rewrote Images And Words' For A Dramatic Turn Of Events.' *Bravewords.com*, 14 Nov 2011.

Conaton, Chris. 'Dream Theater: Black Clouds and Silver Linings.' *PopMatters*, PopMatters, 16 July 2009.

Deeds, Michael. 'Quick Spins: Train of Thought.' *The Washington Post*, WP Company, 3 Dec 2003, www.washingtonpost.com/archive/lifestyle/2003/12/03/quick-spins/6f634e15-2a60-4086-9e18-d30fc3f1fa67/.

Dome, Malcolm. 'The Story Behind The Song: Pull Me Under by Dream Theater.' *Classic Rock Magazine*, Louder, 19 Feb 2016, www.loudersound.com/features/the-story-behind-the-song-pull-me-under-by-dream-theater.

DREAM THEATER Albums Ranked. *Prog Sphere*, 19 Mar 2019.

'Dream Theater Wiki.' *Dream Theater Wiki | FANDOM*,

Eardley, Jon. 'Dream Theater - 'Systematic Chaos' Review.' *Metal Review*,

Everley, Dave. 'Voivod, Dream Theater, Watchtower and the Explosive Birth of

Prog Metal.' *Prog Magazine*, Louder, 14 Feb 2019.

Ezell, Brice. 'Dream Theater: Dream Theater.' *PopMatters*, PopMatters, 16 Oct 2013.

Guarisco, Donald A. 'Funeral for a Friend/Love Lies Bleeding - Elton John: Song Info.' *AllMusic*.

Hatton, Thomas. 'Prog Redemption: Dream Theater, 'Falling Into Infinity'.' *Proglodytes*, 14 Mar 2017.

InsideOutMusicTV, and Roie Avin. 'DREAM THEATER - Interview at the Studio Pt. 1.' *YouTube*, YouTube, 21 Nov 2018.

InsideOutMusicTV. 'DREAM THEATER - Out Of Reach (Track By Track).' *YouTube*, YouTube, 6 Mar 2019.

InsideOutMusicTV. 'DREAM THEATER - Pale Blue Dot (Track By Track).' *YouTube*, YouTube, 8 Mar 2019.

InsideOutMusicTV. 'DREAM THEATER - Room 137 (Track By Track).' *YouTube*, YouTube, 27 Feb 2019.

InsideOutMusicTV. 'DREAM THEATER - S2N (Track By Track).' *YouTube*, YouTube, 28 Feb 2019.

Jones, Sefany. 'Dream Theater's Mike Portnoy Lashes Out At Unappreciative Fans.' *KNAC.COM*, 18 Mar 2012.

LaBrie, James. 'Re: LaBrie's Songs' Meanings...' *JamesLaBrie.com*, 28 Sept 2009.

Ling, Dave. 'Back to the Future: Dream Theater's Images And Words 25 Years On.' *Prog Magazine*, Louder, 21 Feb 2017.

Ling, Dave. 'Dream Theater Albums Ranked From Worst To Best.' *Classic Rock Magazine*, Louder, 1 Aug 2016.

Mackinnon, Eric. 'Peart Named Most Influential Prog Drummer.' *Loudersound*, Louder, 3 Oct 2014.

Maxwell, Jackson. 'Superunknown: 50 Iconic Albums That Defined 1994.' *Guitarworld*, Guitarworld, 16 July 2014.

Mihály, Gergely. 'John Petrucci Interview - 'The Label Didn't Have an Influence on the 'Falling Into Infinity' Album.'' *Rockbook.hu*, 3 Aug 2014.

'Music Videos.' *The Dream Theater World*, 6 May 2016.

Neilstein, Vince. 'DREAM THEATER'S BLACK CLOUDS & SILVER LININGS IS STOCK DREAM THEATER.' *MetalSucks*, 13 July 2009.

'Official Website.' *Dream Theater*, 22 July 2019, dreamtheater.net.

Papeghin, Marc. 'Dream Theater - Honor Thy Father - Movie Samples.' *YouTube*, YouTube, 27 Jan. 2012.

Patrizio, Andy. 'Train of Thought.' *IGN*, 21 May 2012.

Peperoni, Gianluca. 'Chaos in Progress: The Making of Systematic Chaos.' *YouTube*, YouTube, 12 Oct 2016, www.youtube.com/watch?v=HAFrAMvYlS8.

Perspectives, Sonic, and Rodrigo Altaf. 'DREAM THEATER's James LaBrie: 'With 'Distance Over Time' We Tried to Emcompass Our Musical Roots.' *YouTube*, YouTube, 21 Nov. 2018.

Pociluk, Rob. 'Albums Revisited: Dream Theater – 'Falling Into Infinity.'' *Progressive Music Planet*, 4 Aug 2015.

Portnoy, Mike. 'Dream Theater - Scenes From New York/Live Scenes From New York.' *Mike Portnoy.com The Official Website*, Mike Portnoy.

Prato, Greg. 'James LaBrie of Dream Theater.' *Songfacts*, 28 Jan 2019,

Prog Magazine. 'The 100 Greatest Prog Anthems Of All Time.' *Prog Magazine*, Louder, 26 Mar 2018,

Recchia, Philip. 'PORTNOY'S COMPLAINT – DRUMMER: IMPOSTER BEATS ALL.' *New York Post*, New York Post, 13 Apr 2003.

Records, Roadrunner. 'Dream Theater - Track By Track With John Petrucci.' *YouTube*, YouTube, 3 Oct 2013.

Reesman, Bryan. 'Dream Theater Preview Their Self-Titled New Album In NYC.' *Attention Deficit Delirium*, 31 July 2013.

Rivadavia, Eduardo. 'Dream Theater Albums Ranked.' *Loudwire*, 4 Oct 2016.

Rosen, Steve. 'Dream Theater's John Petrucci: 'You Don't Have to Be Afraid'.' *Ultimate Guitar.com*, Ultimate Guitar, 12 Aug 2013.

Smeaton, Bob, director. *'Classic Albums' Elton John: Goodbye Yellow Brick Road*. Eagle Rock Entertainment, 2001.

Songfacts. 'List of Songs by Dream Theater.' *Songfacts*.

Staff, Mix. 'Recent Sessions at Avatar Studios.' *Mixonline*, 18 Apr 2007.

'Stream of Consciousness.' *The Dream Theater World*, 11 Jan 2016.

TWRY Staff. 'Mike Portnoy Quits Dream Theater.' *TheyWilllRockYou.com*, 8 Sept 2010.

Wilson, Rich. *Lifting Shadows: The Authorized Biography of Dream Theater*. Rocket 88, 2013.

Wilson, Rich. 'The Albums That Saved Prog: When Dream And Day Unite.' *Prog Magazine*, Louder, 2 July 2014.

Your Majesty fan-club officiel français de Dream Theater. 'Interview John Petrucci and James LaBrie.' *YouTube*, YouTube, 31 Jan 2019.

Jordan Blum's ultimate Dream Theater Playlist

This will surely spark some controversy – if there's one thing we progressive metal fans are good at, it's debating each other's views – so let me begin by urging you to see the following list for exactly what it is: one man's opinion on the most essential and emblematic Dream Theater tracks. I tried to cover their whole discography, but I obviously prefer some albums over others, so don't be shocked if you see an imbalance there. In particular, and if I'm totally honest with myself, there's nothing past *A Dramatic Turn of Events* that I'd deem indispensable. As always, I'm interested to learn how your playlist would differ!

1. 'A Change of Seasons' (Complete)
2. 'Six Degrees of Inner Turbulence' (Complete)
3. 'Pull Me Under'
4. 'Metropolis—Part I: 'The Miracle and the Sleeper''
5. 'Wait for Sleep'
6. 'The Shattered Fortress'
7. 'Space-Dye Vest'
8. 'Hollow Years'
9. 'On the Backs of Angels'
10. 'Scene Six: Home'
11. 'Scene Seven: I. The Dance of Eternity'
12. 'Scene Eight: The Spirit Carries On'
13. 'The Glass Prison'
14. 'Disappear'
15. 'This Dying Soul'
16. 'The Root of All Evil'
17. 'Breaking All Illusions'
18. 'Panic Attack'
19. 'In the Presence of Enemies - Part I'
20. 'A Nightmare to Remember'

Dream Theater albums ranked from best to worst

As with the playlist, I'm sure the following album rankings will incite some ire (that's always a fun part of being in such a passionate musical community, right?). For the most part, Dream Theater's middle period is their strongest, yet some later albums also appeal more than earlier ones. Likewise, the Mangini-era started off very strong – whereas Portnoy's last couple weren't amazing – so it's really a mixed bag in terms of chronology. Still, there are some obvious high and low points, and I'd love to know how your placements compare to mine!

1. *Metropolis Pt. 2: Scenes from a Memory*
2. *Six Degrees of Inner Turbulence*
3. *Images and Words*
4. *Train of Thought*
5. *Octavarium*
6. *A Dramatic Turn of Events*
7. *A Change of Seasons*
8. *Systematic Chaos*
9. *Awake*
10. *Black Clouds & Silver Linings*
11. *Falling into Infinity*
12. *The Astonishing*
13. *Distance Over Time*
14. *Dream Theater*
15. *When Dream and Day Unite*

On Track series
Queen – Andrew Wild 978-1-78952-003-3
Emerson Lake and Palmer – Mike Goode 978-1-78952-000-2
Deep Purple and Rainbow 1968-79 – Steve Pilkington 978-1-78952-002-6
Yes – Stephen Lambe 978-1-78952-001-9
Blue Oyster Cult – Jacob Holm-Lupo 978-1-78952-007-1
The Beatles – Andrew Wild 978-1-78952-009-5
Roy Wood and the Move – James R Turner 978-1-78952-008-8
Genesis – Stuart MacFarlane 978-1-78952-005-7
JethroTull – Jordan Blum 978-1-78952-016-3
The Rolling Stones 1963-80 – Steve Pilkington 978-1-78952-017-0
Judas Priest – John Tucker 978-1-78952-018-7
Toto – Jacob Holm-Lupo 978-1-78952-019-4
Van Der Graaf Generator – Dan Coffey 978-1-78952-031-6
Frank Zappa 1966 to 1979 – Eric Benac 978-1-78952-033-0
Elton John in the 1970s – Peter Kearns 978-1-78952-034-7
The Moody Blues – Geoffrey Feakes 978-1-78952-042-2
The Beatles Solo 1969-1980 – Andrew Wild 978-1-78952-030-9
Steely Dan – Jez Rowden 978-1-78952-043-9
Hawkwind – Duncan Harris 978-1-78952-052-1
Fairport Convention – Kevan Furbank 978-1-78952-051-4
Iron Maiden – Steve Pilkington 978-1-78952-061-3
Dream Theater – Jordan Blum 978-1-78952-050-7
10CC – Peter Kearns 978-1-78952-054-5
Gentle Giant – Gary Steel 978-1-78952-058-3
Kansas – Kevin Cummings 978-1-78952-057-6
Mike Oldfield – Ryan Yard 978-1-78952-060-6
The Who – Geoffrey Feakes 978-1-78952-076-7

On Screen series
Carry On... – Stephen Lambe 978-1-78952-004-0
Powell and Pressburger – Sam Proctor 978-1-78952-013-2
Seinfeld Seasons 1 to 5 – Stephen Lambe 978-1-78952-012-5
Francis Ford Coppola – Cam Cobb and Stephen Lambe 978-1-78952-022-4
Monty Python – Steve Pilkington 978-1-78952-047-7
Doctor Who: The David Tennant Years – Jamie Hailstone 978-1-78952-066-8
James Bond – Andrew Wild 978-1-78952-010-1

Other Books
Not As Good As The Book – Andy Tillison 978-1-78952-021-7
The Voice. Frank Sinatra in the 1940s – Stephen Lambe 978-1-78952-032-3
Maximum Darkness – Deke Leonard 978-1-78952-048-4
The Twang Dynasty – Deke Leonard 978-1-78952-049-1
Maybe I Should've Stayed In Bed – Deke Leonard 978-1-78952-053-8
Tommy Bolin: In and Out of Deep Purple – Laura Shenton 978-1-78952-070-5
Jon Anderson and the Warriors - the road to Yes – David Watkinson
978-1-78952-059-0

and many more to come!